DRUGS, SOCIETY AND THE LAW

TO ELAINE

Drugs, Society and the Law

Harvey TEFF, MA, LL.M, PhD
Of the Middle Temple, Barrister-at-Law
Lecturer in Law in the University of Durham

SAXON HOUSE | LEXINGTON BOOKS

Published by

SAXON HOUSE, D. C. Heath Ltd.
Westmead, Farnborough, Hants., England.

Jointly with

LEXINGTON BOOKS, D. C. Heath & Co.
Lexington, Mass. USA

ISBN 0 347 01079 2

Printed in Great Britain by Robert MacLehose and Company Limited
Printers to the University of Glasgow

Contents

Table of cases

Roman numerals refer to page references, italic numerals refer to notes at the end of the relevant chapter.

Table of Statutes

Table of Statutory Instruments

Table of Treaties

Acknowledgements

I am particularly indebted to Dr Bernard Hargrove, who supervised the thesis on which this book is based, for his help and encouragement at all stages of the research. I would also like to thank Neil Hornick for several valuable suggestions about the psychological aspects of drug use.

I am pleased to acknowledge the assistance given to me by the Library Staff of the Pharmaceutical Society of Great Britain and the Staff of the Institute for the Study of Drug Dependence.

I am indebted to the Editor of the Bulletin on Narcotics for permission to reproduce Table 1 of Appendix A and to the Controller of Her Majesty's Stationery Office for permission to reproduce Crown Copyright material in Tables 2, 3, 4 and 5, as well as to Information Canada for permission to reproduce the material in Appendix B.

My thanks are also due to Ann Wood and Anne and Bob Sullivan for helping to check the manuscript and to Colin Munro for pointing out a number of places where the text could be clarified. I am also most grateful to the Publishers for all their help.

It is a pleasure to record my gratitude to Brenda Turner for her patient typing of the manuscript and to Louise Sinclair for her tireless secretarial help in the final stages of preparation.

I have endeavoured to state the law as at 1 January 1975.

1 Legal and Social Perceptions

We live in an age in which an enormous variety of drugs are produced and consumed in ever increasing quantities. A correspondingly large literature testifies to the growing interest in the phenomenon of drug taking and its social significance. In England most of this analysis has been undertaken without extensive reference to the law. Scientific and medical treatises abound and the sociological implications of drug dependence are examined at length. When the law has been discussed, it is primarily from the standpoint of sociological enquiry.[1] Lawyers have not been particularly prominent in the debate.

Yet there are very good reasons why they should not be so reticent. Most obviously, this is because many forms of drug use are either prohibited or controlled by the law, so that questions of interpretation arise which require legal analysis: What is meant by 'possession' of a controlled drug? What is the precise burden of proof required to establish possession? And so on. More generally, both the history of drug control in England and its probable future development are closely bound up with the requirements of international law. One cannot, for example, fully appreciate how cannabis has acquired its present classification in domestic law without reference to the international structure of control.

But over and above the legal problems which derive from particular provisions of the law relating to drugs, there are more fundamental issues which, though by no means the exclusive province of the lawyer, exemplify some of the most intractable problems of jurisprudential theory. What is the legitimate function of the law in such matters as the sale and possession of drugs? The extent to which we deem it necessary or desirable to impose legal controls will depend on value judgements as to what constitutes harmful behaviour and as to the acceptability of using the law as a means of regulating it.

How effective can the criminal law be in preventing the use of a commodity for which there is a substantial demand, and where no incentive exists to report the crime to the police? The law is at its least convincing in dealing with what have been called 'victimless crimes'. To begin with, the purpose of legal intervention is not wholly clear. Is *any* control necessary beyond the minimum needed to protect health and prevent exploitation? Even assuming a consensus can be found as to what constitutes danger to health and exploitation, should the law aim at total eradication of certain kinds of drug use or pursue a policy of containment?

When the law purports to penalise mere possession of a desired substance, it is either demonstrably ineffective, or produces secondary consequences arguably more damaging than the commodity itself, as was shown by the history of Prohibition and the growth of organised crime in America. It is not difficult to justify legal control of crimes of violence. But in the case of drugs the law is addressing itself to more intangible and less easily perceived consequences. In trying to prevent people from becoming dependent on drugs or suffering some kind of physical or psychological harm, it imposes a blanket prohibition on *any* use of certain substances. Because, as we shall see, the criteria used by the law to proscribe the use of some drugs while sanctioning others are far from rational, the non-dependent occasional user of an illegal drug is likely to perceive the law as a blunt instrument penalising harmless conduct, which he finds either pleasurable or in some way functional. If he is dependent on the drug in question, then the law appears to be punishing him for his present condition rather than for any deliberate wrongdoing.

Furthermore, partly because drug offences are by their nature difficult to discover and to prove, they have attracted particularly stringent legal controls and are a temptation to procedural abuses, such that allegations of planting and indiscriminate searches are common. Since alcohol and tobacco are freely available, yet widely acknowledged to cause more extensive harm than most illegal drugs, it should not be surprising that the drug laws have become a focus of concern in the civil liberties field in recent years. How this situation has arisen and what alternative policies are feasible will be considered later. At this stage it is sufficient merely to note that dissatisfaction with, and disregard of, individual laws, if widespread, may bring the law in general into disrepute.

The way in which the law regulates drug use cannot then be seen as a self-contained issue, but leads on to wider arguments about the kind of society in which we live and the proper functions of the law within it. Drug use is especially well-suited to prompt consideration of these more general questions, because the very word 'drug' is among the most powerful emotive symbols in our vocabulary. It evokes a sense of mystery and fear; it conjures up the image of the 'opium den' and of moral decay. Because drugs can transform human behaviour they present a challenge to our understanding of human identity and the potentialities of human experience.

The symbolic significance is both complex and ambiguous, since though drugs are primarily taken to relieve pain or to give pleasure, in common usage the term remains pejorative and, as Chein says, 'the predominant associations of the word "drug" emphasise negative, dangerous or undesirable effects, as "under the influence of drugs" or "he was drugged" '.[2] We do not use the term to refer to aspirin or vitamin pills. Nor do we normally label heavy smokers and drinkers, or even diabetics dependent on insulin, as 'drug users'.

This striking dichotomy is constantly apparent in our perception of drug use. It presents a formidable obstacle to a coherent legal framework which tries to respond to society's need for a healthy and effective work force and at the same time cater for a measure of uninhibited, non-rational behaviour during leisure hours.

Drugs are also now a familiar feature of the political and generational battlegrounds, engendering a degree of polarisation which at times seems to preclude constructive debate. One unfortunate consequence is the tendency of legislative bodies to opt for the popular 'solution' of harsher legal controls,[3] instead of trying to adjust to a different perspective on drug use, by seeking a more constructive blend of coercion, treatment and educational approaches and, where appropriate, simple tolerance.

Of the numerous problems to which drug taking gives rise, not the least of them is our attitude towards it. Its constantly shifting nature requires a corresponding flexibility of outlook. The urge to reduce everything to a single 'drugs problem' which can only be solved by imposing criminal sanctions, while no doubt reflecting popular opinion, utterly fails to convey the variety of drug use and drug users and conceals the adverse side effects of any such approach. In short, it ignores the total social and economic context in which drug taking occurs.

Problems of definition and classification

It would naturally be convenient to have a common understanding as to what is meant by a 'drug' and what are the defining characteristics of 'addiction'. But these terms are not susceptible of precise definition and there is continuing controversy over whether particular substances are truly 'addictive' or merely habit forming. Also, as we have seen, our categorisation of them is coloured by emotive responses. Using pharmacological criteria, it would be hard to think of any substance more fittingly described as addictive than alcohol. It is indisputably capable of producing the three characteristics typically deemed to connote addiction: *craving* – an overpowering desire or compulsion to obtain a drug; *tolerance* – the need to take progressively larger quantities to achieve the same effect, and an *abstinence* (withdrawal) *syndrome* – a variety of unpleasant symptoms, including, in the case of alcohol, fever and *delirium tremens.*

Yet social acceptance of alcohol and its effective institutionalisation through the pub and social gatherings have created a marked resistance to perceiving it as a drug at all, let alone an addictive one. This kind of irrational judgement perpetuates a distorted view of the relative gravity for society of different forms of drug abuse. If one had to name a single drug as being most immediately identified in the popular imagination with addiction, it would surely be heroin. Yet the number of heroin addicts notified to the Home Office has never reached 3,000 and the total number known to be taking the drug during 1973 was 866 (there being 3,025 notified narcotic addicts in all, the majority on methadone).[4] Even on a liberal estimate of the number of users not notified to the Home Office, it is unlikely that the total number of heroin addicts in the United Kingdom has ever exceeded 5–6,000. A recent study on alcoholism suggested that there were approximately 700,000 alcoholics in the later stages of the illness and requiring treatment.[5]

A fuller account of the relative harm attributable to the use of particular drugs will be attempted in chapter six, but it is worth noting here that our unwillingness to acknowledge the extent and harmfulness of alcoholism is but one of the more striking of a whole range of conventional misperceptions as to what constitutes drug abuse, which include resistance to the idea that tobacco (containing nicotine) and coffee (containing caffeine) are drugs and undue complacency about the misuse of barbiturates and even aspirin.

Rather than pursue the somewhat sterile question of which drugs are properly said to lead to 'addiction' and which merely to 'habituation', it is proposed here to adopt the approach of the World Health Organisation (WHO) which recommended that use of these terms be discontinued and replaced by 'dependence', defined as: 'A state arising from repeated administration of a drug on a periodic or continuous basis', '. . . its characteristics will vary with the agent involved, but it is a general term selected for its applicability to all types of drug abuse and carries no connotation in regard to degree of risk to public health or need of a particular type of control'.[6]

The main advantage of this approach is that by avoiding the highly emotive expressions 'addict' and 'addiction' we are less tempted to imagine that society can be neatly divided into addicts and the rest when in reality there is a wide spectrum of reliance on artificial aids to living, ranging from an early morning cup of coffee to an intravenous injection of heroin. Such a perspective makes one less disposed to reject out of hand the notion of the 'stabilised addict' [7] capable of leading a satisfactory and productive life on the basis of small regular doses of, for example, the opiate methadone, which is now in fact the standard method of treating heroin addicts in the new British treatment centres.

But even the more neutral concept of dependence is apt to be misleading if it conveys the idea that a drug in isolation, because of its intrinsic properties, is a proper source of concern. For it is the total context of drug use which determines whether or not harm ensues and numerous variables have to be accounted for. The user's personality, his physical and psychological make up, his familiarity with and expectations of the drug may influence the effect on him just as much as its actual properties, as is so strikingly demonstrated by the curative power of placebos and their capacity for inducing side effects and altering performance on standard tests.

The setting in which a drug is taken may also be highly significant. This is true both of the immediate surroundings and the wider cultural context. To drink alcohol at a party or smoke marijuana as one of a mutually sympathetic group will normally have different consequences from taking either when alone or when participating in a clinically controlled experiment. But at a much broader level, the whole cultural background must be considered, embracing conventional social attitudes towards both the drug in question and its users, as well as the nature of legal control.

In addition to these background features, regard must also naturally be paid to dosage levels, duration and frequency of use, and, in some cases, the method of administration. Intravenous injection of heroin produces a much quicker and more powerful reaction than other methods and tends to lead to dependence sooner. An additional hazard here is the possibility of infection due to the shared use of unsterile needles. Indeed in the case of opiates, such as heroin, it is important to realise that some of the greatest dangers are secondary consequences of taking the drug. The risk of infection due to unsterile injections is increased by the user's total involvement with the drug when dependence is marked. Because of the general lack of energy induced, sexual drive and the desire to work are diminished and precautions regarding health and diet are neglected, insensitivity to hunger often leading to severe under-nourishment.

Finally one should not overlook, as a further reason for not treating drugs in isolation, the simple fact they are frequently taken in combination, thus creating problems for diagnosis and treatment. In some instances, of which alcohol and barbiturates is the best known, the combination may prove fatal.

Clearly then, any statement about drugs in general, or even about the effects of particular substances, invites scepticism. It is therefore equally clear that the impossibility of objectively categorising drugs in terms of their effects and relative harmfulness is a major obstacle to a rational legal classification. Since the law tends to reflect prevailing social attitudes it is hardly surprising that it has endorsed some of the commonplace fallacies.

Thus road traffic legislation persists in using the familiar formula 'drink *or* drugs'. The Road Traffic Act 1972, s. 5(1) provides: 'A person who, when driving or attempting to drive a motor vehicle on a road or other public place, is unfit to drive through *drink or drugs*[8] shall be guilty of an offence.'

In commenting on a similar provision in the Road Traffic Act 1930, s. 15(1), where the formula 'under the influence of drink or a drug' was used, a report of a Special Committee of the British Medical Association observed that '. . . the words, "drink or a drug" are tautologous and confusing, as they suggest that alcohol is not a drug'.[9]

That the law envisaged a clear distinction between the two is further shown in *Thomson* v. *Knights:*[10]

A conviction for driving 'under the influence of drink or a drug' was held not to be bad for duplicity (i.e. for implying alternative offences) on the ground that, *though the section* [11] *postulated alternative facts,* [12] they constituted only a single offence, namely driving a motor vehicle while in a state of self-induced incapacity. No suggestion appears in the judgement that drink is capable of being subsumed under the general category of drugs, a formula which would, of course, dispose of the problem.[13]

A more fundamental criticism in the light of what has been said above concerns the choice, prior to the Misuse of Drugs Act 1971,[14] of the tendentious label 'dangerous drugs' to designate the major legislation in the field. Even the current classification, while signifying a more flexible approach, is not free from a similar tendency to place undue emphasis on preconceptions as to the supposed nature of particular drugs.[15]

However, since it is not practicable to classify drugs accurately according to the degree of dependence and 'dangerousness' which they entail, we shall concentrate our attention on those which have figured most prominently in the legislation for purposes of control or are extensively used; more particularly: opiates (such as heroin and morphine), which are all pharmacologically addictive; cocaine (a powerful stimulant often injected with heroin); cannabis; amphetamines (stimulants commonly referred to as pep pills); barbiturates (used as tranquilisers and, except for the short acting variety, addictive); hallucinogens (such as LSD), and alcohol.

If only to highlight the difficulties posed for legal control, it is salutary to note that several easily obtainable commodities which do not immediately spring to mind in the context of drug use can nonetheless be dangerous if so used. Glue, petrol, cleaning solvents, nutmeg, some Morning Glory seeds and certain cough mixtures come into this category. Craving is not easily thwarted.

Notes

[1] E.g. E. Schur, *Narcotic Addiction in Britain and America,* ABP Ltd. 1962; P. Bean, *The Social Control of Drugs,* Martin Robertson 1974.

[2] I. Chein *et al., Narcotics, Delinquency and Social Policy,* Tavistock Publications 1964, p. 336.

[3] Thus in 1973 New York State introduced what is arguably the most stringent drugs legislation in the United States. See the Laws of 1973, Chapter 1051.

[4] See Appendix A, Table 3.

[5] Merseyside Council on Alcoholism. *The Times* 27 September 1973.

[6] WHO Techn. Rep. Ser. No. 287, 1964, 4, 5, 6.

[7] 'Addict' and 'addiction' have become so integral and familiar a part of the whole subject that it is not proposed to dispense with these terms entirely. For the purposes of the relevant legislation a person is defined as an addict, '. . . if, and only if, he has as a result of repeated administration become so dependent on the drug that he has an overpowering desire for the administration of it to be continued.' Misuse of Drugs (Notification of and Supply to Addicts) Regulations 1973 S.I. No. 799, reg. 2(2).

[8] Italics supplied.

[9] *The Drinking Driver,* British Medical Association, 1965, p. 7.

[10] [1947] K.B. 336.

[11] Road Traffic Act 1930, s. 15.

[12] Italics supplied.

[13] The meaning of 'drug' was the subject of judicial interpretation in *Armstrong* v. *Clark* [1957] 2 Q.B. 391, where the Divisional Court held that insulin was a 'drug' within the Road Traffic Act 1930, s. 15(1). Lord Goddard C.J. described a drug as: '. . . a medicament or medicine, something given to cure, alleviate or assist an ailing body', ibid. at p. 394.

[14] The Long Title of the 1971 Act reads: 'An Act to make new provision with respect to dangerous or otherwise harmful drugs and related matters, and for purposes connected therewith.' The Act itself uses the expression 'controlled drugs'.

[15] See pp. 33–6.

2 The Development of Control

The nineteenth century background

Since we are primarily concerned with drugs currently subject to legal control, our natural historical starting point is the opium debate of the nineteenth century. Whilst it is both tempting and illuminating to go back further,[1] it was the traffic in opium which provided the main stimulus towards international control. As Great Britain is a signatory of the relevant international conventions,[2] they provide the framework within which much of the English law operates.

For a balanced perspective, it is necessary first of all to appreciate the state of medical knowledge and social attitudes towards opium during the nineteenth century. Relatively little was known about the dangers of addiction, and it was common practice for doctors to recommend opium and its derivatives for almost all ills. As late as 1889, it was seriously argued by an American doctor that habituation to morphia should be prescribed as a cure for alcoholism,[3] and when, in 1898, diacetylmorphin (heroin) was first produced it was widely believed to be non-addictive.

Opium pills and laudanum (tincture of opium) could be bought cheaply at any apothecary, without prescription, and it is perhaps not surprising that opium was thought of as a universal panacea when it is remembered that the number and variety of patent medicines was far more restricted than today. In a world without barbiturates, amphetamines and the numerous sedatives and stimulants which are now commonplace, the saying attributed to Sydenham in about 1670, 'without opium there would be no medicine', equally exemplified nineteenth century attitudes. Thus cheap patent medicines such as 'Godfrey's Cordial', 'McMunn's Elixir of Opium' and 'Mother Bailey's Quieting Syrup', often containing as much as half a grain of opium to the ounce, were in constant demand, in an age when self-medication and self-diagnosis – primarily with a view to symptomatic relief – were regarded as normal.[4]

Just as patent medicines, or laudanum alone at a few pence per ounce, were literally the 'opiate of the people', the morphine habit was a fashionable cult among the upper classes. The Romantic Movement in the early nineteenth century, notably through the poetry of Coleridge and De Quincey's classic *Confessions of an English Opium Eater,* first published in

1821, helped to foster this cult, but it may well be that De Quincey's influence has been somewhat exaggerated. As Adams[5] pointed out, the key developments of the nineteenth century were of a medical nature – the isolation of morphine in 1804, the invention of the hypodermic needle in the 1840s and the introduction of heroin in 1898.

Opium then, in one form or another, found a considerable measure of acceptance socially and also among the medical profession, especially as it was not until the mid-nineteenth century that safe anaesthetic techniques began to be developed. Indeed, due to their ignorance of its pharmacological effects, doctors frequently prescribed opium to treat painful symptoms which in fact arose from its use.

In the light of this background, it is odd that, as Goulding says:[6] 'So far as one can judge from inadequate statistics and contemporary writing Britain suffered no problem of drug addiction for centuries – and this in spite of virtual freedom from control over sale and supply until little more than a hundred years ago.' It is hardly conceivable that social commentators and historians could have overlooked a problem which often manifests itself in such dramatic ways, especially as the prevalence of alcoholism was well documented.

One can only conjecture that many people died or suffered without their misfortune being perceived as due to an addiction problem. Significantly, when legal controls began to emerge in the middle of the nineteenth century, they were primarily directed against the would-be felon and not seen as a means of combating addiction.

'From the middle of the nineteenth century progressively greater restraints became statutorily imposed over the trade in drugs, not so much because of their capacity to induce dependence as on account of their toxicity and their attraction, for this reason, to those homicidally or otherwise harmfully intent.' [7]

Thus the Pharmacy Act 1868 regulated the supply and retail sale of a number of poisons, including opium and opium preparations. The Offences Against the Person Act 1861 contains several provisions prohibiting the administration of various drugs with criminal intent.[8] But there is nothing to suggest that any of these restraints on supply and administration were a response to a drugs problem as understood today.

The pattern of dependence as then perceived would seem to have been broadly similar to that of the early twentieth century – a few doctors, some therapeutic addicts, and one or two small, self-contained groups such as Chinese opium smokers in the London and Liverpool docks.

> *Chinese to decline £11,000 left in will*
>
> The thoughts of Mr Henry James Newlin turned, as he made his will, to China. After bequests totalling £61,000 Mr Newlin, who died in a Tunbridge Wells nursing home in June, left the residue of his estate, just over £11,000, to 'the People's Republic of China, in token of restitution on behalf of my country for the damages sustained by the people of China in the Opium Wars'.
>
> The Chinese Embassy said today that China did not intend to accept the money.[9]

The 'opium question', which became a matter of considerable public concern, was, of course, in no way directly connected with the control of drugs in England. The issue was originally purely one of trade with China. Put in its simplest form, England sold China opium in exchange for tea, mainly through the agency of the East India Company. The Company began to take part in the trade from the end of the eighteenth century and in 1831, for example, China bought $11 million worth of opium from the 'country firms' of India, which let the East India Company have $8 million (against bills drawn on London) to spend on tea.[10]

Even when the East India Company left China in 1834, the trade continued, as the Indian government had a monopoly of India's opium and regarded its sale as necessary for revenue purposes. Initially, the potential social dangers were not appreciated and the trade was seen purely as a commercial venture. Hence the two notorious 'Opium Wars' of 1839–42 and 1857–58. 'The primary object of both wars was to open up the vast, closed empire of China to Western goods in general.'[11]

But in the 1840s the social effects gradually became more apparent and the moral issue became a matter of public controversy. An anti-opium society was formed, and parliamentary debates took place. The impression gained ground that Britain, especially under the terms of the Treaty of Tientsin of 1858, was forcing an unwilling China to accept imports of opium. It is not easy to determine how far the opposition of the Chinese government was morally based and how far it was due to a fear that excessive expenditure of silver on opium was upsetting the country's balance of trade.

At all events, the whole issue had attained a national importance. Motions condemning the opium trade were put forward in Parliament in the 1870s and 1880s and, though they were defeated, the climate of opinion was perceptibly changing. In 1891 the motion 'that the system by which the Indian opium revenue is raised is morally indefensible' was carried. But this had little practical effect, and the Royal Commission on Opium of 1895 – a report of over 2,500 pages – gave little comfort to the anti-opium movement, maintaining that the harmful effects of opium had been greatly exaggerated and that India could not afford the loss to its revenue which total prohibition of production would entail.

However three years later heroin was introduced and the stage was set for control on an international scale.

The origins of international control

On 30 May 1906, the House of Commons once again carried a motion denouncing the Indo-Chinese opium trade as indefensible, and the hope was expressed that China would co-operate by halting her own opium production, as a first step. In the autumn of 1906, China introduced legislation to end all opium production within ten years, and 'in 1908 Britain agreed to reduce Indian exports to China in proportion with China's own reductions in cultivation and of her imports from other countries'.[12] Accordingly, 'Upon the most authentic information available . . . both the production and the consumption of opium in China had practically ceased by 1913 . . . Simultaneously the Indian Government ended the exportation of opium to China.'[13]

However, while attention was being focussed on the trade in China, the opium problem had been steadily spreading to other parts of the world during the second half of the nineteenth century. The influx of cheap Chinese labour to the West was one precipitating factor. Even as early as 1846, according to Dr H.H. Cane, there were over 117,000 Chinese in the United States, and the equivalent of 53,189 pounds of prepared opium was imported mainly through Chinese traders, only about half of which was estimated to be smoked by the Chinese.[14] Similar patterns emerged in South America and Australia.

> It was the same in Britain. Apart from a few cultured eccentrics, poets and the like, only the lowest class took opium – in its simpler forms. The Chinese can scarcely have been the direct cause here. But the Midland manufacturing towns which had once dreamed of selling vast quantities of their products to China consumed considerable quantities of the only commodity China had wanted. The English lowest class did not necessarily consist of prostitutes and law breakers, but they were poor. Unlike the poor of China they were

always with us, and of little news value. One enterprising reporter in the eighteen seventies interviewed a number of Midland druggists who told him that they sold many pints of laudanum in the evening directly after the pubs closed. This was worth only a few lines of incidental intelligence.[15]

This observation may help to explain the relative lack of reference to opium by social historians of the period.

There is no doubt that opium smoking was common among the Chinese who lived in the 'Chinatown' areas, but 'throughout the nineteenth century the size of the Chinese population in Great Britain remained negligible, and it was only at the turn of the present century that the so-called 'Chinatowns' began to take shape in London and Liverpool.'[16] Not only were the numbers very small,[17] but assimilation was very limited, especially among the old seamen immigrants of the early twentieth century. 'Of all the coloured immigrant communities in Britain, the Chinese are by far the least assimilated.'[18]

At all events, the increase in opium exports to the West and the gradual realisation of the dangers of opium derivatives, especially heroin (intensified by the use of the hypodermic syringe in contrast to the pipe smoking method of the East whereby most of the impurities would be removed by the heat), pointed towards the need for international action, and this was the theme of the Shanghai Conference of 1909.

The International Opium Commission was established, consisting of delegates from countries with interests in the Far East. The use of opium and its derivatives for non-medical purposes was denounced as a spreading evil requiring both domestic and international control, and three years later the Hague International Opium Convention took place.

The Preamble to the Convention of 1912 reads as follows: 'To bring about the gradual suppression of the abuse of opium, morphia and cocaine, as also of the drugs prepared or derived from these substances which give rise or might give rise to similar abuse.'

The Convention represented a unique and revolutionary approach to an international problem, by envisaging state control over the production of and trade in opiates. It is however important to realise that the major stimulus to the Hague Convention was the desire to suppress trade abuses in the Far East. The social danger

> ... was not, except in certain quarters, recognised to be a real problem at all. Though some Eastern administrations were alive to it ... it was not mentioned in the invitations to the Hague Conference which were issued by the President of the United States, and it was

only the insistence of some governments, including our own, that secured its inclusion in the Agenda of the Conference.

The general want of appreciation of its importance is reflected in, and partly accounts for, the vagueness and indecisiveness of this first attempt to deal with it. Years of study by the Opium Advisory Committee of the League of Nations, first appointed in 1921, were required to bring to light and impress upon the World the extent of the evil, its disastrous consequences and the nature of the traffic by which it was fed. Even to our own Government, the facts connected with British trade in the drugs before the War were very imperfectly known. No statistics existed.[19]

Initially, the admirable sentiments expressed at the Convention had little practical effect. As indicated above, the gravity of the problem was by no means fully understood. Inevitably there was hostility to the proposals and their encroachment on national sovereignty by those countries with a vested interest in the drug traffic, as is demonstrated by the equivocal formula of 'gradual and effective' steps towards drug control introduced in order to increase the number of signatories.

The outbreak of the First World War in 1914 led to an increase in scale of the drug traffic and of drug use by soldiers and civilians alike. The restrictions which had been imposed and maintained by the Chinese government merely served to foster illegal production and smuggling. But there was at least a growing awareness of the complexity and enormity of the problem and the corresponding need for a comprehensive form of international control, embracing detailed regulations and supervision and requiring extensive and continuous research.

Responsibility for the control of dangerous drugs was handed to the League of Nations, and ratification of the Treaty of Versailles was deemed to involve ratification of the Hague Convention in 1912. A twelve month time limit was imposed on signatories within which to enact domestic legislation to give effect to the Hague Convention, and it was in this way that the Dangerous Drugs Act 1920 emerged as the first major[20] attempt in English law to tackle the problem.

An outline of legislation and developments, 1920–70

In the words of the long title, the Dangerous Drugs Act 1920 was 'An Act to regulate the Importation, Exportation, Manufacture, Sale and Use of Opium and other Dangerous Drugs'. Part 1 of the Act dealt with raw opium, part 2 with prepared opium, and part 3 primarily with cocaine, morphine and diamorphine (heroin). Provision was also made whereby new drugs or derivatives with substantially similar effects could be made subject to the Act by Orders in Council.[21]

A system of import and export licensing was established and it was made an offence to possess the drugs in question without authority. Prescriptions were introduced, as well as detailed regulations on safety precautions and keeping records. Medical practitioners' records were to be open to inspection by regional medical staff of the Ministry of Health and those of wholesale chemists and pharmacists by Home Office inspectors and the police. Thus a relatively elaborate structure was established in conformity with the control requirements of the Hague Convention.

The terms 'addiction' and 'drug addict' were not mentioned in the Act. A registered medical practitioner was authorised to possess and supply the drugs only 'so far as is necessary for the practice of his profession . . .'.[22] This inevitably led to controversy over the limits of legitimate medical practice, already the subject of litigation in the American courts in their attempts to interpret similar provisions in the Federal Narcotic Law 1914 (The Harrison Act).[23]

While there were initially a number of prosecutions for minor contraventions of the record keeping requirements of the Act,[24] the Home Office, in the absence of some clear guiding principles, did not seek to have actions brought against doctors who continued to supply addicts.[25] In order to clarify the position, the Departmental Committee on Morphine and Heroin Addiction was set up in 1924, with Sir Humphry Rolleston as chairman, and its report,[26] published in 1926, in practice served as the basis of the law for some forty years.

The Committee concluded that

> . . . morphine or heroin may properly be administered to addicts in the following circumstances, namely, (a) where patients are under treatment by the gradual withdrawal method with a view to cure, (b) where it has been demonstrated, after a prolonged attempt at cure, that the use of the drug cannot be safely discontinued entirely, on account of the severity of the withdrawal symptoms produced, (c) where it has been similarly demonstrated that the patient, while capable of leading a useful and relatively normal life when a certain minimum dose is regularly administered, becomes incapable of this when the drug is entirely discontinued.[27]

Thus no outright ban on prescribing to addicts was advocated. Whether the proposed criteria existed in a given case would be a matter for the individual practitioner to decide,[28] and the Report also suggested certain precautions for the treatment of addicts, such as a preference for institutional treatment for gradual withdrawal[29] and circumstances in which a second opinion was desirable.[30]

It is highly significant that the Committee was composed of eminent physicians and that all the witnesses were also members of the medical profession. Thus, from the outset, addiction was viewed in this country first and foremost as a medical problem, 'as a manifestation of disease and not as a mere form of vicious indulgence'.[31] The contrast with the origins of control in America, where the Prohibition campaign to ban alcohol progressed side by side with a punitive approach to drug use, is particularly illuminating.[32] To supply addicts in accordance with the three criteria proposed by the Committee was to be regarded as 'treatment' and not the mere 'gratification of addiction'.

The 'British System'

The Rolleston Committee's interpretation of the legislation as outlined above forms the basis of what has become known as the 'British System'. This title is certainly misleading in so far as it implies a methodical and comprehensive scheme for the control of drug abuse, when in fact the approach has been essentially pragmatic throughout.

Thus, as Bewley puts it:

> Before the last war, there were in this country very few known addicts to opiates. The majority were either doctors, nurses, pharmacists – people with access to drugs – or a few people who had been originally treated for some chronic painful condition and who had in the course of treatment accidentally become addicted to the drug. There were very few of the type of addict who first becomes addicted by obtaining drugs from another addict. In these circumstances the system worked very well, and there were many arguments, mostly in the United States, as to whether it was because of this system that there was so little addiction in this country. In fact, I think that the so-called British System really was a group of administrative practices that grew up when there was very little addiction.[33]

What has remained a constant, however, is the medically oriented approach to the problem, inspired by the humane attitudes contained in the Rolleston Report, and contrasting sharply with some of the excesses associated with the development of control in America, in particular some of the individual state legislation.[34]

Certainly there was relatively little significant legislation in England until the 1960s, apart from that dictated by international commitments. Thus the Geneva Convention of 1925 required governments to provide the newly created Permanent Central Opium Board with annual statistics on the production of opium and coca leaves, and filled in some of the gaps left by the Hague Convention of 1912, notably by establishing the system of import certificates and export authorisations. Limited control of Indian hemp (cannabis) was also introduced. The Geneva Convention of 1931 further regulated the manufacture and distribution of narcotic drugs. Both of these conventions were incorporated into English law by the Dangerous Drugs Acts of 1925 and 1932 respectively.

The Pharmacy and Poisons Act 1933 was passed to control poisons, and the Poisons Rules have been issued under it. It has provided limited legislative control over barbiturates, in that they can be sold only on the prescription of a doctor, dentist or veterinary surgeon.[35] Yet there was no further major legislation directly concerned with drug addiction,[36] other than the Dangerous Drugs Act 1951 itself merely a consolidating Act, until the 1960s.

As late as 1961, partly in reliance on the encouraging Home Office statistics,[37] the Interdepartmental Committee on Drug Addiction (The Brain Committee) felt able to conclude that:

> In Great Britain the incidence of addiction to drugs controlled under the Dangerous Drugs Act, 1951, is still very small and traffic in illicit supplies is almost negligible, cannabis excepted. This is mainly due to the attitude of the public and to the systematic enforcement of the Dangerous Drugs Legislation.[38]

How far was this optimism – to be belied a mere four years later when the reconvened Committee produced its Second Report – justified at the time? Certainly there was ample support for it in the statements of most experts writing about the period, from the Rolleston Committee onwards:

> This evidence has all tended in the same direction, and the collective effect is remarkably strong in support of the conclusion that, in this country, addiction to morphine or heroin is rare.[39]

> The number of addicts in Great Britain is of the order of hundreds rather than of thousands. The number actually known to exist from official records is about 700.[40]
> The British system of control is admitted by other countries to be

> second to none. It has reduced drug addiction in this country to the smallest proportions.[41]
>
> From time to time, the Home Office has received confirmation of its opinion that the degree of hidden addiction is small. One of the leading physicians in the country, who lives and practises in a large provincial conurbation, asked over seventy local practitioners if they had a drug addict among their patients. None of them had. The physician himself was aware of one case in the district, which was of therapeutic origin. The chief constable of a provincial seaport (a city where, if drug addiction flourished at all in the United Kingdom it would certainly be found) in response to allegations about the existence of vice and drug addiction in the city, and in particular among seamen of Asiatic origin, conducted a most thorough enquiry and found no evidence whatever of drug addiction . . . .
>
> There are one or two minor pointers which suggest the same conclusion. For some years the metropolitan police isolated the figures for dangerous drugs in respect of theft from unattended motor vehicles. This practice was discontinued because the number of cases was so small that the information was worthless. The pre-war practice of keeping statistics of all drug addicts admitted to prisons fell into partial disuse for the same reason. A recent survey of admissions to the principal prisons in Great Britain revealed less than two dozen addicts who were admitted in the two years ending December 31 1954 . . . The 'criminal' addict, i.e., the addict who is a confirmed criminal apart from his drug addiction, is virtually unknown in the United Kingdom.[42]

Similar conclusions are arrived at by Schur[43] and Wilkins,[44] and no evidence has since come to light to refute them, though, as already noted, one must bear in mind the relative ignorance concerning drug dependence until recent times.

The value of statistics in assessing the prevalence of addiction

Before trying to evaluate the official Home Office statistics and other estimates made by experts in the field, we need to consider in general terms why accurate figures about drug addiction are so hard to obtain.

The only official figures that we have are the Home Office annual record of persons known to be addicted to narcotic drugs specified formerly in the Dangerous Drugs Acts and now in the Misuse of Drugs Act 1971. This list is kept partly to fulfil the international obligation to make annual returns to the United Nations and also to provide an estimate of the size of the problem for domestic purposes. Previously its primary source consisted of routine inspections of retail pharmacies made by the police, who report regular and unusual supplies to the Home Office, whereupon further inquiries may be made by regional medical officers from the Ministry of Health to establish the legitimacy of supply. This information is supplemented by other police inquiries and voluntary reporting by hospitals, social workers and pharmacists. Now compulsory notification by doctors forms the basis of the figures.

It should be made quite clear that there has never been a system of registration with the Home Office. The constantly referred to 'registered addict' entitled to dangerous drugs on prescription is a mythical figure. The decision whether or not to prescribe was, until 1968, left to the individual practitioner, and though most doctors did in fact inform the Home Office there was no compulsion to do so. It was only in 1968 that a system for 'notification' to the Home Office was introduced[45] and that the supply of heroin and cocaine to addicts was restricted to licensed practitioners working in treatment centres.[46]

The Home Office figures relate only to those addicts known to have been taking drugs during the previous year, and exclude those in prison, abroad, permanently or temporarily cured and, of course, any obtaining their supplies illicitly. As Dr Bewley points out,[47] this means that three groups of users were not accounted for:

1 Addicts in the early stages who obtain all their drugs from addict friends or on the black market.
2 Permanent addicts obtaining drugs in the same way and not coming to the notice of the police.
3 Those who are temporarily removed from the register for the reasons given above.

Not only is it impossible to know the extent of illicit importing, but also the number of addicts who have obtained supplies as a result of over-prescribing. There is considerable evidence of over-prescribing by a few individual practitioners prior to the setting up of the treatment centres,[48] in part, at least, due to the practical difficulties which faced a busy general practitioner in trying to assess the correct prescription, or adjustment of dosage, for a given addict.

Two further factors must be borne in mind. First, as most addicts on the Home Office index have been addicted for about a year when first noted, the recorded totals have always been approximately a year behind the true figure. Also, the method of compiling the index was altered in 1945 (and again in 1969: See Appendix A Table 2). Prior to 1945, a name was only taken off the list if the person was not known to have taken prohibited drugs for ten years. After 1945, as we have seen, only those known to have taken drugs in the previous year were noted. In view of the very high relapse rate in addiction, it is unfortunate that the Brain Committee in 1961 did not allow for a number of names having been removed from the list.

Apart from these specific points, it is also necessary to recognise certain variables which are a general feature of criminological investigation, such as differential publicity, reporting, prosecution and even definition of 'addict', in short the kind of imponderables which make problems 'arise' in those areas where they are investigated. A striking example in the present context is the study of Rathod and de Alarcon on teenage heroin users in Crawley New Town, during 1966–67.[49]

By actively employing a wide range of sources of information – the probation service, the police, their own patients, a survey of hospital patients treated for jaundice, and a search of casualty department records of overdoses of hypnotic and stimulant drugs – they uncovered ninety-two cases of heroin users among boys aged 15–20 years, as compared with the eight cases reported to the Home Office by general practitioners. On the other hand, '. . . in the two years 1969–70 out of 95 deaths of addicts only 4 had not been previously known. So it appears reasonable to say that it is unlikely that a large pool of unknown opiate users exists at present.'[50]

The official estimates for opiates and cocaine are thus necessarily inadequate, though they do give a useful guide to general trends in the incidence of addiction.[51] Estimates for other drugs are a matter of speculation, though some pointers do exist. In the case of marijuana and amphetamines, the number of prosecutions and convictions, and quantities seized, as well as information from mental hospitals and prisons, are useful indications up to a point; as, in the case of barbiturates, are the number of deaths from overdoses and the number of admissions for poisoning and addiction, as well as general population surveys. It is by the use of such methods that Bewley produced his estimate of the incidence of drug misuse in the United Kingdom in 1966.[52]

An attempt to assess the significance of such statistical data as we have will be made in a later chapter,[53] when changes in the social patterns of addiction will be examined. But a cursory glance at the tables and figures in Appendix A will suffice to reveal certain clear trends, even granted the inadequacy of the figures. Thus the initially gradual increase in the number of known addicts in the mid-fifties followed by a sharp rise in the mid-sixties contrasts with the relative stability of the previous twenty years; and there has been a marked increase in the use of heroin, and, more recently, methadone. Perhaps most striking has been the alarming rise in the number of non-therapeutic addicts, together with a corresponding change in age distribution. (Appendix A Tables 2, 3 and 4.)

Post-war developments

The Second World War saw an increase in illicit trade, in particular as regards opium offences. Many of these were committed by seamen and did not constitute a serious or permanent problem. It was not until 1955 that a significant increase in non-therapeutic addiction began to emerge and even then its implications were not foreseen.

Indeed it is interesting that in the same year the Government's attempt to proscribe the use of heroin failed, largely due to the opposition of the medical profession. In America such a ban had been imposed as early as 1924, but here the Government's proposal was viewed as an unwarranted interference with the independence of the profession. It would seem that this was at least as important a consideration as the contention that heroin was medically irreplaceable.

That the Government ultimately had to give way over what became a minor political issue is a measure of the degree to which the drug problem has consistently been regarded as a matter primarily for decision by doctors. It may also reflect the lack of a serious drug addiction problem at the time, or at least of any grounds for believing that there was one.

Certainly the official position in 1955 gave no cause for alarm. The Home Office figure was only 335, and the Annual Report to the United Nations stated: 'The illicit trafficker is unknown, although some addicts may occasionally procure more than their own requirements in order to supply their friends.' [54]

As Lindesmith observes,[55] the fact that very few addicts were being sent to prison at this period – from 1952–55: 6, 16, 11, 11 respectively – is one reason for believing that few concealed addicts existed, since the need to maintain a supply would sooner or later make a prison sentence likely. However, two doctors to whom he spoke in 1955 estimated that, for every addict known to the authorities, there were ten unknown addicts. Despite the dismissal of these figures by Government officials and other doctors, they are a further indication of the uncertainty surrounding this issue.

It is now apparent that by the end of the 1950s, for a variety of reasons, the use of opiates and other drugs was reaching disturbing proportions, and the confidence expressed in the first Brain Report in 1961 was found to be misplaced. The Drugs (Prevention of Misuse) Act 1964 was passed to prevent the unauthorised possession and unlicensed importation of various substances, notably amphetamines, amphetamine compounds, and (as from August 1966) LSD and mescaline. The Act was primarily a response to the increasing attraction of 'pep' pills for teenagers, especially Drinamyl, but it was also aimed at curbing the irresponsible use of substances such as Dexedrine, which had been much used as an appetite suppressant.

There was however no control over manufacture or supply; nor were chemists required to keep records of prescriptions. In these circumstances, over-prescribing, forgery and theft from retail chemists and warehouses have been common,[56] though both manufacture and over-prescribing have recently diminished as a result of voluntary restraints.

Meanwhile, the Single Convention on Narcotic Drugs 1961 had codified the existing treaty law. It was implemented by the Dangerous Drugs Act 1965 which (together with the Dangerous Drugs Act 1967) controlled the opiates, their derivatives, cocaine and cannabis. Offences against the Acts were made punishable, on indictment, by a fine not exceeding £1,000 and/or ten years imprisonment.

In 1965, in its second report, the Brain Committee had to concede that it was dealing with a substantially new situation. The main recommendations of the first report had been to advocate institutional treatment of addicts – though not compulsory committal – and to reject (a) abrupt withdrawal treatment; (b) registration of addicts; (c) the establishment of medical tribunals to investigate circumstances in which a doctor's authority to possess and supply dangerous drugs might be withdrawn; and (d) any further statutory controls on prescribing.[57]

The Committee concluded,[58] *inter alia,* that there had been 'a disturbing rise in the incidence of addiction to heroin and cocaine, especially among young people, mainly as a result of "over-prescribing" . . . by a small number of doctors'; that 'all addicts to dangerous drugs should be notified to a central authority';[59] and that special treatment centres be set up, and that heroin and cocaine should only be prescribed to addicts[60] by doctors on the staff of these centres. The establishment of an advisory committee to keep under review the whole problem of drug addiction was also proposed.

Some of these recommendations have since been implemented. Thus notification of addicts was introduced in February 1968[61] and the first treatment centres established in April 1968.[62] The Advisory Committee on Dangerous Drugs was set up in the same year under the chairmanship of Sir Edward Wayne.

But the suggestion that compulsory *treatment* be introduced was expressly rejected.[63] Nor has the recommendation in the second report for compulsory detention of addicts who wish to discontinue treatment originally undertaken voluntarily been adopted. In a sense, however, both are already possible. Under the provisions of the Mental Health Act 1959 a given addict might be classified as suffering from 'psychopathic disorder', a notoriously vague category.[64]

However the Committee's main concern was the method of prescribing, and there is no doubt that opinion in the medical profession was divided by the early sixties as to what constituted good or desirable medical practice. There was evidence that addicts could obtain heroin and cocaine easily from certain doctors, who were prepared to prescribe increased doses, without the precaution of either obtaining a second opinion, as advocated both by the Rolleston Committee[65] and the first Brain Committee,[66] or inquiring whether the addict could remain stabilised on a non-progressive dose, let alone encouraging 'a prolonged attempt at cure'. It was in these circumstances that the special treatment centres were established.

In the last few years growing public anxiety has been reflected in increased police powers. Admittedly arrest without warrant on reasonable suspicion of possessing opiates was authorised by the 1920 Act, and several widely framed local 'stop and search' powers have existed for many years.[67] But in respect of drugs further points arise. First, as a consequence of the Criminal Law Act 1967, anyone believed 'with reasonable cause' to be 'about to commit' the offence of possessing cannabis (and, now that the 1971 Act is in force, most amphetamines) is liable to summary arrest, since a term of five years imprisonment is possible for these offences.[68] Also there is the controversial 'stop and search' power introduced in the Dangerous Drugs Act 1967,[69] which enables police to search persons without a warrant on reasonable suspicion of possessing any of the controlled drugs. This sensitive area was explored at length in the Deedes Report,[70] whose majority recommendation for retention has prevailed.[71]

It was against this background of mounting alarm and constant press coverage that two leading cases, *Warner* v. *Metropolitan Police Commissioner*[72] and the *cause célèbre* of *Sweet* v. *Parsley*[73] demonstrated the anomalies to which a strict liability approach can give rise. For it has not proved easy to find a formula which is appropriate for the large scale heroin trafficker without attaching a disproportionate degree of criminality to mere possession of less harmful drugs or to occupation of premises where they are found.

These two cases, as well as directly influencing certain provisions of the Misuse of Drugs Act 1971, are of fundamental importance in criminal law as a whole. Without some appreciation of their wider significance it is impossible to understand either the decisions themselves or judicial interpretation in drugs cases generally.

The central issue concerns the extent to which criminal liability may be imposed in the absence of fault. Common law crimes have almost invariably required proof of *mens rea,* that is, some element of intention, knowledge, or recklessness on the part of the accused in relation to the prohibited conduct. But in the case of crimes created by statute – such as drugs offences – the position is far from clear. Acts of Parliament do not state in terms whether or not *mens rea* is a constituent element of offences they create and the matter is left for judicial interpretation. Where the statute is silent or unclear on the point it is open to the courts in construing a particular provision to hold that the offence is one of strict liability.

One's instinctive reaction is to recoil from the notion that a person who is not blameworthy may ever be found guilty of a criminal offence. One would expect examples of it to be extremely rare and compelling. Unfortunately, no really consistent pattern has emerged, either as to the type of case that has attracted strict liability, or as to the criteria of interpretation and policy used to justify it.

Sometimes narrow points of construction have been decisive, such as the absence of the word 'knowingly' from the section of the Act, especially where it is present in other sections, or in comparable sections of similar previous Acts. Sometimes more attention is paid to broader policy issues such as the perceived social purpose of the statute and the practical difficulty or administrative inconvenience of proving fault in certain offences.

But once one enters the realm of policy, justifications are put forward for strict liability which differ strikingly from one another. On the one hand many, but by no means all, of the regulatory offences inescapable in a modern industrial society – for example the unintentional distribution of impure food and minor traffic offences – are treated as criminal on a strict liability basis as a matter of convenience. Here the principle is invoked as a means of automatic processing of conduct 'not criminal in any real sense', and not involving severe punishment or any pronounced stigma. On the other hand, there are cases in which the judges have stressed the need to protect the public from the social harm attaching to what seems to be a fairly arbitrary range of conduct, from dangerous driving to drugs and pollution.[74]

The lack of a consistent rationale has made the concept of strict liability peculiarly vulnerable to shifts in judicial attitude, even over comparatively short periods of time. Thus whereas in 1966 the Court of Appeal had held dangerous driving to be an offence of strict liability,[75] a mere five years later it overruled its previous decision and decided that fault has to be proved.[76]

In regard to drugs, a major reason for imposing strict liability in several cases in the 1960s – both for unlawful possession and for responsibility for premises where drugs were used – was the judicial view of drug taking as a grave social menace. The Lord Chief Justice, Lord Parker, made the point explicitly in *Yeandel* v. *Fisher:*

> . . . this statute is dealing with the very important matter, particularly today, of dangerous drugs. I certainly take judicial notice of the fact that drugs are a great danger today, and legislation has been tightening up the control of drugs in all its aspects.[77]

A few months later, in *Lockyer* v. *Gibb,*[78] he made it clear that he regarded the social danger as sufficient reason in itself for not requiring proof of fault. Judicial abhorrence of drug use of any kind is frequently forcefully expressed in the course of a summing up or on passing sentence,[79] and it was perhaps unfortunate that the first House of Lords case on an issue of general significance in the criminal law, which is so bound up with judicial perceptions of its aims and functions, should have been concerned with drugs. Lord Guest, for example, argued that to require *mens rea* would create 'a drug pedlar's charter'.[80]

At first sight it is surprising that whereas in *Warner,* as we shall see, the House of Lords (apart from Lord Reid) were prepared to accept a strong measure of strict liability, in *Sweet* v. *Parsley,* where application for leave to appeal to the Lords was delayed until after their decision in *Warner,* there was a spirited reassertion of the presumption in favour of *mens rea*! It is true that *Warner* concerned possession while *Sweet* v. *Parsley* was about the responsibility of an absentee landlady for premises where drugs were taken, and that the court justified its refusal to impose strict liability in *Sweet* v. *Parsley* by a narrow construction of the relevant section.[81] But it is only realistic to assume, as is implicit in Lord Reid's judgement, that the alarming implications of a finding of guilt for anyone responsible for premises used by others, and the publicity which attached to the original conviction of Miss Sweet, who lost her job as a teacher, had a marked influence on the court's approach.

It is difficult to see what is to be gained by imposing strict liability, with all that it may entail, in addition to the sentence itself, by way of stigma and adverse consequences on people who cannot be said to be criminals in the ordinary understanding of the word. It is admittedly plausible to argue that the need to protect the public in the face of grave social dangers should in certain areas of the law relieve the prosecution of the full burden of proving *mens rea.* But it is by no means clear either that all kinds of drugs cases present grave social dangers, or that strict liability is the only alternative to putting the entire burden of proof on the prosecution. Many of the cases have concerned possession of minute quantities of cannabis and it is only by virtue of a blanket condemnation of all drugs, or an unargued assertion of the dangers of escalation from 'soft' to 'hard' drugs, that such an approach could be justified on the basis of protecting the public.

The other matter is of more general application, and was discussed both in *Warner* and *Sweet* v. *Parsley.* We are not faced with an either/or situation as regards proof. It may sometimes be appropriate for the criminal law to place an evidential burden on the accused, such as the need to prove, or at least tender credible evidence of, honest and reasonable belief in the lawfulness of his conduct. A formula of this kind has found partial acceptance in the Misuse of Drugs Act 1971,[82] and has the merit of penalising the kind of behaviour which strict liability is said to deter, without having the same potential for working injustice.

The possession cases

The case law on possession provides an object lesson in how such injustice can arise. Notoriously elusive as a legal concept, and not suggestive of positive criminal conduct, 'possession' is hardly calculated to create any pronounced sense of guilt when, for example, it concerns a minute quantity of cannabis. It is strange, to say the least, that in an area where the question of the 'victimless crime' is in issue the accused has less protection than in a whole range of demonstrably more serious offences. Yet, as we shall see, the House of Lords decision in *Warner* had precisely that effect and, especially as interpreted in *R.* v. *Marriott,*[83] and later in *Searle* v. *Randolph,*[84] gave a very restricted meaning to the mental element required for possession in the dangerous drugs legislation.

In *Marriott,*[85] forensic analysis revealed 0·03 grains of cannabis resin adhering to the tip of the blade of the defendant's penknife. He was convicted of unlawful possession of cannabis resin,[86] following the judge's direction that, if he were knowingly in possession of the penknife, he was automatically in possession of the cannabis, even if unaware that there was foreign matter of any kind on the penknife. He successfully appealed, on the ground that the prosecution had to prove that he had reason to know at least that there was something foreign on the knife.

That the Court of Appeal rejected the trial judge's direction is not noteworthy in itself; what is of interest is its purported formulation of the relevant principle in *R.* v. *Warner*:

> . . . for the purposes of this present appeal, the result of *R.* v. *Warner* may, broadly speaking and we hope with accuracy, be stated in this way: If a man is in possession, for example, of a box and he knows there are articles *of some sort* inside it and it turns out that the contents comprise, for example, cannabis resin, it does not lie in his mouth to say: 'I did not know the contents included resin.' On the contrary, on those facts he must be regarded as in possession of it . . .[87]

Similarly, in considering whether knowledge of the existence of 'some foreign matter' on the blade could ground liability, the court, rather more cautiously, observed: 'Perhaps the law does go as far as that.' It is submitted that in *Warner,* Lord Reid, Lord Wilberforce and Lord Pearce did not 'go as far as that', whereas Lords Morris and Guest went further.

Warner differed from *Marriott* in being a 'package' or 'container' case. The accused claimed that he believed that a parcel in fact containing amphetamines contained scent.

Lord Reid (who dissented from the majority's strict liability approach) maintained that '. . . if *mens rea* has not been excluded, what would be required would be the knowledge of the accused that he had *prohibited drugs* in his possession.'[88] Even if the offence were strict, he continued, it would still be necessary to prove that the accused had 'in his possession' what were in fact prohibited drugs, and, if the case fell to be decided on this narrower ground, his lordship was content to accept the analysis of Lord Pearce and Lord Wilberforce on the relevant test for 'possession'.

In fact Lord Wilberforce did not formulate a definition, but indicated that he thought a descriptive approach more helpful. In essence his view was that control was strong evidence of possession, obliging the defendant to furnish an explanation. It is, however, clear, from his observations on the Canadian case of *Beaver* v. *The Queen,*[89] that he regarded honest belief that a package contained innocent substances as a defence. With perhaps unwarranted optimism, he also observed: 'I see no difficulty in making clear to the jury what is required in order to establish possession', adding, 'on this point I desire to associate myself with the observations of my noble and learned friend Lord Pearce.' [90]

In these circumstances it is unfortunate that Lord Pearce's approach is somewhat puzzling. In a key passage he says: 'I think that the term "possession" is satisfied by a knowledge only of the existence of the thing itself and not its qualities.' [91] Had he stopped there, it would have been possible to equate his position with that of the Court of Appeal in *Marriott.* But he continues:

> Though I reasonably believe the tablets which I possess to be aspirin, yet if they turn out to be heroin I am in possession of heroin tablets. This would be so I think even if I believed them to be sweets. *It would be otherwise if I believed them to be something of a wholly different nature.* [92]

And again, 'If the accused knew that the contents were drugs or were tablets, he was in possession of them though he was mistaken as to their qualities.' [93]

Leaving aside the question of whether sweets and heroin tablets can properly be said to be species of the same genus, it is quite clear that Lord Pearce envisaged liability only where the accused had some knowledge (or, as appears elsewhere in his judgement, constructive knowledge) of the 'kind of thing the contents were'. In short, whereas *Marriott* suggests that knowledge that a container has contents may suffice to ground liability, the view of Lord Pearce in *Warner* – effectively the majority view – is that knowledge of the kind of contents is necessary, however that may be delimited in a particular case.

Lord Morris maintained that the prosecution must prove possession by the defendant of something which was in fact a prohibited substance, but that even 'if he wrongly surmised that a box was empty which in fact had things in it, possession of the box . . . would involve possession of the content.' [94]

Lord Guest observed: 'For my part I can see no halfway house between the offence being absolute in the sense that mere possession of the container constitutes the offence and the offence only being constituted by knowledge in the full sense.' [95] He rejected the latter approach on the ground that it would lead to wide scale evasion of the Act. It is their views which the original direction in *Marriott* reflects.

Lord Guest's all or nothing stance has much to commend it in principle, but neither of his tests seems desirable in practice. Strict liability is particularly inappropriate for a possessional offence in an area where social stigma is so pronounced and the credibility of the law itself is in issue.[96] Yet proof that the accused knows that he has a substance which is a prohibited drug (and arguably this implies knowledge of its chemical constituents) is an unrealistic requirement, especially when illicit and lawfully obtainable tablets may closely resemble one another.

What is surely needed is a test which gives the defendant a meaningful opportunity of denying responsibility for the substance in question, and the emphasis would often be on surrounding circumstances rather than on the precise nature of particular tablets.

The recent case of *R.* v. *Irving*[97] illustrates the point. An amphetamine tablet was found in the accused's bottle of stomach pills. Amphetamines had been prescribed for his wife, who, he claimed, must have put one in the bottle by mistake when refilling it with stomach pills. He was convicted on the basis that if he was knowingly in possession of the bottle, he was *ipso facto* in possession of the contents. The Court of Appeal quashed the conviction, holding that he could not be in possession of a tablet 'slipped into' the bottle. But suppose that she had completely refilled the bottle with a prohibited drug similar in appearance to his stomach tablets? A test based purely on knowledge that he had tablets would have led to a different result.

For the purposes of the decision in *Marriott* the court had merely to extract from *Warner* a simple proposition: knowledge that a container has contents is a *necessary* prerequisite for liability. It unfortunately created the impression that it was also sufficient. Section 28 of the Misuse of Drugs Act 1971, whatever its other shortcomings as a formula, provides a more satisfactory test by making possession lawful where the accused can prove that he '. . . neither knew of nor suspected nor had reason to suspect the existence of some fact alleged by the prosecution which it is necessary for the prosecution to prove . . .' One such fact would be that the substance in question was a controlled drug.[98]

Thus, instead of liability hinging on questionable distinctions between kind and quality, or on the chance factor as to the contents of a package, the emphasis is placed squarely on the state of mind of the defendant. That some such formula is timely is further demonstrated by the Divisional Court's decision in *Searle* v. *Randolph.*[99]

In this case the court took the view that 'the law does go as far as' had been conjectured in *Marriott,* and does impose liability simply on the basis of knowledge that '*some* foreign matter' is in one's possession. A search of the defendant revealed thirty-six cigarette ends. One contained three milligrammes of cannabis and there were traces in two others. He was charged with unauthorised possession,[100] and initially acquitted on the ground that though he was aware that he had the cigarette ends, it had not been proved that he knew or ought to have known that they contained any foreign substance.

The prosecutor's appeal was allowed on the basis that the difference between a cigarette end composed of tobacco and one filled with a substance including cannabis was the same kind of distinction as that between an aspirin and a heroin tablet. It was therefore only necessary to prove that he possessed a cigarette end which contained a measurable quantity of cannabis. *Marriott* could be distinguished on the ground that there the accused was unaware of the foreign matter on the blade, whereas in *Searle* v. *Randolph* he knew that he had the cigarette end which was in fact the drug.

After this decision it is hard to see precisely what mental element was left in the concept of possession, before the 1971 Act came into operation, if a person who genuinely believed that he had an ordinary cigarette could be convicted of possession of cannabis. One comes back to the strange distinction between nature and quality made by Lord Pearce in *Warner,* strange partly because his particular examples seem in fact to relate to nature rather than quality.

Since the whole issue is concerned with the *legal status* of the substance in question, how can any rational distinction be drawn along the lines suggested by Lord Pearce? The obvious inference from his examples is that the primary criterion for liability is similarity of appearance to a controlled drug, such that the possessor is put on his guard. This would seemingly explain *Searle* v. *Randolph,* but is irrational in that it may have no bearing whatsoever on what he believed or even on what he ought to have suspected. Once it is conceded that he *believes* the substance is innocuous, there is no relevant distinction between, for example, cigarette ends and cigarette cards. The fact that many people are unaware of the physical appearance of even the commonest controlled drugs merely adds to the anomaly.

As Professor Smith points out,[101] we seem now to have erected a distinction between 'container' cases – where possession of the container is only *prima facie* evidence of possession of the contents – and other cases, where knowledge that one has a substance imports liability, subject only to the tenuous distinction made by Lord Pearce. If one may be permitted a note of scholasticism in an area which seems to thrive on it, is it not arguable that *Searle* v. *Randolph* is itself a 'container' case, in that a small quantity of cannabis, surrounded by tobacco, is enclosed in a cigarette paper? It is after all the defendant's knowledge as to the *contents* of the cigarette end which is strictly in issue.

Even though the above problem is resolved by the Misuse of Drugs Act 1971, such is the fluidity of the concept of possession that no statutory formula will cater for every contingency, as the recent case of *R.* v. *Buswell*[102] has shown. The defendant was given a prescription for seventy amphetamine tablets. He put them, or so he believed, in the pocket of his jeans, which his mother later washed. Consequently, he assumed that any unused tablets had dissolved, and he obtained a new prescription from his doctor. Ten months later he found the missing tablets while clearing out a bedroom drawer, and was subsequently prosecuted for unlawful possession,[103] when the police were searching the house in another connection.

He was convicted on three grounds: that the new prescription displaced the legal right to possession under the original one; that the period of treatment envisaged by the first prescription had long since passed, and that the original tablets had become abandoned property, so that his rediscovery amounted to a new possession, not founded on a prescription and therefore unlawful.

The first two grounds were summarily disposed of by the Court of Appeal. Indeed, had they not been, one wonders how many thousands of medicine cupboards containing the odd amphetamine tablet, left over from a long forgotten slimming course, or prescribed to relieve anxiety, would lay their owners open to the same charge. It is also interesting that neither of these two grounds was argued in *R.* v. *Ewens.*[104] In this case a bottle containing five Drinamyl tablets fell from the defendant's pocket while he was being examined by a doctor at a police station. His defence that the drugs 'came from some prescription from some doctor at some time'[105] failed only on the evidential point that he was unable to discharge the onus of proving this assertion which was a matter peculiarly within his own knowledge. Since only five tablets were left, it is a reasonable inference that the period of any supposed course of treatment would have been at an end.

As regards the third ground in *Buswell's* case – that the original tablets had been abandoned – one is again faced with the task of defining the mental element necessary for possession. In order to *acquire* possession there is ample evidence that one must be aware of the physical presence of what, in the event, is a proscribed drug.[106] But the law is naturally not so strict about the requisite mental element for *retention* of possession. Thus:

> There is no need to ask what is necessary to 'retain' possession, since once the plaintiff is held to have acquired possession, he continues to

> be entitled in law to the benefit of the possessory rule, until he 'loses' possession, for example when he abandons the chattel . . .[107]

Thus, in *Buswell,* the Court of Appeal decided that possession had not been lost as the original tablets in fact remained in his care and control throughout. It is submitted that this is the only reasonable conclusion when one considers the main criteria that have been used to indicate possession in both civil and criminal law.

To begin with, the defendant had control over the room in which the tablets were and presumably the intention to exclude others from it, as well as possession of the drawer [108] in which they were found. The law abhors a vacuum in possession [109] and the situation is not one in which anybody else is staking a claim. Where there is any element of doubt the law is reluctant to draw the conclusion that the loser of an article has abandoned it.

The only apparent ground for maintaining that he did abandon the tablets is his positive belief that they had been destroyed, on which he acted by asking for a new prescription. Yet the dictum that: 'If I put refuse in my dustbin outside my house I am not abandoning it . . .' [110] suggests that very cogent proof is needed. Above all, the context of medical treatment argues forcefully against possession having been lost. This becomes clear if, as Harris has suggested, [111] the judges will apply their concept of the purpose of a particular rule when other factors are evenly balanced. If someone, more especially an addict, as Buswell was, has been prescribed pills, possibly to be taken several times a day, what could be more natural on mislaying them than to ask immediately for a replacement? To construe such behaviour as abandonment, when it would be the obvious course to take even if one were not absolutely sure that the tablets had been lost, would be most odd.

It is submitted that the Court of Appeal reached an eminently practical solution, and it is somewhat surprising that leave to appeal to the House of Lords was given (though not ultimately exercised). It is already difficult enough to find persuasive arguments to justify possessory offences. People would be highly mystified to learn that they had become criminals when they were foolhardy enough to delve deep into their medicine cupboards.

Responsibility for premises where drugs are found has revealed similar difficulties. If Miss Sweet's conviction for 'being concerned in the management of . . . premises used' [112] for the purpose of smoking cannabis had been upheld by the House of Lords

> . . . hundreds of thousands of people who sub-let part of their

premises or took in lodgers or were concerned in the management of residential premises or institutions were daily incurring a risk of being convicted of a serious offence in circumstances in which they were in no way to blame.[113]

The simple explanation of section 5 (b), [114] as Lord Reid observed, is that it was copied from an identical provision in the Dangerous Drugs Act 1920 relating to opium. There, strict liability, comparable to that under the Licensing Acts, could be justified as a policy measure, to regulate an institutionalised activity taking place in 'opium dens'. The notion that Parliament consciously intended a similar result for cannabis is highly implausible. But the interpretation put on section 5 (b) by the House of Lords – that, for there to be liability, the 'purpose' in respect of smoking cannabis had to be that of the management, and not that of the user – is far from convincing, and the impression remains that the decision was reached 'in spite of the clear implications of the words of the Act'. [115] Under the new Act, the occupier or person concerned in management is liable only if it is proved that he permits such activities 'knowingly', so that negligence will not suffice.[116]

The Misuse of Drugs Act 1971[117]

Undoubtedly the new Act brings a fresh approach to bear on problems of control. Its main features are: an attempt to classify controlled drugs according to their 'relative harmfulness'; a distinction between offences of simple possession and possession with intent to supply; novel defences to reduce the element of strict liability, and more stringent sanctions against over-prescription.

The drugs are classified in three groups, [118] and penalties are related to the class of drug in question as well as to the type of offence. Broadly speaking, Class A – comprising those drugs deemed most harmful – consists of opiates, some hallucinogens (notably LSD), and injectable amphetamines; Class B includes various other amphetamines, and cannabis, and Class C contains 'pep pills' considered less dangerous. Flexibility and the means to deal speedily with urgent problems are ensured by provision for amendment of the lists by Order in Council, following recommendations from the newly established Advisory Council, which will keep the whole situation in the United Kingdom under review.

A new offence of being in possession 'with intent to supply' [119] is created, carrying a maximum sentence on indictment of fourteen years imprisonment and/or an unlimited fine in respect of Class A and Class B drugs (and five years and/or an unlimited fine for Class C). The maximum sentence for possession alone is reduced to seven years for Class A; five years for Class B (i.e. including cannabis), and two years for Class C.

To combat over-prescription, the Home Secretary may, if a tribunal so recommends, prohibit prescribing or supplying 'in an irresponsible manner', [120] subject to the practitioner's right to make representations which must be referred to an advisory body. In cases of urgency the Home Secretary may give temporary directions – initially operative for six weeks – provided a panel of three doctors considers that 'reasonable grounds' exist.[121]

The mechanics of control

The Government decided not to await the outcome of the agreement being worked out on similar lines by the United Nations Commission on Narcotic Drugs – the Convention on Psychotropic Substances 1971. Does domestic policy need to be closely linked, as it has been in the past, to the international structure?[122]

It is obvious that the international system of control has certain built-in limitations. Drug abuse is a volatile phenomenon, strongly influenced by national, cultural and social patterns. International procedure is inevitably slow, and the attempt to cater for countries with widely differing drug problems makes it difficult to deal adequately with their individual needs,[123] or changing attitudes towards given drugs.

Yet, despite these drawbacks, the regulation of production and of trafficking must initially be approached on an international basis. Scientific developments and modern methods of communication make it relatively simple to manufacture and smuggle many of the substances in question. The Convention on Psychotropic Substances emphasises this central need for co-operation by requesting parties to make serious offences extraditable, [124] and by requiring courts to take into account drug offences in other countries for sentencing purposes. Co-ordinated action against illegal drug traffic is also envisaged by the Common Market countries.

An interesting example of broad judicial interpretation, influenced by the international nature of trafficking, occurred in the *Director of Public Prosecutions* v. *Doot.* [125] Five Americans had made an agreement concluded in Belgium or Morocco to import cannabis resin into England for re-export to America. Their initial conviction for conspiracy was quashed by the Court of Appeal,[126] on the ground that, the essence of the offence being the agreement, the English Courts have no jurisdiction when that agreement is completed abroad. But the House of Lords reversed this decision, holding that there is jurisdiction if an agreement made abroad is subsequently performed, wholly or in part, in England. The conspiratorial agreement remains in being until terminated by performance or abandonment and the conspiracy is treated as a continuing offence.

To what extent is the new Act a satisfactory blueprint for future developments? No doubt some classification on the basis of 'relative harmfulness', however imperfect, is inevitable. Certainly the provision for speedy adjustment to the designated categories should prove helpful in counteracting new forms of abuse. However, initial classifications tend to become entrenched. Thus lighter penalties for possessing cannabis were previously resisted on the ground that any reduction would be interpreted as an official seal of approval.

The Explanatory Memorandum to the Bill did not indicate which criteria of 'harmfulness' were deemed most important in selecting and classifying the controlled drugs. Nor has this been clarified in parliamentary debate. What, for example, is the relative weight to be attached to social disapproval, capacity to induce dependence, and potential for inducing anti-social behaviour?[127]

Admittedly the task is far from easy, as is shown by the difficulties the courts continue to experience[128] in trying to define a 'noxious thing' for the purposes of the Offences against the Person Act 1861. A distinction has been drawn between a recognised 'poison' and other substances which, though harmless when taken in small quantities, may be noxious in large quantities. Thus in *R.* v. *Hennah,*[129] a small harmless dose of cantharides was held not to be a 'destructive or noxious thing', whereas in *R.* v. *Cramp*[130] half an ounce of oil of juniper, sufficient to act as a powerful stimulant and cause vomiting, was deemed dangerous for a pregnant woman, and a 'noxious thing' within the statute.[131] But it was also suggested that to administer a recognised 'poison' may be a statutory offence even if the quantity is too small to be harmful.[132]

Most recently, in *R.* v. *Weatherall,* two-thirds of a barbiturate tablet (Tuinal) added without the drinker's knowledge to a cup of tea, causing mild sedation and, possibly, slight shock, was held not to be noxious. (A normal dose would have been 1–3 capsules.)

What is instructive about these cases is the essentially emotive and unscientific difference of approach to 'poison' and to 'noxious things'. Granted that the Statute is fixed with the phrase 'poison or other noxious thing', there is still no logical reason for applying a nominalist approach to poison and a functional approach to noxious things. It is submitted that a functional approach is always to be preferred in categorising drugs. In this respect, the omission of the word 'dangerous' from the short title of the 1971 Act and its use of the term 'controlled drugs' are useful first steps.[133]

The absence of barbiturates from any of the categories has been strongly criticised.[134] Popularly believed to be harmless, they are still over-prescribed by some doctors; are currently being misused by a small number of multiple drug users, who inject them intravenously; can cause severe physical dependence; and, when taken with alcohol, may lead to death.[135] Admittedly it is difficult to control drugs which have well-established medical uses. Perhaps social acceptance of the sleeping pill has reached a point where – as with alcohol – greater restrictions are simply deemed impracticable; for about seven per cent of all National Health Service prescriptions are for barbiturates. But, though there is a strong case for notification and control of supply for the severely dependent and those who inject intravenously, a recommendation to this effect has not been implemented.

Hallucinogens such as LSD which are included in Class A do not produce physical dependence.[136] Fears that they could produce chromosome damage may have initially been exaggerated, but have not been entirely dispelled.[137] Undeniably LSD is a very potent drug, with unpredictable effects, capable of causing severe panic reactions and psychosis unless taken under strictly controlled conditions. Whilst it seems undesirable to associate LSD in the public mind with opiates, few would dispute the need for extreme caution in view of the possible dangers, as illustrated in *R.* v. *Lipman,*[138] now accentuated by the availability of the drug in tablet form.

The treatment of cannabis is somewhat perplexing. It is designated as a Class B drug and therefore possession carries a lighter maximum penalty than that for heroin, presumably acknowledging a distinction between 'hard' and 'soft' drugs. Yet the sanctions against occupiers of premises where it is smoked, and for possession with intent to supply, are the same as for heroin. The latter provision is particularly anomalous in a country where there is no large scale black market run by professional criminals, and the line between possessor and 'pusher' is not easy to draw.

Given this situation, as well as the absence of established norms for correct doses and the difficulties of proof involved, the Wootton Committee concluded[139] that a distinction between possession and possession with intent to supply was unworkable. It is suggested that if a possessory offence is to be retained further consideration should be given to the approach advocated by Michael Schofield in his Note of Reservation to the Report, [140] namely, the adoption of a scale of penalties varying according to the quantity in possession. Such a system operates in several American states and though it has its drawbacks – for example it has been interpreted as an invitation to distribute in small amounts – it has the merit of greater clarity; could help to achieve more consistency in sentencing policy in a field where it is conspicuously absent, and arguably act as a deterrent to large scale trafficking.

The increased maximum penalty for supplying heroin and the reduced penalty for possessing cannabis represent a more balanced scale of relative punishments. But only the wildly optimistic could imagine that such changes will have more than the most marginal effect on drug problems. They simply serve to highlight the inadequacy of orthodox methods of dealing with drug offences. Indeed, one of the chief impressions which emerges from the numerous parliamentary debates on the subject is a lack of confidence in the efficacy of legal controls.

A novel and controversial feature of the Act is the defence provided in section 28 to charges *inter alia* of possession and possession with intent to supply. The Law Commission, invited to devise an appropriate formula, adopted a solution mooted in the House of Lords in *Warner* and in *Sweet* v. *Parsley,* involving a shift in the onus of proof. It is now open to the accused to prove 'that he neither knew of nor suspected nor had reason to suspect' facts which the prosecution must establish, one such fact being that the substance in question is a controlled drug.[141]

Several questions arise. [142] How, in the absence of a special verdict, is the judge to know for sentencing purposes which of the three guilty states of mind has been established? Why is the section limited to certain categories of offences, namely production, supply and possession, the cultivation of cannabis and some opium offences? Should not the defence be available, for example, in cases of importation? Why does the section not apply to offences by occupiers, whose conduct, as is recognised in the penalties provided, would often be more blameworthy than that of someone in possession of a minute quantity of a controlled drug? Under section 8 the burden remains on the prosecution to prove that the occupier 'knowingly' permitted unlawful activities. Further, though it has been said that section 28 '. . . is not intended to catch a merely negligent person', [143] the phrase 'had reason to suspect' is open to just such an interpretation.[144]

When one tries to determine the rationale of control and the best means of effecting it, numerous difficulties are apparent. It is disingenuous and wholly unrealistic to adopt the attitude that if there were no drugs there would be no drug dependence. Equally it seems irresponsible to argue that heroin addiction is simply a slow form of suicide and as such not within the province of the law. Between these two extremes we have to try to establish what are the most effective points of control.

To prevent illicit manufacture is a virtually hopeless task, and quantities of opium far in excess of the world's medical needs continue to be produced. In the nature of things, new synthetics will emerge and private experimentation will continue. The enormously high profits of drug trafficking and the ease with which many of the substances can be smuggled and prepared are formidable obstacles to effective international control.

Control at the point of legitimate supply, however, is more feasible, and the most valuable feature of the new Act may prove to be its attempt to deal with over-prescription. Fears that the wide powers given to the Home Secretary constitute an unjustifiable infringement of the doctor's 'right to prescribe' can be discounted. Not only do the provisions have the approval of the British Medical Association, but the individual practitioner has adequate safeguards under the enacted procedure.

Nonetheless, the proper interpretation of 'irresponsible prescribing' may pose problems, [145] and above all a mechanical approach must be avoided. For if the 'grey' market is totally removed a black one will almost certainly take its place. Also, as became apparent when heroin was restricted to prescription at treatment centres, many addicts will rapidly move from one form of drug to another.

The extensive police powers of search and arrest are restated in sections 23 and 24. They are said to be justified by the present and potential scale of drug abuse, difficulties of detection, and the absence of aggrieved informants. But they have been under attack from several quarters, and in particular the right of search prior to arrest has been condemned as an undue encroachment on privacy and civil liberty, [146] responsible for much resentment of the police.

The Deedes Report clearly accepted the proposition that there is a distinction between detention for the purpose of search, and arrest, [147] and it is presumably intended in section 23 (2) (a). Whether this accurately represents the law is open to question, since the mechanics of search would seem to imply arrest. At all events, the police commonly believe that search prior to arrest is permissible on wider grounds than afterwards, though this is precisely what gives credibility to allegations of random and discriminatory searches.[148]

It is noteworthy that the Committee felt obliged to recommend that 'particular modes of dress or hair style should never by themselves or together constitute reasonable grounds to stop and search', [149] and that legislation ought to state explicitly that the test of reasonableness is objective. [150] Perhaps it is unrealistic to concentrate on the niceties and obscurities of powers of search, which inevitably reflect a continuous conflict between public policy and the rights of the individual. But it remains a cause for concern that the 'generation gap' should be enlarged by singling out drug abuse as an area of extensive police powers, especially as only the minor offender is likely to be caught in this way. The contrast with the more elaborate procedures of the 'breathalyser law' under the Road Traffic Act 1972 [151] and the extensive case law interpreting it is very much in point.

Notes

[1] See e.g. T. Bewley, 'Control of Drug Dependence', *The Medico-Legal Journal,* vol. 37, part 1, 1969, pp. 7–9, on the control of tobacco in the seventeenth century.

[2] The most recent being the Single Convention on Narcotic Drugs 1961, and the Convention on Psychotropic Substances 1971.

[3] J.R. Black, 'Advantages of substituting the morphia habit for the incurably alcoholic', *Cincinatti Lancet-Clinic,* vol. 22, 1889, pp. 537–41, in A. Lindesmith, *Addiction and Opiates,* Aldine Publishing Co. 1968, pp. 211–12.

[4] See A. Hayter, *Opium and the Romantic Imagination,* Faber and Faber 1969, ch. 1 and cf. Chein *op.cit.* pp. 353–55 and see pp. 114–17.

[5] E.W. Adams, *Drug Addiction,* Oxford University Press, London 1937, pp. 23–25.

[6] R. Goulding, 'The Statistics of Drug Addiction', *Medicine, Science and the Law,* vol. 8, no. 4, 1968, pp. 266–67.

[7] Goulding, ibid., p. 266.

[8] E.g., s. 22, 23, 24, 58, 59, and see p. 35–6.

[9] *The Times* 1 September 1972.

[10] J.M. Scott, *The White Poppy: a History of Opium,* Heinemann 1969, pp. 83–84.

[11] Ibid., p. 42.

[12] Ibid., p. 127.

[13] L. Eisenlohr, *International Narcotics Control,* Allen and Unwin, London 1934.

[14] J.M. Scott at p. 128.

[15] Ibid., pp. 129–30.

[16] Kwee Choo Ng, *The Chinese in London,* Oxford University Press 1968, p. 5.

[17] Estimates of Chinese population in England and Wales according to Census Reports were as follows: 1851 – 78; 1861 – 147; 1871 – 202; 1881 – 665; 1891 – 582; 1901 – 387; 1911 – 1,319. Ibid., p. 6.

[18] Ibid., p. 88.

[19] Sir Malcolm Delevingne, 'The international background to the dangerous drugs acts'. Ch. 6 of *Poisons Law* by H.N. Linstead, pp. 136–37.

[20] Stricter wartime controls were introduced in the Defence of the Realm Regulations 1916, No. 40B, (as amended) to halt the increased trafficking in cocaine in London, and the Defence of the Realm (Consolidated) Regulations 1917, which were primarily aimed at preventing the export to Japan of British-made morphia, which was then apparently smuggled into China.

[21] Dangerous Drugs Act 1920, s. 8(2).

[22] Dangerous Drugs Regulations 1921, No. 865, reg. 11.

[23] See p. 90.

[24] The Dangerous Drugs and Poison (Amendment) Act 1923, was passed to reduce the penalties for inadvertent breach of these regulations.

[25] Report of the Departmental Committee on Morphine and Heroin Addiction 1926, HMSO paras. 15, 16.

[26] Hereinafter referred to as the Rolleston Report.

[27] Rolleston Report, para. 51.

[28] Cf. The Duties of Doctors and Dentists under the Dangerous Drugs Act and Regulations, DD 101, 6th ed., London, 1956, para. 7: 'The authority granted to a doctor or dentist to possess and supply dangerous drugs is limited by the words "so far as may be necessary for the practice or exercise of his profession". In no circumstances may dangerous drugs be used for any other purpose than that of ministering to the strictly medical or dental needs of his patients. The continued supply of dangerous drugs to a patient solely for the gratification of addiction is not regarded as "medical need".'

[29] Rolleston Report, para. 52.

[30] Ibid., para. 53.

[31] Ibid., para. 27.

[32] See p. 90. The Harrison Act, because it was passed as a tax measure, was enforced by the Treasury Department, which was also the enforcement agency of the National Prohibition Act.

[33] Bewley, op.cit., p. 12. Cf. L. Wilkins: 'It may be fair to summarise

what has been called the "British System" as a lack of system.' 'Some sociologic factors in drug addiction control' in D.M. Wilner and G.G. Kassebaum (ed.), *Narcotics,* McGraw-Hill Inc., New York 1965.

[34] See p. 86.

[35] See Poisons Rules 1972 (as amended). See also Poisons Act 1972.

[36] The relevance of the Criminal Justice Act 1948, s. 4 and the Mental Health Act 1959, will be considered later, see p. 78–9.

[37] See Appendix A, Table 2.

[38] Drug Addiction, Report of the Interdepartmental Committee, 1961, HMSO, para. 67(1), and see paras. 24, 25 and 54.

[39] Rolleston Report, para. 23, and cf. para. 24.

[40] Report to the League of Nations by His Majesty's Government for 1935. Traffic in Opium and Other Dangerous Drugs. Quoted E.W. Adams, *Drug Addiction,* 1937, p. 37.

[41] Delevingne, op.cit., p. 144.

[42] John H. Walker, British delegate to the United Nations Narcotics Commission addressing a special committee of the Canadian Senate in May 1955. Reproduced in Daniel Subcommittee Hearings, part 5, p. 1862. Quoted A.R. Lindesmith, *The Addict and the Law,* Indiana University Press 1967, pp. 166–67.

[43] *Narcotic Addiction in Britain and America* 1962, p. 118.

[44] 'Some Sociologic Factors in Drug-Addiction Control', at p. 141.

[45] Dangerous Drugs (Notification of Addicts) Regulations 1968, No. 136 (see p. 147). See now, Misuse of Drugs (Notification of and Supply to Addicts) Regulations 1973. The term 'notification' was suggested by the Brain Committee in its Second Report in 1965, partly to avoid giving the impression implicit in 'registration' of entitlement to an approved quantity of drugs. See para. 18.

[46] Dangerous Drugs (Supply to Addicts) Regulations 1968, No. 416. Now repealed. See previous note.

[47] Recent Changes in the Pattern of Drug Abuse in the United Kingdom, *Bulletin on Narcotics* vol. 18, No. 4, 1966, p. 2.

[48] *Drug Addiction:* The Second Report of the Interdepartmental Committee, the second Brain Report, paras. 11, 12, HMSO 1965.

[49] Rathod and de Alarcon, *British Medical Journal,* vol. 2, 1968, p. 549. Quoted in Laurie, *Drugs,* pp. 131–133.

[50] 'Dangerous Drugs and the National Health Service', in News and Notes Supplement to the *British Journal of Psychiatry* June 1972, p. 8.

[51] E. May, after interviewing officials at the Home Office and the Department of Health and Social Security in 1970 noted that '. . . no one suggested that the number of "unknowns" is as large as the numbers

listed . . . The highest estimated for unreported opiate use was 25 per cent.' *Dealing with Drug Abuse,* A Report to the Ford Foundation, Macmillan 1972, pp. 385–86. And see Appendix A, Tables 2 and 3.

52 See Appendix A, Table 1.

53 See ch. 6.

54 *Summary of Annual Reports of Governments relating to Opium and other Narcotic Drugs, 1955.* United Nations Commission on Narcotic Drugs. Geneva. E/NR1955/Summary, p. 50.

55 A. Lindesmith, 'The British System of Narcotics Control', in *Law and Contemporary Problems,* vol. 22, 1957, p. 142.

56 See the Report of HM's Chief Inspector of Constabulary for the Year 1970, HMSO, p. 48.

57 First Brain Report, para. 67.

58 Second Brain Report, para. 43.

59 Ibid.

60 'Addict' is defined so as to exclude a person who requires a drug for the relief of organic disease. Ibid., para. 17.

61 See note 45. Also p. 147.

62 See note 46. Also pp. 91–5 for an account of these centres.

63 Cf. first Brain Report, para. 28, and Rolleston Report, para. 52.

64 Ss. 4, 26, 60. Cf. Criminal Justice Act 1948, s. 4. See ch. 4, especially pp. 78–80.

65 See paras. 79–85.

66 See para. 45.

67 The most notable being the Metropolitan Police Act 1839, s. 66.

68 I.e. an 'arrestable offence' s. 2(1) (5).

69 S. 6(1).

70 'Powers of Arrest and Search in Relation to Drug Offences', HMSO 1970.

71 Misuse of Drugs Act 1971, s. 23(2).

72 [1969] 2 A.C. 256. See also A.L. Goodhart, (1968) *Law Quarterly Review* vol. 84, p. 382.

73 [1970] A.C. 132.

74 *R.* v. *Ball and Loughlin* (1966), 50 Cr. App. Rep. 266; *Warner,* [1969] 2 A.C. 256 and *Alphacell Ltd.* v. *Woodward,* [1972] 2 All E.R. 475, respectively.

75 *Ball and Loughlin,* see above.

76 *R.* v. *Gosney* [1971] 2 Q.B. 674.

77 [1965] 3 All E.R. 158.

78 [1966] 2 All E.R. 653.

79 E.g., 'You all played with dirt. You dabbled in this ghastly, filthy

trade and you involved young girls whom you corrupted in order to carry this rubbish for you.' Lawson, J., on sentencing four men for smuggling cannabis resin. *The Times* 9 May 1973.

80 [1969] 2 A.C. at p. 301.

81 See pp. 32–3.

82 See p. 37.

83 [1971] 1 All E.R. 595 (C.A.).

84 [1972] Crim. L.R. 779.

85 This analysis substantially reproduces the author's casenote in 1971, 34 M.L.R. 585.

86 Contrary to the Dangerous Drugs (No. 2) Regulations 1964, reg. 3 and the Dangerous Drugs Act 1965, s. 13.

87 [1971] 1 All E.R. 595, 597. Italics supplied.

88 [1969] 2 A.C. 256, 279. Italics supplied.

89 [1957] S.C.R. 531.

90 [1969] 2 A.C. 256, 311.

91 Ibid., at p. 305.

92 Ibid. Italics supplied.

93 Ibid., at p. 307.

94 Ibid., at p. 290.

95 Ibid., at p. 300.

96 Edmund Davies L.J., in delivering the judgement of the court, referred to '. . . *the grave offence* of being in unlawful possession of the minute quantity of cannabis resin' (italics supplied). The quantity in question was the equivalent of 1/333 of a single cannabis cigarette.

97 [1970] Crim. L.R. 642.

98 S. 28(3) (b).

99 [1972] Crim. L.R. 779.

100 Contrary to the Dangerous Drugs Act 1965, s. 13.

101 [1972] Crim. L.R. 780.

102 [1972] 1 All E.R. 75.

103 Contrary to s. 1(1) of the Drugs (Prevention of Misuse) Act 1964, which provides that '. . . it shall not be lawful for a person to have in his possession a substance for the time being specified in the schedule to this Act [in this case amphetamines] unless (a) it is in his possession by virtue of the issue of a prescription by a duly qualified medical practitioner . . . for its administration by way of treatment to him . . .'

104 [1966] 2 All E.R. 470.

105 Ibid., p. 471.

106 See *R.* v. *Smith* [1966] *The Times* 17 August; *Lockyer* v. *Gibb* [1967] 2 Q.B. 243; *Warner* v. *Metropolitan Police Commissioner* [1969]

2 A.C. 256; *R.* v. *Irving* [1970] Crim. L.R. 642; *R.* v. *Marriott* [1971] Cr. App. R. 82; *Searle* v. *Randolph* [1972] Crim. L.R. 779.

107 D.R. Harris, 'The concept of possession in English Law', *Oxford Essays in Jurisprudence* (ed. A.G. Guest), ch. 4, p. 73.

108 Cf. the old larceny cases, e.g. *Cartwright* v. *Green* (1802) 8 Ves. 405; *Merry* v. *Green* (1841) 7 M. & W. 623.

109 Cf. *R.* v. *Buswell* [1972] 1 All E.R. 75 *per* Phillimore, L.J. at p. 78: 'Presumably it has not been in a state of limbo.'

110 *Williams* v. *Phillips* (1957), 41 Cr. App. R. 5, *per* Lord Goddard C.J. at p. 8.

111 Cf. note 107 above.

112 Dangerous Drugs Act 1965, s. 5(b).

113 *Sweet* v. *Parsley* [1970] A.C. 132, *per* Lord Reid, at p. 150.

114 'If a person . . . (b) is concerned in the management of any premises used for any such purpose as aforesaid; he shall be guilty of an offence against this Act.'

115 *The Times* (Leader), 1 August 1969.

116 S. 8(d). See also *R.* v. *Souter* [1971] 2 All E.R. 1151.

117 This account substantially reproduces extracts from the author's article on 'Drugs and the Law', 35 M.L.R. 225. See also R. Card, 'The Misuse of Drugs Act 1971', Crim. L.R. 1972, p. 744.

118 S. 2 and Sched. 2.

119 S. 5(3).

120 S. 13(2).

121 S. 15(1), (2), and Sched. 3.

122 For an interesting account of the relationship between the international control system and domestic legislation, see P. Bean, *The Social Control of Drugs.*

123 Still less with problems arising in particular parts of a country. S. 17 of the Misuse of Drugs Act 1971 empowers the Home Secretary to require a practitioner or pharmacist, practising in an area where there appears to be a social problem caused by extensive misuse of drugs, to furnish him with particulars of supply.

124 Art. 22(2) (b); cf. Misuse of Drugs Act 1971, s. 33: conspiracy to commit an offence against any enactment relating to controlled drugs is to be treated as an extraditable offence, within the Extradition Act 1870, Sched. 1.

125 [1973] 1 All E.R. 940.

126 [1972] 2 All E.R. 1046.

127 The long title of the Act refers to 'dangerous or otherwise harmful drugs'. In the Third Reading in the House of Lords, Lord Windlesham said

that the intention was 'to classify drugs according to their potential danger and the extent of their misuse.' H.L. Deb., vol. 316, no. 77, col. 1017.

128 See e.g. *R.* v. *Weatherall* [1968] Crim. L.R. 115 C.C.C.

129 [1877] 13 Cox C.C. 547.

130 (1880) 5 Q.B.D. 307.

131 Offences against the Persons Act 1861, s. 58.

132 *R.* v. *Cramp* (1880), 5 Q.B.D., 307, pp. 309–10.

133 Cf. the observation of Scrutton, L.J., on the alleged distinction in the law of tort between things dangerous *per se* and *sub modo:* 'Personally, I do not understand the difference between a thing dangerous in itself, as poison, and a thing not dangerous as a class, but by negligent construction dangerous as a particular thing. The latter, if anything, seems the more dangerous of the two; it is a wolf in sheep's clothing instead of an obvious wolf.' *Hodge & Sons* v. *Anglo-American Oil Co.* (1922) 12 Ll. L. Rep. 183, at 187.

134 In several of the Debates. See also the correspondence column of the *British Medical Journal* vol. 1, 1970, at p. 817. Statutory control is through the Poisons Rules formerly issued under the Pharmacy and Poisons Act 1933. See n. 35 *supra.* They may be sold only on prescription, but there is no offence of unlawful possession.

135 Barbiturates are second only to carbon monoxide as a cause of death from self-poisoning: 'On the State of the Public Health', DHSS 1970, HMSO. They account for approximately 2,000 deaths each year.

136 See *Non-Medical Uses of Drugs:* interim report of the Canadian Government's Commission of Inquiry, the Le Dain Commission, Penguin 1971, pp. 106, 170.

137 Ibid., pp. 104–05.

138 [1970] 1 Q.B. 152.

139 *Cannabis:* Report by the Advisory Committee on Drug Dependence. The Wootton Report, 1968, HMSO, para. 86.

140 Ibid. at pp. 36–7, paras. 5, 6. But see also H.C. Deb., vol. 798, no. 87, col. 1456.

141 See p. 29.

142 See [1970] Crim. L.R. 245–48.

143 The Solicitor-General, H.C. Deb., vol. 808, no. 53, col. 623, 10 December 1970.

144 But see *R.* v. *Hudson* [1966] 1 Q.B. 448, and [1972] Crim. L.R. 757–61.

145 The phrase is adequate to cover slimming-clinics which prescribe excessive quantities of amphetamines.

146 The minority view on the Deedes Committee. Cf. Lord Stonham: 'I

can say now that I well recall how astonished I was that this particular proposal excited so little opposition.' H.L. Deb. vol. 315, no. 55, col. 257.

[147] Para. 109.

[148] See p. 140.

[149] Para. 155 (V).

[150] Para. 155 (VI).

[151] Ss. 8, 9.

3 Causes of Dependence

Introduction

'. . . The question, "Why did you start using narcotics in the first place"? should never be asked. It is quite as irrelevant to treatment as it would be to ask a malarial patient why he went to a malarial area.'[1]

This trenchant observation of William Burroughs, while a valuable corrective to excessive concentration on causal aspects of drug dependence, is also an over-simplification. To reduce dependence to a purely medical issue, though an advance on the equation of addiction with criminality, is misleading if it is intended to suggest that it can be 'cured' as one might mend a broken leg, or even treat malaria. Precisely because we are talking about dependence, we are also talking about potential relapse, and the reasons for initial dependence and for relapse may both be closely related to underlying personality and/or social factors. Malaria is not strictly analogous to heroin addiction, for example, because relapse does not have a comparable psychological basis and can often be prevented by eradicating the parasite. Only if we have a clear picture of what produces dependence can we even begin to pronounce on how to alleviate, cure, or prevent it, whether compulsory measures and punishment are acceptable and, if so, for whom.

Another possible drawback of dispensing with the question 'why'? is that to do so draws a veil over issues of personal responsibility, which may need to be resolved for legal purposes. Thus the initial reason for taking drugs might be thought highly relevant to decisions in jurisdictions where it is an offence merely to *be* an addict,[2] and also arguably in offences of possession.

Certainly, as long as responsibility remains a central concept in the criminal law, the causes of dependence may vitally affect the question of sentence in drug related offences. There is clearly a case for distinguishing between the 'therapeutic' and 'non-therapeutic' addict as regards acts done under the influence of drugs, for purposes of mitigation. But it is not clear how far the distinction should be taken.[3] One must bear in mind that *continued* (as distinct from initial) dependence may arise from a combination of the original reasons and an acquired craving which can become such a powerful autonomous factor that the moral issue becomes blurred and also the criminal law loses all value as a deterrent.

It is obvious that people may become dependent on different (or even the same) drugs for diverse reasons, and that the search for some all-embracing explanation is doomed to failure. In fact 'cause' is a rather misleading and perhaps pretentious word to use, given that dependence may arise accidentally and often seems to be the chance manifestation of some deep seated personality disturbance, which could have just as easily revealed itself in other ways.

We may never be able to ascertain the 'causes' of dependence with any precision; indeed the unreliability of many addicts as a source of information poses an immediate problem as to what constitutes acceptable evidence. But even if the search for a unifying theory be futile, social changes in recent times, and such statistical information as we possess, do suggest some general trends and the possibility of constructing typologies that may prove operationally useful. What follows does not purport to be more than an impressionistic survey of the more deep rooted causes and precipitating factors leading to addiction.

Sources of dependence

Medical

One obvious classification of addicts, to be found in the Home Office statistics, is into those of therapeutic and of non-therapeutic origin. The term 'therapeutic addict' requires some clarification.

The Rolleston Committee defined 'addict' so as to exclude '. . . a person . . . requiring the continued use of a drug for the relief of the symptoms of organic disease . . .',[4] and this approach was followed by the second Brain Committee.[5] But in its first report the Brain Committee had distinguished between three groups of addicts:

> There are drug addicts who have been introduced to the practice when physically healthy with drugs procured by illicit means or in the course of their professional work . . . There are those who, having been given a drug of addiction as the appropriate treatment for a painful illness, continue to be dependent on it when the original necessity for its use has disappeared. And there is a third group of those who are unable to abandon a drug rightly or wrongly prescribed for some physical or mental ailment which itself persists. Opinions may well differ as to whether those in the last group should be regarded as addicts, except in a technical sense, and where the line should be drawn between addiction to a drug and its appropriate medical use.' [6]

It is difficult to see why those in the second group should not also be deemed 'therapeutic addicts', in so far as dependence has been initially caused by medical treatment. It is submitted that for legal purposes they should be treated as such, in all cases where craving has become autonomous.

Home Office figures for persons addicted as a result of medical treatment remained consistently around 300 for several years and were down to 207 for 1973.[7] A measure of opiate dependence is a calculated risk of legitimate medical treatment, sometimes, as with terminal cancer, being the lesser of two evils.

More serious, because less excusable medically, is the extent to which dependence has been caused by irresponsible prescribing of amphetamines and barbiturates. Medical opinion is becoming increasingly sceptical of the value of amphetamines except for certain rare conditions, and is more alive to the dangers of over-prescribing barbiturates, though the temptation is not always easy to resist, given their proved efficacy and in the context of an overworked National Health Service.[8]

Properties of the drug

A drug such as heroin if taken in sufficient quantities can cause dependence by virtue of its intrinsic properties, irrespective of the motivation of the user. It is therefore reasonable to assume that when the addictive quality of the drug itself is very marked, and especially if the subject is ignorant of this, personality and environment may be of minimal significance as compared with chance factors such as the availability of the drug.

Even when the user is intellectually aware of the potential danger, he may find it difficult to visualise himself in a condition where he cannot remain master of his fate. With heroin he may underestimate its potency; with barbiturates the shift from habituation to addiction may be imperceptible, and in the case of alcohol it is quite common for someone to be unaware that he is an alcoholic.

William Burroughs, one of the most articulate literary advocates of drug use, has no doubt as to the primacy of drug over personality in causing heroin addiction: 'There is no more a pre-addict personality than there is a pre-malarial personality . . . The whole addict personality can be summed up in one sentence: the addict needs junk . . . You see, junk is a personality . . .'[9]

This artistic insight may for many degenerate into a convenient rationalisation, a means of avoiding responsibility by assuming the role of martyr. But it serves as a reminder that, whatever the complexities that go to make up addiction in individual cases, the properties of the drug itself must never be overlooked.

Personality of the user

'As far as I can see, there is no solid evidence yet for the view that there is a recognisable personality which you can label beforehand as liable to turn to drug addiction. I believe it may be to a large extent a matter of chance.'[10]

One cannot quarrel with this more circumspect version of Burroughs' attitude, but it does not rule out the possibility that some common predisposing personality factors may exist, in respect of a given drug, in a given society, at a particular period of time. Here, for example, is an extract from a recent account of the 'typical' heroin addict:

> In Britain the heroin and cocaine addict . . . is most likely to be a male under the age of twenty-five. Males outnumber females in the ratio of 5 to 1 or 7 to 1, depending on the area . . . Many have a somewhat higher intelligence than the average, but their educational attainments and knowledge are well below standard for their intelligence. They tend to have either personality maladjustments or an emotionally disturbed family relationship background or both. The more poorly motivated to come off their drugs are usually emotionally shallow, self-centred and have a very low tolerance of frustration.[11]

Such characteristics however are equally common in other deviant groups. Also, as Stimson has shown,[12] heroin addicts do not fall into a single category. More specifically, in the case of the 'junkie', one is often struck by a marked exhibitionism, the flaunting of the 'junkie' image, reflected in the ritualism of 'fixing' and refusal to sterilise needles. But there comes a point when it is impossible to decide how far such behaviour is a secondary consequence of heroin use or a defiant acceptance of society's hostile labelling. Yet to speak of exhibitionism is merely to describe outward conduct. What is often seen simply as publicity seeking is frequently a desperate cry for help, a need to reduce oneself to a condition so pitiable that someone has to give assistance. In fact, because the pattern of disintegration commonly resulting from heroin addiction is often so much more drastic than with other forms of dependence, and notoriously so, it is interesting to speculate how far there are personality links with suicide.

In a sense, taking heroin may be a form of long drawn out suicide.[13] A kind of continuous suicide attempt in which you know you will have the dubious pleasure of surviving. Certainly there is evidence that drug addicts are particularly vulnerable to suicide. Stengel,[14] having cited alcohol and drug addiction as typical criteria of an impending suicidal act, adds: 'The relative frequency of drug addiction among doctors is probably one of the reasons why suicide is more common among them than in a comparable group of the general population.'[15] Attempted suicide is no longer a criminal offence.[16] Whether we should treat a life style which for practical purposes is a prolonged suicide attempt in the same way for legal purposes will be considered later.[17]

Junkies tend to congregate in self-contained groups, and constitute an identifiable subculture. Barbiturate use does not lend itself to such solidarity, and therefore no clear personality pattern is perceived. But, if one discounts the minority cult of injecting tablets, there is, perhaps, one 'typical' barbiturate addict. It is the woman in her late forties or fifties who has initially obtained the drugs on prescription, frequently because of difficulty in coping with the menopause. Loneliness, frustration, tension and insomnia would be common characteristics; a vicious circle may be established in which sedatives are taken to alleviate the strain of social contact, but increased inhibition, due to the drug, makes such (desired) contact even less likely.

Barbiturates are easily obtainable and the process of addiction is relatively slow, and difficult to observe. Consequently they have acquired a kind of respectability. You cannot really define yourself as a barbiturate addict in the way made possible by the ritualism of heroin abuse. In spite of this, it may not be fanciful to pursue the suicide analogy suggested above and see barbiturate addiction as a muted, subconscious death wish, akin to heroin abuse, if less dramatic.

The link between amphetamines and personality type is, on the available evidence, probably more tenuous still, especially since they are taken for such a wide range of reasons:

> There is . . . a sharp contradiction between observers as to the role of personality. Thus, whereas Durrant asserts that psychopathy, immaturity and personality defects, such as inadequacy and homosexuality, are consistently found to be a background of (amphetamine) addiction, Scott and Willcox, examining a large series of boys and girls admitted to a remand centre, found that there were no major differences in personal factors between those adolescents who were taking amphetamines and those who were not.[18]

A salutary caution also comes from the Advisory Committee on Drug Dependence:

In the present state of knowledge it appears to us that all generalisations about the personalities and histories of drug-takers, and the factors conducive to drug-taking, must be treated with considerable reserve. Most of the available evidence consists of unsystematic observations and subjective impressions of those drug-takers who happen to have come to the notice of doctors, social workers or the courts; while the few scientific surveys that have been undertaken have unavoidably been restricted in scope. Even within the limited sphere of those who take only, or mainly, amphetamines or amphetamine compounds, evidence derived from the fifteen-year old who makes a few experiments with purple hearts is not necessarily transferable to the youth who fortifies himself with pep pills before engaging on a criminal enterprise or sitting for an examination, to the lorry driver about to embark on a long-distance journey, the regular consumer of Drinamyl, or the habitual injector of methylamphetamine.[19]

With cannabis the picture is much the same:

Whether, or how far, particular features of personality conduce to the establishment of the cannabis habit is a highly contentious question, as much so as in the case of alcohol . . . The temperamental qualities most often cited as predisposing are anxiety, impulsiveness, shyness combined with a longing for social contacts, immaturity, emotional instability and various neurotic and psychopathic features. They are clearly unspecific.[20]

The effects of the drug are less predictable than in the case of those considered above, and in any case marked dependence is rare in England. Moreover, to stress personality factors in the abstract, as it were, is to ignore the role of learning to perceive the experience as pleasurable in ensuring continued use, as Becker has convincingly demonstrated.[21] In varying degrees this is also true of other drugs, of which alcohol is a familiar example.

Hallucinogenic drugs, in particular LSD, can be conveniently considered together with cannabis in this context, and the search for personality factors seems equally fruitless, partly because one cannot use the concept of dependence with any confidence. It is unusual for someone to wish to take LSD often, and in the rare cases where a psychological dependence is established, personality changes may be so drastic that, as with most drugs to a lesser extent, it becomes very difficult to disentangle predisposing factors from consequences of abuse.

It is often asserted that LSD use, like cannabis use, is particularly prevalent among students, intellectuals and entertainers in the world of pop music. Certainly both drugs are strongly associated with the 'hippy' movement and the idea of experimentation with a view to aesthetic and spiritual experience. But such generalisations are of very limited value. In the first place, they obscure the fact that use of these drugs is gradually spreading among the population at large. Secondly, it is doubtful if they tell us more about personality than about fashion and availability. In the course of the twentieth century cannabis has been popular among sailors and the criminal underworld in dockland areas, among jazz musicians in the Twenties and Thirties and, more recently, among West Indian immigrants. One can hardly expect to find a common personality thread in the midst of so much cultural diversity.

Social setting

> We are only at the very beginnings of our attempts to explain the causes of drug dependence, though perhaps we know enough to say that an affluent and highly competitive society produces strains and anxieties, dissatisfactions and unhappinesses which leads many people to look for an avenue of release other than the traditional ones of alcohol and tobacco.[22]

Society's image of addiction, and social attitudes towards drug taking, are themselves significant pointers as to who actually become addicts. Thus social disapproval encourages someone who is predisposed or inclined to reject conventional values to fit into the very category to which society has assigned him. Contrasting reactions towards alcohol and other drugs provide a case in point.

> Perhaps because most people can identify with the alcoholic more readily than the drug taker, perhaps because they can *understand* it more readily than drug taking, perhaps because alcohol is so traditional a 'prop' in our society, perhaps because as an industry it employs thousands of people and has evolved one institution – the pub – with which the vast majority of the population are familiar, alcoholism is seen as an illness, an unfortunate condition, a fate best avoided. But it has lost the nineteenth century overtones of moral degradation and despair. This aura has passed to the drug addict.[23]

On one level, then, addiction can be seen as an expression of protest by the alienated. But when one considers the extent to which our society is itself committed to drugs of one form or another, this becomes a gross over-simplification. The above contrast between alcohol and other drugs is merely the most obvious example. There are probably as many people dependent on placebos as there are heroin addicts. In 1946, Jellinek found that 52 per cent of a tested group were satisfied by the placebo effects of dummy aspirin tablets.[24] Indeed, social attitudes towards aspirin provide a most instructive starting point for an understanding of how far drug taking in general is a natural feature of modern western social life:

> Aspirin has no hypnotic action and therefore is valueless for treatment of insomnia alone, and it is definitely contra-indicated for the treatment of any symptoms arising from the stomach. . . . In spite of this 7·8–14 per cent of the symptoms for which aspirin was self-administered were in this group.[25]

Professor Wilson concludes that

> abuse of aspirin, and the subsequent dependence on aspirin which may develop from it, are characterised by a psychic dependence originating from the culture pattern which accepts tablet taking as a fact of modern society. Indeed the fact that members of the family, cultural and work groups of the individuals in whom aspirin dependence has been described, took aspirin, was advanced as a justifiable reason for these patients to start taking aspirin themselves. Such reasoning clearly indicates the relationship between the development of drug dependence and the occurrence of drug abuse in society, between the pharmacodynamic actions which can be produced by a drug on an individual when it is consumed in unnecessary quantities and the persuasive effect of widespread advertising on a gullible society of actual and potential drug users.[26]

The point is further illustrated by our complacent acceptance of excessive prescribing. Thus a recent survey in Hartlepool of 500 homes[27] revealed 43,000 unwanted drugs, of which 16,000 acted on the brain and nervous system. Sir Derrick Dunlop commented: 'It is probable that approximately two and a half million tablets or capsules were available in that town, which if it is representative of Britain would represent one and a quarter billion unwanted items in the United Kingdom, at a basic National Health Service cost of about £6,600,000.'[28]

Our readiness to accept drugs as a standard form of treatment for numerous illnesses is obviously due in large measure to their actual efficacy. How far this is accounted for by the drug's constituents must in many cases be conjectural, as experiments with placebos indicate. Given the high incidence of psychosomatic illness,[29] it is clear that expectation of cure is often of prime importance. It may well be that the excellent results achieved in the 1930s with antibiotics such as penicillin aroused expectations of 'cure' through drugs in general, which have not proved fully justified.

Certainly the public's ever-increasing knowledge about drugs and their effects has helped to promote their use. Whether the influence of the mass media in this respect has been creditable is highly questionable. Up to a point one can discern a simple economic model in which supply and demand for a given drug are functions of the information available about them.

The commercial basis of advertising pharmaceutical products has long been a matter of controversy, and its dangers increase as techniques of persuasion become more sophisticated. The marketing of Drinamyl ('purple hearts') – discredited as a long term appetite suppressant and regarded with increasing scepticism generally – affords an interesting example.

Thus Dr Dale Beckett:[30]

> The principle of advertising is that you find an image, say sex or the purple heart. . . . When the purple heart image was being sold it was pushed very hard, and we completely failed to get a view of the advertising information which was sent to the firm before they put this image out.

And Dr Connell:[31]

> The attractiveness and the way in which a medication is presented is an important aspect of drug-taking, and this applies to therapeutic levels, and to addict or dependency levels. The Press have suggested that this is a mystique factor when discussing the so-called heart-shaped (really triangular) Drinamyl tablet which was later discontinued and replaced with a round blue tablet of the same colour.

In fact, an investigation of Drinamyl dependent patients,[32] using the triangular blue tablet and an equivalent white round tablet, showed that some patients were formulation dependent, that is, significantly influenced by the shape and colour of the tablet. It should be noted that it is not only patients who are susceptible. 'It seems to me astonishing', commented Dr Goulding,[33] 'that the purveying of very effective and dangerous drugs to a learned profession should have to take the form of persuasive, dramatic and glamorous advertising . . . The advertisers would not indulge in this if it did not work.'

The plain fact is that the pharmaceutical industry is now such a powerful economic force that it is unrealistic to expect the impact of its advertising to diminish. Commercial competition and scientific advances have led to an enormous increase in the number of drugs on the market, and impressionability is unlikely to be materially reduced.

In addition to the effects of direct advertising on drug taking habits, one must consider the indirect influence of the mass media by way of sensationalist accounts, condemnatory or otherwise, which glamorise drugs and may foster, or at least reinforce, a desire to experiment and to emulate.

We have no hard data on the relationship between the incidence of drug dependence and sensationalist accounts in the press, films or television. Much controversy exists over the degree of influence which pop stars may exert over young people because of press and television coverage of their opinions, though it is impossible to say whether or not drug abuse has increased because of a surfeit of publicity. [34] But it seems reasonable to suppose that the kind of link exists which has been found in several studies of imitative crime and violence – namely, that a predisposition towards some kind of deviant behaviour may take the form of drug abuse, as a response to a recently publicised incident.

Equally difficult to evaluate is the influence of the 'folk rock' music of the mid-sixties with its oblique reference to drugs and its musical effects designed to heighten psychedelic experience, as well as the role at the time of the 'underground' press in propagating drug use. [35] In both media drug advocacy has since become more restrained.

On a more general level still, the effect of modern communications on the quality of people's lives and the demands of a technological society provide strong, not necessarily consciously understood, pressures towards drug taking. Keniston, an American psychiatrist, has described these pressures in American society as 'stimulus flooding and psychological numbing', [36] which lead to drug taking either in order to conform ('instant efficiency') or to 'drop out' ('instant rest').

> Thus, to survive with calm and intactness in the modern world, we all require an armor, a protective shell, a screen, a capacity to 'close off', ignore, or deny our attention to the many stimuli of our physical and social world. Such numbing is necessary and useful for most of us, most of the time.

Keniston observes that it is very easy for this numbness to lead to a deadening of response, which, especially in the case of students (the context of his paper), highlights the gap between social pressure for cognitive professional competence on the one hand and the private search for meaning on the other.

> . . . the feeling and fear of psychological numbing leads to a pursuit, even a cult, of experience for its own sake. And the use and abuse of psychoactive drugs by students is closely related to these two themes in student values.[37]

The changed socio-economic status of youth

One feature of the relative affluence of post-war Britain has been the increasing significance of the young as an economic and social force. In 1959 the Home Office index did not record a single heroin addict under the age of twenty. In 1968 the figure was 709. The Drugs (Prevention of Misuse) Act 1964 was, as we have seen,[38] primarily a response to amphetamine abuse by young people gathering in coffee bars, dance halls and clubs. There is ample evidence, revealed almost daily in press reports, that use of prohibited drugs is now mainly confined to the young, in striking contrast to the situation well into the 1950s, when therapeutic addicts over fifty years of age comprised the vast majority (some 85 per cent), and about 10 per cent of the rest were occupational addicts.

This emergence of the young as an economic and social force is surely a vital aspect of the whole subject. The changing nature of the 'drug scene' parallels the trends in popular music, by providing a new means of self-awareness and a realisation of influence which has reached international proportions, while at the same time opening up another field in which a teenage market can be exploited and manipulated.

As Michael Schofield argues:[39]

> . . . In the past, young people were most influenced by adult groups in close proximity – his family, his neighbours, his workmates and so on. Now the most influential factor is a separate teenage mythology which is countrywide and even international.

Whereas in the past youth's social defiance has taken forms which the older generation could come to terms with – modes of dress, attitudes towards sex, language, music, political activity – '. . . drug-taking is an altogether different matter which the rest of society has found far more deeply bewildering and disturbing.'[40] It is not an activity which (except in the case of alcohol) parents could ever visualise indulging in themselves.

Drug taking then has become one of several ways of expressing generational conflict. Because of the particular abhorrence with which it is conventionally viewed, it is an ideal symbol of alienation. Young people may manifest this 'outsider' role by taking drugs for much the same reasons as they may become juvenile delinquents: the sense of danger and challenge, a search for identity, group activity analogous to the psychology of the gang, a means of expressing freedom from parental domination or parental indifference – drug taking is for many a fashionable form of social deviance.

The immediate environment

Granted that many young people will turn to drugs as a means of challenging accepted social values, are there any features of their immediate environment which may partially account for, or reinforce, such behaviour?

Family background

As regards family history, the broken home pattern, associated with numerous forms of social deviance, also emerges from several studies, mainly American, on drugs. Gerard and Kornetsky (1954),[41] investigating thirty-two male opiate addicts under twenty-one years of age, found that in 41 per cent of cases, death of a parent, divorce or separation had taken place before the subject was ten years old, and that 60 per cent of the fathers played a minimal role or were actively punitive. Chein (1964)[42] confirmed previous American research[43] to the effect that very many heroin addicts in large cities come from slum areas where the family lacks solidarity, consistent affection and care.

The absence of a warm relationship with a father figure with whom a boy could identify has been a very common feature of these studies. Chein noted this, as more recently did Fort (1967).[44]

There is relatively little English research, but fairly general agreement that poor family relationships are a significant factor in drug taking. A study by the Addiction Research Unit (1968) ('Heroin Use in a Provincial Town') found that in nine out of thirty-five cases the parents of heroin users were either divorced or separated or not both alive. Linken[45] found that of twenty-seven cases of university students who, since 1958, have sought advice for emotional difficulties in which drug taking (mostly cannabis) formed a part, 48 per cent had suffered parental loss in some form.

It is true that Scott and Willcox (1965)[46] in their study of fifteen year olds in a remand home found little to differentiate amphetamine users from non-users. But, first, it is not being suggested that the findings above are specific to drug users, and, secondly, they did note that the more dependent users had grossly unfavourable home backgrounds.

However, the dangers of complacently accepting the common assumption that broken homes are more likely to produce addicts can be seen from Dr Wiener's findings in *Drugs and Schoolchildren.*[47] Having investigated (in 1968) over one thousand subjects aged from fourteen to nineteen, from schools in the London area, he found no significant differences as regards parental separation, size of family or degree of family privacy between the drug users and the controls. Further, though the drug users felt that their parents were more lenient, they did not feel less close to their fathers than the controls.

The occupational addict

Members of the medical and related professions are particularly at risk, partly because drugs are so readily available to them, and, in some cases, because of predisposing factors. Similarly, 'those whose work brings them into contact with alcohol have the highest rates for alcoholism and the alcoholic diseases. Publicans and barmen, waiters and others in the catering trade, brewers and distillers, coopers and draymen all have high rates.'[48]

The Home Office figures show a disproportionately high incidence among medical personnel relative to the total number of addicts:

	1954	1959	1964	1966	1968	1969	1970	1971	1972	1973
Total number of addicts	317	454	753	1349	2782	2881	2661	2769	2944	3025
Medical and allied professions	72	68	58	54	43	43	38	44	33	29

It is however noticeable that the actual number has decreased very gradually, despite the sharp general rise in addiction. Naturally it is impossible to say how accurate these figures are, since such persons, being more susceptible to social stigma than the general population and at the same time better able to conceal their drug taking, do not always come to light.

At all events, such evidence as we have suggests that occupation in itself is a rather limited indicator of dependence. Hewetson and Ollendorf (1964), in a preliminary survey of 100 London heroin and cocaine addicts,[49] listed 12 jazz musicians, 12 casual labourers, 6 prostitutes, 4 seamen, 3 postgraduates, 2 industrial chemists, 2 nurses and 59 semi-skilled workers, with no particular trade predominating. The experience of the treatment centres suggests an equally wide range of social background:

> The addicts in the clinics are as fair a cross-section of people as you might find in a London bus – skinheads to architects. An antique dealer, a garage mechanic, a shop assistant and an art student were one doctor's patients one afternoon last week.[50]

The medical adviser

Over-prescription was undoubtedly a serious source of heroin addiction before the establishment of the treatment centres. The second Brain Committee concluded that 'the major source of supply has been the activity of a very few doctors who have prescribed excessively for addicts'[51] and that 'not more than six doctors have prescribed these very large amounts of dangerous drugs for individual patients. . . .'[52]

The present system, limiting the prescription of heroin and cocaine to 'maintenance doses' at treatment centres, has only partially solved this problem. Since it is not pharmacologically possible to estimate accurately the correct dose, and there are not many doctors experienced in the field anyway, some over-prescription persists.

But even to limit prescription, in the face of demand, creates new difficulties. Multiple drug use is common, so that confining heroin to the centres has 'caused' an increase in the injecting of other substances – in particular methedrine, and more recently barbiturates. New methadone addicts have appeared, since this drug is used by most centres to wean patients off heroin, and is also still available on ordinary prescription.

Potentially the most serious threat implicit in the new approach is the danger that it will create a large scale black market. The price of illicit heroin has shot up from £1 a grain before the centres began to as much as £20, and conditions are ripe for organised distribution in Britain by the Mafia.[53]

Finally we may note again that irresponsible prescription of barbiturates and amphetamines has led to much dependence in the past, but that the medical profession is now far more alive to the dangers.

Reference groups

A survey on 2,500 juvenile delinquents at a remand centre near London[54] revealed that nearly one-third had taken drugs illicitly and that most of these had begun to experiment with them when they were about fifteen and a half years old. It also seems that contacts made at school, in the street and at places of entertainment were more instrumental than family background in prompting addiction. What then is the role of peer groups in precipitating addiction?

Nowadays, an adolescent's most influential reference group is far more likely than in the past to be that of his peers rather than his elders. The desire to identify with, and be accepted by, a group is obviously a strongly felt need for most young people, and if the group in question takes drugs then the newcomer will be impelled to do likewise. Not only is it a means of finding acceptance, it may even be a prerequisite of membership. For in the case of drug taking in general, the group must take precautions against the exposure of its illicit activities, and in particular with cannabis the act of smoking is normally a communal activity, where non-participation may provoke hostility and tension.

Wiener[55] discovered three main patterns in the leisure activity of his drug users as compared with the controls: more time was spent in mixed peer group company; they saw themselves as more disobedient, had less respect for property and were more impulsive; they knew more drug takers, had more favourable attitudes towards drugs and knew more about them. 'All three patterns tend to indicate that factors in the subjects' immediate environment play a very important part in determining drug use.'[56]

The initial contact

In examining the way in which drugs come on to the market, it is necessary to distinguish between the situation in America, where there is a highly sophisticated hierarchical distribution structure – the importer, the kilo-connection, the connection, the weight dealer, the street dealer and the pusher[57] – operated by criminal organisations, and the as yet much looser system of supply in England. Since heroin is illegal in America, there is a thriving black market which turns the addict into a 'status criminal'. One recent estimate suggests an average daily cost of about thirty dollars a day to support the habit.

The following extracts from an article[58] on heroin abuse in some American schools give an indication of the extent of the problem:

> Many teachers are afraid of addicts and terrified of pushers: 'You don't tangle with a suspected pusher – it's dangerously big business.'

> For many child addicts the best way of supporting their habit is to come into school as a pusher . . . Besides the school's regular students who may push drugs in the lavatories, parking lots and corridors, inner city schools are plagued with outsiders, often drop outs from other schools who come in sometimes merely for warmth and to see their friends, but often these days to deal in drugs.

Certainly there has been little evidence to suggest the presence of large scale organised drug rings in Britain. In 1969, Laurie maintained[59] that

> . . . so far no real black market with a criminal organisation importing and distributing drugs exists in Britain. The Mafia, via their representatives in the Channel Islands, have made one or two tentative attempts to sound the market . . . As long as addicts are able, without too much difficulty, to get nearly as much heroin as they need, no solid opening for a black market can exist.

As we have seen, the restriction of heroin prescription to treatment centres with the consequent huge increase in the price of illicit heroin may easily alter the situation. Predictions of Mafia control can no longer be dismissed as fantasy, now that its activities are being hampered by the American authorities, and there are growing signs of infiltration of British gaming clubs, which could prove to be the financial base for control of the drug market.

As yet, then, the 'pusher' is less significant and menacing in England than has sometimes been asserted. The term is anyway misleadingly emotive in so far as it is applied to the addict who sells his surplus to maintain his own supply. In this sense, all addicts are 'pushers' or potential 'pushers', but without necessarily implying random distribution of drugs, or a regular practice of trying to initiate the unsuspecting.[60] There has naturally always been a ready market among those addicts who have shunned legal prescription as a symbol of being 'really hooked', and are afraid of being marked for life by this contact with officialdom, a fear which the present system seems unlikely to dispel.

On the other hand, the non-addict 'pusher', the small time criminal who obtains his supplies from criminal gangs, is a recognised figure in the criminal underworld,[61] and the indications are that his role will become increasingly significant. Nor does he necessarily limit himself to opiates:

> First contact with amphetamines is frequently made in the following manner. Young people coming into London from unemployment areas, especially Scotland and Ireland, in search of work and accommodation find that neither are as easy to find as had been

> assumed. After these people have started work it will be two weeks before they get paid; their landlords want two weeks' rent in advance; rents are far higher than had been anticipated; many finding neither work nor accommodation, are caught in a vicious circle whereby they cannot find employment because they have no accommodation, and cannot find accommodation because they have no employment; without a fixed address they cannot obtain National Assistance. They know little or nothing of social work agencies and become desperate because they do not know where to turn for help. They 'sleep rough' in parks until the weather gets too cold; they sleep in derelict houses until the police chase them out and they end up in seedy and delinquent all-night cafes and clubs from where they get turned out if they fall asleep. They therefore become easy game for the 'pusher' and the dealer in black market amphetamines and other pep pills who come up to a sleepy kid and ask him if he wants something to keep him awake, cheer him up, give him a lift.[62]

However, one must be wary of the 'pusher at the gates of every school' explanation of drug initiation, for several reasons. To begin with it encourages irresponsible press reporting.[63] More importantly, to cast the small time dealer as the central villain of the piece is an all too convenient illustration of the scapegoat principle. In so far as there is a black market it exaggerates his importance, while *his* suppliers are kept in the background, and at the same time it serves to relieve the community at large from a sense of social responsibility.

In any event, to concentrate exclusively on the exploitation of the innocent is to ignore the extent to which drug taking arises in circumstances of mutual trust and may constitute an accepted social pattern. An obvious example is the increasing use of cannabis. It is also interesting to compare with the form of initiation just cited another social worker's description of a pattern of drug taking not uncommon in the more colourless provincial towns of England:[64]

> In contrast to the self-styled beats, these boys do not consider themselves to be rebels, though they do seem to regard themselves as a group apart – 'sharper' in all respects than those denied membership. Drugs are as much a part of the culture of this group as their mode of dress and the music they prefer. Yet the great majority of them use drugs only at the weekend, or perhaps once during the week when they go to a discothèque or a party. They are almost all pillheads – i.e. they use drugs in pill form . . . .
>
> . . . 'Terry' began his flirtation with drugs in much the same way as

> his contemporaries. He began as a weekend junkie, simply using the pills as a means of enabling him to keep awake all night on Saturday and listen to the music . . . .

It would seem that once one is accepted within the charmed circle of drug takers, it is possible to obtain practically any preparation, from cannabis to heroin, within a few hours. In such circumstances, one is

> constantly at risk through being in contact with the drug scene. Also it is clear, that, while under the influence of the pills, the sense of responsibility and proportion tends to become blurred and the temptation to experiment, in a congenial setting, becomes great. . . . The real tragedy is that the youngster can pass from being a weekend junkie to being a full time one so imperceptibly that not even he is aware of the transition.'

It is not however suggested that the transition is arbitrary:

> As a youth worker, I have met, and dealt with, a large number of young people who have taken drugs in the 'social' way I describe. Yet only a very small percentage of these have been led into more serious involvement. These were all boys with problems in relation to their environment or in coming to terms with their own personal situation. Perhaps they would once have run the risk of becoming alcoholics. Now they run the risk of becoming drug addicts.

An aspect of technological society

It is not easy to be a drug addict on the village green. It becomes easier in an urban and more anonymous area. It is easiest of all in the total anonymity of central London, where the proliferation of addicts in Piccadilly Circus, some beyond all hope of rehabilitation, testifies to a population expansion and weakness of social structure such that needs are not catered for and the individual's activities go unheeded.

At a time when increasing attention is being paid to the evils of pollution, it should not be overlooked that drug dependence can be viewed as a pollution model, as a spill out of modern technology. The ever-expanding pharmaceutical industry has supplied us with a volume and variety of drugs which would have seemed inconceivable fifty years ago, a symbol of the stresses and 'side effects' of life in a technological age.

We have already referred to Keniston's theory of 'stimulus flooding and psychological numbing' which, in crude terms, lead some to 'drop out' with tranquilisers and others to try to compete with stimulants. In different ways both reactions support the observation that 'drugs can be a spurious way to fill the gap between aspiration and capacity.'[65] The drift into 'retreatism' and addiction by young people unable to take advantage of the opportunities seemingly open to them, described by Cloward and Ohlin,[66] is relevant in this context. In a world where Man's survival is precarious, yet at the same time potential material achievements seem limitless, the 'non-achievers' are more susceptible to the attractions of drugs.

It would however be an incomplete and unduly negative interpretation to suggest that the stresses of a technological society fostered drug taking solely because of an inability to adapt to its demands. The growth of automation, and predictions of 'enforced' leisure; the decline of traditional religion, and the failure of the scientific age to provide alternative human values; the processes of dehumanisation and depersonalisation which seem inextricably bound up with scientific and medical progress, have all contributed to a questioning – in some cases a rejection – of material values.

Drug taking as a reaction against materialism, as part of a spiritual quest, may at present only be a minority pursuit, as typified for example by the 'hippies'. But the vision of Huxley as long ago as 1932, in *Brave New World,* in which it became an integral social activity, should not be discounted. On the contrary, precisely because the obvious dangers of drug addiction rightly evoke strong feelings, it becomes important to examine the constructive possibilities of drug use – which may or may not lead to dependence – in a society which seems likely, for whatever reasons, to foster such use.

Recognition of the deeper implications of drug use can be found in the Canadian Interim Report of the Commission of Inquiry into the Non-Medical Use of Drugs (the *Le Dain Report*):

> By cause we understand not merely the immediate, direct motivations for a particular drug experience, but the larger social significance of the phenomenon – how it relates to various aspects of life today – family relations, education, work, institutions, and conditions of life generally. In what ways is it a response to the problems of modern living? What are its philosophical or spiritual implications? What does it say about our value structure? How does it reflect the way people think about the future?[67]

And again:

> . . . there is no doubt that a search for self-knowledge and self-integration and for spiritual meanings are strong motivations

with many. We have been profoundly impressed by the natural and unaffected manner in which drug users have responded to the question of religious significance . . . It may be an exaggeration to say that we are witnessing the manifestations of a genuine religious revival, but there does appear to be a definite revival of interest in the religious or spiritual attitude towards life.[68]

Availability and the element of chance

In the constant search for causes it is all too easy to neglect the mundane chance factor. This does not necessarily imply that dependence is entirely fortuitous, but rather that if drug taking is frequently merely one way among many of meeting adversity, it follows that when unfortunate personal circumstances and the availability of a drug happen to coincide, dependence may result with the minimum of positive motivation.

In the television documentary 'Gale is Dead', widely acclaimed for its sensitive, dispassionate portrayal of the life of a drug addict, Gale described how on the day of her release from Holloway she was provided with thirty shillings, a room in a hostel, and a job to begin that evening as a petrol pump attendant. Some friends at the hostel, former fellow inmates at Holloway, persuaded her to go with them to Piccadilly, instead of going to work on her first day out of prison. There they gave her heroin. . . .

These facts are not untypical. The Borstal boy, just released, who has heard others discussing drugs is similarly vulnerable. Indeed, sheer ignorance as to the possibility of addiction in general, and of the kind or strength of drug taken, is a ground for considerable concern.

Thus, 'Chinese' heroin (believed to come mainly from Hong Kong) which consists of heroin adulterated with substances such as caffeine or talcum powder, ranges in strength from 40–70 per cent, as compared with the pure drugs available at the treatment centres. The user, therefore, literally does not know what he is taking, and may in any event be totally ignorant of what would be a safe dose for someone with his tolerance level.

Allied to the availability of drugs as a causal factor is the 'contagion' aspect. Alarcon has shown that among 58 heroin users in Crawley New Town, aged 15–20 years old, 48 were initiated by other Crawley youths, and that in one route of transmission, 32 users could be traced to the original initiator.[69] In the same way, it has been shown[70] that the influx of Canadian and American heroin addicts in the late fifties and early sixties – to avoid harsher laws – partially explains the increase in Home

Office figures at that time. But it is unlikely that their presence had more than a short term effect.

The drug traffic

One-third of the cases dealt with by Interpol now concern drugs. Modern methods of communication allow for flourishing international drug rings and individual smuggling on a scale inconceivable in previous generations. The narcotics processing laboratories in the Marseilles area, once the major source of heroin for America, are notorious, and agents from the American Bureau of Narcotics have conducted intensive investigations there for several years, with the net effect of shifting the main centre of operations to Rio de Janeiro. America has also brought considerable economic pressure on source countries such as Turkey and Mexico.[71]

Britain's 1970 report on narcotics to the Interpol General Assembly indicated that the two most significant developments in drug traffic here have been the organised smuggling of cannabis and the appearance of 'Chinese' heroin. In 1967 there was only one conviction in England for possession of 'Chinese' heroin. In 1968, the year that prescription of heroin was first restricted to treatment centres, there were thirty-five. In 1973 customs officials seized more than nine tons of cannabis valued at over £8 million and more than 20 million amphetamine tablets. In particular there has been a big increase in the smuggling of liquid cannabis, which is far more potent than the resin.

Detection of drugs poses immense problems – LSD, for example, has been passed in the gum of postage stamps and envelopes – and with the growing number of illicit laboratories and synthetic drugs the traffic seems likely to grow larger still. Moreover, the increased popularity of foreign travel, including holidays to countries such as Turkey and Morocco, has been responsible for an increase in individual smuggling. Reinforced by the cultural diversity resulting from immigration, travel has presumably both encouraged the circulation of drugs and a questioning of a system of values which regards alcohol as acceptable and other drugs as taboo.

The role of the law

In his introduction to *Narcotics, Delinquency and Social Policy* Chein writes (in the context of drug addiction in America):

> We saw the law as setting the framework of the problem, but we did not start with any suspicion that the law might be in any way contributing to the existence of the problem . . . It did not occur to

us at the time to question the fundamental premise of the commonsense view, namely, that the motivation of such actions exists independently of the risk and of the conditions that make these actions risky. It did not occur to us to ask how much drug-taking behaviour would not take place were it not for the challenge of the risk; the attractiveness of the forbidden; the glamour of defying authority . . . and the inducements to drug use motivated by vast profits made possible by the very effectiveness of the law enforcement agencies and the operation of the economic law of supply and demand.[72]

In England, the law does not designate the addict as a 'status criminal', nor is there the possibility of profits on a comparable scale. On the other hand, illegality must intensify curiosity and account for much of the glamour attaching to certain drugs. Further, by implicitly attaching stigma to addiction and 'standing for' opposition to drug taking, the law can increase the latent alienation or exhibitionism of some addicts and serve as a focus for hostility.

This hostility towards legal authority is inevitably reinforced by the mechanics of legal control. Search and arrest procedures are necessarily sensitive matters, but peculiarly so in the case of drugs, since the ease of concealment entails stringent regulations, and the conventional image of the drug user opens the way to charges of discriminatory practices.[73]

At a more specific level, by classifying both heroin and cannabis as 'dangerous drugs' (only partially rectified by the Misuse of Drugs Act 1971) the law has made it more likely that they will be obtainable from the same source, and may marginally influence the person who, having taken cannabis without ill effects, is tempted to imagine that heroin is not dangerous. (The view that there is frequently a 'progression' from cannabis use to heroin addiction will be considered in a later chapter.)[74]

What would have happened in America if the 'British System' had been applied is a matter of pure speculation. Legal methods of control probably reinforce the identity of the addict far more than they create it. The law, and police practice in enforcing it, cannot in themselves 'cause' dependence; but they can be instrumental in establishing and fortifying a subcultural milieu of protest.

Conclusions

In its Final Report, the Le Dain Commission observed that 'We cannot begin to think and act effectively in the field of prevention unless we can come to some consensus about motivation and other related factors which influence the cause of non-medical drug use.'[75] We seem, then, to be faced with the dilemma that it is necessary to establish causes in order to decide on policies, but that the 'causes' which have been discovered are not specific to drug use.

If one reverts to the point that drugs are initially taken for pleasure or to relieve pain, or simply from curiosity when they are available, this should occasion no surprise. One would expect a proportion of initially casual users to drift into continued use almost imperceptibly, seeking continued pleasure or relief from pain. It is partly because drug dependence is now perceived as one of our specific social problems that we tend to expect it to have well-defined specific causes, in some way differentiated from the causes of other forms of behaviour. But if one thinks of the notion of dependence in its widest connotations there are no grounds for such an assumption. We seldom trouble to ask why people become 'addicted' to dangerous sports such as mountaineering, or adopt dangerous life styles, and when we do the conventional answer is that they are responding to a challenge in what is felt to be a legitimate, even natural, way.

In this respect, the thesis which Weil puts forward in *The Natural Mind*[76] is of considerable interest. He argues that the desire to alter consciousness periodically is an innate, normal drive, observable from early infancy in the pleasure derived from whirling and becoming dizzy. In this light, illegal drug use is merely one means of continuing a natural developmental sequence, so that to search for specific causes of it as indicating deviant behaviour would be misguided from the outset.

What does seem to emerge from the bewildering diversity of 'causes' suggested above is that a great deal of drug dependence strongly reflects desires and pressures of which the individual subject to them is often only dimly aware. The question 'How, or why, did you become an addict?' suggests a conscious motivation which may simply not exist.

To acknowledge that there is a strong element of drift into drug use is not to deny that a proportion of drug users have serious problems for which society must try to find the answers. Nor does it imply that inquiry into causes is fruitless. First, it surely suggests that criminal sanctions are less appropriate to drug *use* than has been thought in the past, both because the deterrent value of the law is less apparent when the behaviour it seeks to prevent lacks conscious motivation and because the moral justification for imposing penalties is weaker. Secondly, in so far as the drift to drugs is a function of availability, it points to the need for strong measures of control to limit that availability. This implies strict legal controls over illicit supply, as well as restraint in the advertising and production of certain substances.

The fact that indicators of drug dependence are non-specific merely means that we must concentrate our efforts, as the Le Dain Commission points out, on providing the social alternatives to drugs which will enable those who are vulnerable to serious forms of dependence to cope with the low self-esteem, boredom and stress which they experience, and counteract any inclination to try to solve such problems by a resort to irresponsible drug use.

Notes

[1] D. Odier, *The Job: Interview with William Burroughs,* Jonathan Cape 1970, p. 152.

[2] E.g., in several American states, such as Oklahoma which imposes a mandatory sentence of not less than 90 days for a first offence. But the Supreme Court has held a California Statute, which makes it a misdemeanour to 'be addicted to the use of narcotics' unconstitutional: *Robinson* v. *California* 370 U.S. 660 (1962).

[3] In *R.* v. *Lipman, The Times* 11 October 1968, Milmo, J., in passing sentence, is reported as saying: 'You did this when you had deliberately taken a dangerous drug [LSD] promoting hallucination *in order to give you pleasure.'* (Italics supplied.)

[4] P. 9, para. 21.

[5] P. 7, para. 17.

[6] P. 11, para. 36.

[7] See Appendix A, Tables 2 and 3.

[8] Department of Health and Social Security Report No. 124, (1970), pp. 3–4 (amphetamines), p. 18 (barbiturates).

[9] *The Job,* op.cit., pp. 148–9.

[10] Professor W. Paton, 'Drug Dependence', *The Listener* 14 November 1968, p. 643.

[11] N. Imlah, *Drugs in Modern Society,* Geoffrey Chapman Ltd. 1970, p. 94.

[12] G. Stimson, *Heroin and Behaviour,* Irish University Press 1973, where he distinguishes four types: 'Junkies', 'stables', 'two-worlders' and 'loners'.

[13] See Menninger, *Man against Himself,* Harcourt, Brace, New York 1938.

[14] E. Stengel, *Suicide and Attempted Suicide,* Penguin 1964.

[15] Ibid., p. 52.

[16] Suicide Act 1961.

[17] See pp. 107–19

[18] Dept. of Health & Social Security, Reports on Public Health and Medical Subjects, No. 124, HMSO 1970, p. 7.

[19] DHSS, The Amphetamines and Lysergic Acid Diethylamide (LSD), Report by the Advisory Committee on Drug Dependence, HMSO 1970, pp. 12–13, para. 33.

[20] DHSS No. 124 (see n. 18), pp. 37–38.

[21] H. Becker, 'Becoming a Marihuana User', *American Journal of Sociology* vol. 59, 1953; reprinted in *Outsiders,* Free Press 1963.

[22] D. Downes, 'Drug takers and the community', in *Behind the Drug Scene,* British Medical Association 1970, p. 24.

[23] Ibid., p. 22.

[24] See *Adolescent Drug Dependence,* ed. C.W.M. Wilson, p. 153.

[25] Based on NOP survey on Home Medication, Aspro-Nicholas Products, 1965, quoted Wilson, p. 152, and see pp. 105.

[26] Ibid., pp. 153–4.

[27] Quoted Imlah, p. 118.

[28] Ibid.

[29] See *Medicine and Society: the changing demands for medical care,* OHE 1972.

[30] Quoted Wilson, pp. 278–79.

[31] Ibid., p. 270.

[32] Wilson and Beacon [1964], Wilson, p. 271.

[33] Ibid., p. 279.

[34] In *R.* v. *Jagger* [1967] 51 Cr. App. R. 473, at 476, Lord Parker C.J., referring to the responsibilities of a pop star, said that it was '. . . only natural that those responsibilities will carry a higher penalty.'

[35] In *Calder (John) Publications Ltd.* v. *Powell* [1965] 1 Q.B. 509, it was held that *Cain's Book* might properly be found obscene because it '. . . highlighted, as it were, the favourable effects of drug-taking, and, so far from condemning it, advocated it, and that there was a real danger that those into whose hands the book came might be tempted at any rate to experiment with drugs and get the favourable sensations highlighted by the book.'

It is interesting that French Law has made it a specific offence to portray drugs in a favourable light: Loi n. 70–1320 du 31 décembre 1970, art. 630. In common law jurisdictions, the general offence of counselling might be invoked, as was the case in Canada when an 'underground' paper was convicted of encouraging the cultivation of marijuana: *R.* v. *McLeod & Georgia Straight Publishing Ltd.*, 12 C.R.N.S. 193 (B.C.C.A.).

[36] K. Keniston, 'Drug use and student values', in *Drug Awareness*, Avon Books 1970, p. 115.

[37] Ibid., p. 119.

[38] Cf. p. 22.

[39] *Behind the Drug Scene*, Family Doctor Publications, British Medical Association, London 1969, p. 5.

[40] Ibid., p. 6.

[41] Psychiatric Quarterly vol. 29, 1955, pp. 458–86, quoted Wilson, pp. 426–27.

[42] *Narcotics, Delinquency and Social Policy.*

[43] E.g. Drake and Cayton [1945], Spinely [1953], quoted Wilson, p. 428.

[44] 'Heroin addiction among young men', in O'Donnell and Ball, *Narcotic Addiction*, New York 1966

[45] Quoted Wilson, p. 162.

[46] 'Delinquency and Amphetamines', *British Journal of Addiction* vol. 61, no. 1/2, 1965, pp. 9–27.

[47] Longman 1970, pp. 116–18.

[48] N. Kessel and H. Walton, *Alcoholism*, Penguin 1969, p. 72.

[49] *British Journal of Addiction* vol. 60, 1964, p. 110.

[50] V. Brittain, 'How the Drug Clinics Work', *The Times* 18 August 1970.

[51] P. 6, para. 11.

[52] Ibid., para. 12.

[53] See p. 62.

[54] R. Cockett, *Drug Abuse and Personality in Young Offenders*, Butterworths 1971.

[55] *Drugs and Schoolchildren*, pp. 157–58.

[56] Ibid., p. 159.

[57] See *Dealing with Drug Abuse:* A Report to the Ford Foundation, Macmillan 1972, Staff Paper 4: 'The Economics of Heroin', p. 290.

[58] V. Brittain, *The Times* 13 March 1970: 'Teenage heroin epidemic that has alarmed U.S.'.

[59] *Drugs*, Penguin Books 1968, p. 158.

[60] Selling to maintain one's supply was found to be the chief incentive in a study of 22 drug 'pushers' in the United Kingdom, by MacSweeney and Parr, *Nature*, 31 October, vol. 228, 1970, p. 422, quoted, *The Times* 31 October 1970.

[61] See S. O'Callaghan, *Drug Addiction in Britain*, Robert Hale & Co. 1970, ch. 8.

[62] Wilson, p. 500, Mrs. J. Piepe, a social worker.

[63] A much-publicised allegation in 1969 that an ice-cream vendor was selling drugs to children outside a local school was subsequently found to be false.

[64] S. Yeger, 'Weekend Junkies', *New Society* 19 February 1970.

[65] Dr Rakoff: submission to the Canadian Commission of Inquiry into the Non-Medical Use of Drugs, Interim Report, p. 162.

[66] *Delinquency and Opportunity: a Theory of Delinquent Gangs,* Free Press, 1960. See also D. Matza, *Delinquency and Drift,* J. Wiley 1964.

[67] Ch. 4, 'Some causes of non-medical drug use', p. 153 para. 137.

[68] Ibid., p. 157, para. 329. See pp. 130–3.

[69] Paper to Royal Medico-Psychological Association, quoted *The Times* 7 May 1969.

[70] Lady Frankau, 'Treatment in England of Canadian Patients Addicted to Narcotic Drugs', *The Canadian Medical Association Journal*, vol. 90, no. 6, 8 February 1964, pp. 421–24, quoted, Lindesmith, p. 184.

[71] *The Sunday Times* 27 September 1970. See also pp. 127–8.

[72] Pp. 6–7.

[73] See pp. 38–9.

[74] See pp. 164–8.

[75] At p. 32.

[76] A. Weil, *The Natural Mind,* Jonathan Cape 1973.

4 Sanctions and Treatment

Any suggestions as to the best methods of dealing with addicts reflect certain assumptions about the dependent condition itself. The equation of addiction and criminality has strongly influenced American policies, especially on opiates, whereas the British approach owes much to the belief that an addict is primarily someone in need of treatment.

Broadly speaking, there are three basic ways in which a society can classify addiction. It can label it as criminal and meriting punishment; as an illness, either in its own right, or as symptomatic of some underlying disturbance, in which case treatment with a view to cure or maintenance is indicated; or simply as the expression of an alternative life style, to be tolerated, perhaps disapproved of, but not seen as necessitating any formal societal reaction.

To label the addict a criminal and punish him *for* his addiction is rather like singling out one section of the community and making it subject to strict liability.[1] This is not to say that compulsory measures for addicts are in all circumstances necessarily unacceptable, but merely that an exclusively punitive approach is even more negative in their case than for conventional criminal categories. The justification of a deterrent function is unmaintainable, and criminal behaviour is fostered, as the American experience shows, by this identification with criminal subcultures, reinforced there by the need to resort to theft to support a drug habit.

To equate addiction with illness facilitates a more progressive and humane approach. But, at the same time, under a humanitarian guise, inflexible measures are possible, which are more insidiously punitive, because constitutional safeguards seem superfluous and the régime is often taken for granted.[2]

To label someone as ill is to imply that he needs treatment and that we should try to cure him. As noted earlier, to speak of addiction as an illness is misleading if it fosters the belief that the medical condition can be treated and a cure effected without reference to social factors. Further, it perpetuates a conveniently artificial division between addicts and 'normal' members of society, and discounts the possibility that the notion of cure as applied to conventional illnesses may be inappropriate to the addict's needs and society's reasonable expectations of him.

An example of the orthodox English view can be found in the very first paragraph of a recent Home Office report on rehabilitation:[3]

> The aim of rehabilitation *must* be to re-educate the individual to live without drugs and to assume or resume a normal social life. All concerned with the problem of drug addiction *must* therefore have this purpose clearly in mind from the time when the addict first comes into contact with any of the services, statutory or otherwise, which operate in this field.

However laudable the motives, this is surely an unduly restrictive approach, which stems from the belief that the addict belongs to a clearly defined group, wholly separate from society at large. Even if it is valid to argue that the severely dependent young heroin addict belongs to a distinct and recognisable subculture, it is still legitimate to ask whether we should think of (and treat) him primarily as someone apart, or rather as someone who represents in an extreme form the need for dependence of all members of society. It is suggested that the latter view accords more with the reality of how many people become addicts, and is likely to prove more operationally fruitful. Discarding the stereotype is a first step towards acknowledging the need for individualised treatment.

It should be stressed that no attempt is being made here to minimise the very real clinical difficulties involved in the treatment of addicts, or to deny that on a very concrete level drug dependence poses a medical problem. But it is not solely a medical issue; nor, for that matter, one which is susceptible of a uniformly approved medical approach, even in the case of a particular drug, such as heroin.

The history of methadone maintenance in the treatment of heroin addiction affords a simple illustration of the failure to disentangle the medical from the social and moral aspects of drug control. The violent opposition which it initially aroused in America – in particular the narcotic blockade treatment of Dole and Nyswander[4] – seems to have been based on an emotive objection to a form of treatment which involved the continued administration of drugs and the substitution of one, albeit lesser, type of dependence for another, as much as on purely medical considerations.

Criticism on these lines has come from widely differing sources. Not only has the World Health Organisation adopted a cautious attitude, partly for this reason,[5] but '. . . some black militants are opposed to methadone maintenance because they regard it as a device to keep the black community "drugged and enslaved".' [6]

There are, of course, legitimate arguments for caution in advocating the use of methadone, such as the danger of its indiscriminate prescription fostering a primary methadone dependence problem in the illicit market. But the fact remains that the nature of the opposition to methadone use has in the past been moralistic and contrasts sharply with the conclusions of a well-researched modern American investigation:

> . . . its essential efficacy is as well-established as anything in this field can be. It is now generally acknowledged that methadone is medically safe, acceptable to many heroin addicts, and effective and administratively feasible for large scale programmes.[7]

The relative success of Dole and Nyswander has done much to make it more acceptable and there are now over 200 methadone clinics in the United States. As of December 1971, the Food and Drug Agency estimated that 40,000 to 50,000 Americans were on methadone maintenance. Prolonged low dosage substitution (though not high dosage blockade) is now the standard treatment for heroin addicts at the new British centres.

Moreover, the long history of drug use suggests that solutions aimed at the total abandonment of drugs of dependence are probably unrealisable and would have disastrous social consequences. A report by the Le Dain Commission observes that in the treatment of opiate dependence '. . . a significant majority of those who achieve permanent abstinence develop a substitute dependence of some kind, such as alcoholism, excessive eating or dependence on a therapeutic community.'[8] Beyond some generally agreed minimum level of medical treatment, we may discover that to perceive drug taking as part of a life style to be accommodated within the existing social structure is the most appropriate, practical and convenient attitude – 'solving' the drug 'problem' by achieving a different social perspective on drugs.

These general observations must be qualified. To begin with, punishment and treatment are not at all points mutually exclusive, nor can any single reaction to drug use be deemed uniquely appropriate without full consideration of the type of drug, kind of addict and other variables to which numerous references have been made. But, to avoid constant qualifications, this chapter will be primarily concerned with ways of dealing with non-therapeutic heroin addicts, without pre-judging whether they ought to rank as prominently as they do in the scale of public concern over drugs.

The role of compulsion

If our spectrum ranges from the punitive, through the treatment orientated, to the permissive, the legitimacy of compulsory measures becomes a crucial issue. Unfortunately, political and emotive overtones have produced an unwarranted dogmatism about the acceptability of compulsion as such, instead of a reasoned debate on whether the medical desirability of such a drastic step may, in some circumstances, outweigh its social hazards. To evaluate current proposals it is first necessary to outline the present legal position.

Compulsory and persuasive powers are already extensive. Thus, of some 3,000 admissions of drug addicts to psychiatric hospitals in 1968, 459 were admitted under compulsory treatment orders, mostly under the Mental Health Act, but some under Section 4 of the Criminal Justice Act 1948.[9]

Under the latter Act (as amended by the Criminal Justice Act 1972), a court may make it a condition of a probation order that the offender should have treatment (residential or otherwise) for a specified period of up to three years. The evidence of one doctor, approved under Section 28 of the Mental Health Act 1959, is needed, that the offender's condition requires and may be susceptible to treatment, but is not such as to justify a hospital order.

Admittedly a probation order cannot be made without the consent of the offender, but it is only realistic to regard the consensual element as nominal in many cases. Section 4 orders are in fact increasing in number, and are likely to continue to do so if existing pressure on prison facilities and alternative policies aimed at reducing the prison population result in an expansion of the probation service.

Under the Mental Health Act 1959, mental disorder is defined as 'mental illness, arrested or incomplete development of mind, psychopathic disorder and any other disability of mind'.[10] Compulsory hospital admission may arise in emergency, under an observation or treatment order, or a hospital order made by the courts.

Section 25 provides for admission and detention for up to twenty-eight days for observation, on the written recommendation of two doctors that the patient is suffering from a mental disorder and that detention is desirable to protect him or others.

The same procedure authorises admission and detention for treatment under Section 26 when a patient is suffering from mental illness or, if under twenty-one, from psychopathic disorder. The latter is defined as 'persistent disorder or disability of mind which results in abnormally aggressive or seriously irresponsible conduct . . . .'

A person convicted on indictment[11] (other than where the penalty is fixed by law) who, on the evidence of two doctors, suffers from mental illness or psychopathic disorder to a degree warranting detention may be detained under a hospital order, provided that a particular hospital is willing to admit him within twenty-eight days and that such an order is the most suitable method of disposing of the case. A magistrates' court has power to remand him for examination and medical reports, though in committal proceedings it cannot technically 'order' the preparation of medical reports on someone remanded in custody for trial.

Now it is clear from the widely framed definitions of mental and psychopathic disorder that heroin addicts and persons suffering from, for example, a psychosis following an LSD 'trip' can be, and sometimes are, admitted under these headings. Equally, drug taking, as we have seen, is often a secondary aspect of mental disorder of some kind. It is therefore apparent that, without any amendment to the existing law, more addicts could be compulsorily detained and treated. The real obstacles are pressure on beds and problems of priority.

Once the issue of compulsion is seen as an aspect of the wider problems of hospital admission, the arguments for further powers take on a somewhat abstract and superfluous air. There is no reason to suppose that this pressure will diminish in the near future, or that addicts will ever rank high on the scales of priority for admission.

The second Brain Report did suggest compulsory detention of addicts who wanted to discontinue treatment originally entered into voluntarily.[12] Also, one can easily understand the frustration of the clinician at the ease with which hospital patients can obtain outside supplies. But the suggestion was not taken up in any of the subsequent legislation, although proposals for compulsory measures have recently come from several quarters – notably the Magistrates' Association, a few psychiatrists, and several members of Parliament.

The matter was considered at some length during the Third Reading of the Misuse of Drugs Bill 1970[13] when W.F. Deedes, MP, moved an Amendment to Clause 10 in the following terms:

> On the recommendation of two doctors approved under section 28 of the Mental Health Act 1959 to prohibit, for a stated period, administration or supply of controlled drugs for out-patient treatment to a named person and to authorise:–
>
> (a) compulsory detention either for observation or assessment for not more than 28 days.
>
> (b) compulsory detention for treatment in secure conditions for not more than one year.

In support of this proposal he cited a memorandum produced by the Magistrates' Association which called for greater control on two main grounds: first, that spreading drug dependence involves a degree of proselytisation, so that more control of the few is justified to protect the many at risk – really a form of quarantine based on the contagion model of drug dependence; secondly, that compulsion is indicated in cases where the motivation for cure vacillates. On these grounds they proposed the establishment of a centre for therapeutic treatment with a secure perimeter and a liberal hospital régime.

As was pointed out in the debate, a major difficulty concerns satisfactory criteria for applying such measures. On what grounds are we entitled to single out addicts for this kind of treatment from the whole range of social deviants? How wide a definition of 'addict' is envisaged? Would it, for example, include the vast number of chronic alcoholics? The power of the police under the Criminal Justice Act 1972 to take someone arrested for drunkenness in a public place to an approved medical centre for alcoholics stops short of compulsory treatment. The Government proposes to establish 'detoxification centres' at which medical or social treatment will be available on a voluntary basis. However, though not technically in custody, an offender who refuses treatment and leaves such a centre will remain liable to be charged with an offence.[14] One can hardly introduce a procedure with formidable social and constitutional implications on the basis of such a vague criterion as vacillating motivation for cure.

It is doubtless true that some addicts who are not responsive to psychotherapeutic techniques do benefit, at least in the short term, from more stringent methods. It is also true that many will not spontaneously seek treatment. But, in the absence of compelling evidence,[15] the onus of proof must surely lie on those who propose schemes entailing deprivation of liberty.

The claims made for the involuntary measures introduced in post-war Japan, to combat amphetamine abuse and heroin addiction,[16] are so striking that they cannot be discounted in any discussion on the merits of compulsion. But caution about an outcome apparently so different from the familiar pattern is reinforced by a natural reluctance to generalise from experience in so distinctive a cultural setting.

Before the Second World War drug dependence was very rare in Japan. From 1946 to the mid-fifties, abuse of stimulant drugs, notably amphetamines, reached such proportions that, in 1954 over 53,000 offences against the Amphetamines Control Law 1951 were recorded, and it was estimated that at one stage more than 1 million people were dependent.[17] Penal measures were consequently strengthened, and a nationwide drive to end amphetamine abuse was launched in 1955.

It was extremely thorough. The problem was tackled on several fronts – stricter control of trafficking, education of the public via the mass media, publicity in schools, factories, prisons and clubs, and greatly increased expenditure on treatment and hospital services. Under the Mental Hygiene Law 1951, addicts deemed dangerous to themselves or others were to be treated in mental hospitals, or, if accommodation was lacking, could even be confined to their homes. Consequently in 1958 only 268 offences against the Amphetamines Control Law were recorded.

What is missing from this picture of a remarkable decline in amphetamine abuse is adequate information as to the long term consequences for drug abuse generally. Even from Nagahama's highly favourable account one might infer the existence of multiple drug use. Thus:

> At the same time that measures to control stimulant drug-taking were becoming effective, leading to a decrease in the number of users, there was a marked increase in the incidence of narcotic drug-taking, especially heroin.[18]

Admittedly he then states that an anti-narcotics campaign – employing substantially similar methods – virtually eradicated heroin addiction by 1966. But the account is rather sketchy and one is justified in being sceptical of statements such as: 'The treatment period in hospital has been increased to 70–80 days, in hope of obtaining a complete cure.'[19] On the other hand, a programme which claims that its relapse rate[20] is a mere 14 per cent deserves closer investigation.

Perhaps the explanation is primarily cultural, reflecting a highly disciplined and law abiding society, where the combination of social stigma, severe measures, and an efficiently organised, expensive campaign proved exceptionally successful. If so, it provides further support for the view[21] that, in the case of heroin, the addictive qualities *of the drug itself* have often been exaggerated.

A society reluctant to accept such an intensive programme but dissatisfied with the results of voluntary measures, must recognise that its lack of consistency and continuity of approach has its disadvantages. It was suggested earlier that the debate on compulsion and voluntarism has tended to degenerate into doctrinaire assertions on moral acceptability, without reference to the particular phase of addiction in question. But while there is obviously a distinction to be drawn between, for example, the mechanics of withdrawal and the process of rehabilitation, the idea that an addict may be subject to compulsion at one stage, and then be expected to adjust painlessly to a voluntary rehabilitative régime, may be as psychologically naive as to expect a long term prisoner to feel at ease in the outside world immediately on release. Cure and rehabilitation are ideally to be seen as aspects of the same process, and it is not easy 'to make this division between creative willing rehabilitation and enforced detention for cure.' [22]

It is interesting that the Commons debate on compulsory treatment followed discussion of a proposal raising fundamentally similar issues – spot checks on schoolchildren for evidence of drug taking. [23] However well-intentioned, this would surely have been a misguided measure of social defence, likely to have caused many more difficulties than it would have resolved as to the respective roles of parents, teachers and the law. Even if the technical problems involved in identifying and quantifying certain drugs could be overcome, such informed research as we have on drug taking by the young[24] does not justify such a step.

Practical problems in the treatment of addiction

The question of compulsion clearly has implications reaching far beyond the particular case of drug dependence. But several problems peculiarly associated with drug addicts tend to limit the amount of money and resources expended on them, whether for purely clinical treatment or for the various other facilities, such as hostels and halfway houses, that they may require.

Reference has already been made to the reluctance of psychiatric hospitals to admit addicts, and it is hardly surprising that they come low down on the list of medical priorities. There is an almost total lack of institutions built specifically for the purpose of treating addiction. Given that hospitals are overcrowded and understaffed, addicts are perforce placed in wards together with the psychotic and the incontinent. Because of the nature of their 'illness', addicts are often unco-operative with staff as well as alienated from them. Disturbances late at night and intimidation of nurses in casualty departments by heroin addicts are familiar occurrences in the larger central London hospitals, and special police protection has been introduced.[25]

Even where there are special addiction units attached to hospitals the medical profession tends to regard them as 'poor relations' and, as is indicated by the following extracts from letters written to the *Lancet,* in 1968, the case for better facilities fares badly in terms of cost effectiveness:

> It has become increasingly unfashionable in our profession to consider economics in treating our patients . . . . The cost of treating

heroin addiction is particularly great. The expenses of running one particular drug-addiction treatment clinic apparently work out at £30 per addict out-patient attender per month. In addition the cost of daily prescriptions for narcotic drugs is not inconsiderable. The capital expenditure (apart from the running costs) on the various in-patient, out-patient, and research units for narcotic addiction recently built or building must run to many hundreds of thousands of pounds; while the cost to the community of the several hundreds of heroin addicts who are convicted by the courts every year can only be guessed at. The great majority of 'junkies' are permanently on national assistance or sickness benefit.

It seems that the cost to the community of treating or 'maintaining' heroin addicts . . . will be between £2 million and £3 million in 1968 . . . .[26]

The alleged treatment of drug addicts by psychiatrists is merely another example of the lack of humility on the part of psychiatrists and their refusal to face what must be a painful fact to them – namely, that there are conditions which are not amenable to their 'treatment'. There is not the slightest evidence that any form of treatment administered by psychiatrists is statistically significantly better in curing drug addicts compared with what can be expected without such treatment. Neither on the grounds of economy nor logic are there any reasons for treating drug addicts in the National Health Service. Their treatment should be primarily penal and in the hands of the Prison Medical Service and not in the hands of psychiatrists in the National Health Service. Lord Chief Justice Parker once said that addiction units should be set up attached to prisons; it is a pity that this has not been implemented instead of wasting money on the so-called psychiatric treatment of drug addiction in the National Health Service.[27]

Needless to say, such sentiments are even more prevalent among the general public, and there are strong local pressures against establishing clinics, especially if run on fairly radical lines. The fate of the Salter Unit at Cane Hill is a case in point.

Further difficulties stem from the dependent condition itself and the doctor/patient relationship peculiar to it. Whereas most 'ordinary' patients have a positive desire to recover, the heroin addict is often resigned to his fate. In so far as he has adopted a distinct life style, he confronts the doctor with the formidable task of offering an alternative plausible in the addict's own terms.

This lack of motivation is seen as crucial by those who stress the value of group therapy techniques in reorienting the addict. It may be significant that organisations such as Alcoholics Anonymous and Synanon originated in America, where the social pressures to join such groups are more marked than in this country, complemented, perhaps, by a greater readiness to lay bare one's personality. The contrast between the openness of the American attitude towards alcoholism at work and the typically more guarded, or wilfully blind, approach in Britain is instructive:

> ... American companies have done disproportionately more not only to recognise the problem but also to introduce policies to inhibit its effects. Several companies ... prohibit the use of alcohol in their canteens and dining rooms both in the United States and the United Kingdom. But, more significant, it has now become a recognised public relations exercise for an American company to publicise its 'alcohol programme.'[28]

It also has to be said that medical expertise in the field of drug addiction has not in the past been very noticeable in England. Few doctors could have claimed expert knowledge before the treatment centres were set up and some of these have been convicted of criminal offences and professionally disciplined. The doctor/addict relationship is delicate and complex and there is a shortage of responsible and informed practitioners able to devote adequate time to it.

At the most basic level, it is very difficult to assess dosage with any accuracy on the spot. The doctor may not know initially whether the patient is on heroin at all or, if he is, how much, and how regularly he has been taking it. Nor will he know, without a urine test, whether he is taking other drugs, and even with such analysis certain drugs remain undetectable. If the doctor seems hostile or under-prescribes, the addict will turn to the black market, and addicts almost invariably ask for excessive amounts, to sell, to pass on to friends, or simply as a function of their insecurity.[29]

The doctor must therefore be particularly perceptive and dedicated. The addict may well be deceitful, perhaps displaying self-inflicted needle marks; he may be persuasive, pitiful, pleading, while obtaining drugs from other sources at the same time. The strain imposed on the doctor who ran the risk of disapproval by the general public and loss of professional esteem, meant that, before the treatment centres were established, the 'junkie' doctors and a few dedicated men were virtually the only ones to treat addicts at all. In the potentially impersonal atmosphere of a clinic, assessing dosage, and the establishment of a firm, yet understanding, doctor/patient relationship could prove even more difficult than in the surgery.

However, even if a good relationship is established, it is only a beginning. To the extent that it is accurate to call heroin addiction a 'chronic relapsing disorder' it demands a comprehensive programme, from withdrawal through to aftercare and rehabilitation. An addict will face different problems at different stages of his treatment. Hence the function of the treatment centre is now crucial. It could easily degenerate into a mere prescribing centre, an 'off-licence' for drugs; or, ideally, become the focal point for co-ordinating the various services required.

For to deal successfully with addiction in a given area requires co-operation between the different bodies with which the addict may come into contact – the treatment centre, the police, the court, the probation service etc. Whilst all of these institutions are in principle concerned for his welfare, some have other, possibly overriding, aims which may conflict with it. Whereas the doctor is treating the addict, the court is 'treating' addiction, and will often resolve any conflict it senses between the individual and the defence of the general community in what it conceives to be the latter's interest.

Some progress has been made by means of liaison programmes. In particular, Birmingham has fostered co-ordination between its police drug squad and the addiction unit at All Saints Hospital, which helps to account for its success in dealing with heroin addiction. Liaison committees have also been formed in many parts of the country, modelled on a scheme introduced in Bradford, which incorporates local doctors, probation officers, the police, and interested professional and voluntary organisations. Information is gathered about the local drug 'scene' which may indicate particular measures for that area.

The case for differential policies in particular localities is implicitly stated in Section 17 of the Misuse of Drugs Act 1971 which enables the Home Secretary to obtain details from doctors and pharmacists 'if it appears . . . that there exists in any area in Great Britain a social problem caused by the extensive misuse of dangerous or otherwise harmful drugs in that area . . . .' It is to be hoped that this kind of co-operation will become nationwide as a first step towards the dissemination of accurate knowledge about drug use and treatment methods as well as helping to introduce more uniformity of sentencing.

Methods of dealing with addicts

Criminal sanction

In England, as we have seen, it is not a crime to be an addict, nor would any conceivable purpose be served by making it one. No one would dispute that the criminal law has an important role in combating traffic in certain drugs, but to castigate addiction as a 'status' crime could only have disastrous consequences.

The point is repeated merely to underline the contrast with America, where heroin is banned and, in approximately one third of the states, [30] addiction *is* a crime (or falls within a statutory definition of vagrancy and disorderly behaviour) in some cases carrying a mandatory minimum prison sentence. The net effect is to 'criminalise' a segment of the population by making it wholly dependent on criminals as a source of supply, forced to steal in order to support a drug habit; vulnerable to secondary infection through fear of any contract with authority or, alternatively, having to act as police informers under threat of prison.

Compulsory treatment in prison

There is no standard procedure in English prisons for dealing with offenders who are also addicts. The prison medical officer has authority to act as he thinks appropriate. This can mean abrupt withdrawal, but gradual withdrawal, with oral methadone, is much commoner.

Prison medical officers will normally contact the offender's previous doctor or hospital, though this clearly desirable precaution is not invariably taken. One comes back to the perennial problem of overworked staff in prison hospitals, where conditions are often little better than in the prisons themselves.

Withdrawal from the drug alone can never be more than a short term expedient. But this is not to say that withdrawal in a coercive background is necessarily unacceptable, for so much depends on the subsequent treatment of the addict.

Vaillant's twelve year follow-up study [31] of 100 American voluntary patients and prisoners sent to Lexington Hospital and discharged in 1953–55 is illuminating on the efficacy of compulsion. He found that:

(a) in the long term, those who were voluntarily re-admitted after 1953 fared little better than those who underwent abrupt withdrawal at home;
(b) prison without parole was not significantly different in terms of success from voluntary treatment; and
(c) the most effective treatment was a sentence of more than eight months followed by more than a year's parole.

Furthermore,

> . . . the likelihood that significant abstinence would occur after

prolonged involuntary imprisonment followed by prolonged involuntary supervision was *fifteen* times greater than after voluntary hospitalisation.

Vaillant did not conclude that *punishment* was intrinsically beneficial for the addict, but rather that prolonged imprisonment was beneficial in so far as it enabled the addict to have therapy over a long period, and that addicts may respond more favourably to coercive therapy than to more orthodox psychotherapeutic techniques. The exacting régimes of Synanon, Phoenix House and Daytop Village [32] give some support to this view, reinforcing the case for rethinking the role which compulsion might usefully play at different stages of various treatment programmes.

However, there remains the major qualification that most prison régimes are in practice especially primitive for addicts. Facilities are lacking and little more is achieved than withdrawal and perhaps a modicum of treatment for those who would not normally seek it voluntarily.

Civil commitment

If it is accepted that addiction is more akin to illness than to crime, there is no compelling reason to confine treatment within a criminal law or punitive context. Several American states did in fact have rudimentary civil commitment schemes at the beginning of the century, but they were rarely used in practice, since compulsory detention was not possible in the absence of a criminal charge.

Reflecting the relative lack of success in Lexington and Fort Worth, and envisaged as a possibility in *Robinson* v. *California* (1962), [33] the move towards civil commitment in America really took root in the early 1960s in California and New York, and a Federal Commitment Law was also passed in 1966. [34] If it is too early to speak of concrete achievements, at least the official recognition of the futility of exclusively punitive measures is welcome.

Basically, civil commitment means a court-ordered confinement in a special treatment facility, followed by supervised out-patient treatment in the community. If the addict remains drug free he is finally discharged; if not he is reconfined. The commitment period is indeterminate, subject to a maximum (usually three years). The confinement phase normally consists of withdrawal and therapy; in the out-patient stage there are various supportive services and, usually, periodic testing for drugs.

Existing programmes permit the involuntary commitment of non-criminal (as well as criminal) addicts, merely on proof that they are addicted to narcotic drugs, or even, in some jurisdictions, if in 'imminent danger of becoming addicted'. In support of this controversial power, analogies are drawn with the mentally ill and the spreading of a contagious disease, confinement being deemed justifiable in the interests of the community's safety and health.

There are several disquieting features of such an approach. The two standard justifications for confining the mentally ill are that they constitute a danger to themselves or to others, and/or that they are in need of care and treatment. But to invoke 'danger' on proof of addiction, without more, is to perpetuate the myth that addicts constitute a dangerous class as such, without requiring the kind of evidence needed before confining the mentally ill. To argue that they are in need of care and treatment is more plausible, with the proviso that false expectations of cure are easily aroused.

As with any form of social defence where the criteria for intervention are suspect, there are also serious dangers that administrative powers will be abused. The problems are neatly summed up in the *American Task Force Report* on Narcotics and Drug Abuse:

> the façade of benevolence generally associated with civil commitment programmes does not avoid the danger that such programmes can be used as a means of circumventing ordinary criminal safeguards in order to remove 'Undesirables' from society and to keep them in custody for long and indefinite periods during which there is little expectation of providing efficacious treatment.

And again:

> It does not seem unfair to conclude that as long as there is no evidence to show that existing methods for treating addiction hold out a reasonable prospect for cure, civil commitment is but a euphemism for imprisonment.[35]

This criticism seems particularly applicable to those states where committed addicts are subject to the control of the correctional and not the public health authorities. In the California programme more than 90 per cent of the addicts have been involuntarily committed after conviction; many live in prison-like conditions, and their three years of 'after care' differs little from parole. Despite the optimism of the authorities, there has been some disillusion, and a former Chief of Research for the programme concluded that '. . . the rehabilitation success of the civil addict programme with group therapy seems to be no better than that of the regular prison programmes for addicts in California.'[36]

The analogy with contagious diseases frequently made in order to justify commitment is superficially attractive but usually overstated. It is a good example of the emotive distortion so common in discussion about drugs. The typical use of the word is to describe a commonly fatal disease such as typhoid or smallpox which spreads by contact alone, and to which the population at large is vulnerable without taking any positive steps to contract it. It should be readily apparent that to apply the term to drug use entails an unwarranted extension of meaning.

Involuntary commitment of addicts convicted of crime at least presents no problems of the legitimacy of custodial measures. The difficulty here concerns the form which treatment may reasonably take if it is to be an acceptable alternative to imprisonment. Prison sentences are normally fixed, whereas treatment, if it is to be meaningful, should be indeterminate. Thus, under the California programme, treatment in lieu of imprisonment is for an indeterminate period of between 3½ and 10 years, however short the prison sentence might have been.

The objection is not, in principle, to the extra length of confinement. It arises, again, because of the lack of successful treatment methods and, in practice, because of the prison-like conditions which such an addict is likely to endure throughout his stay.

In the case of voluntary commitment, at a pre-conviction stage, of addicts on a criminal charge, a converse problem has arisen. Not surprisingly, many accused simply choose the shorter régime. Since the existing treatment programmes for volunteers last for three years at most, the 'worst' offenders, in the sense of those who anticipate a longer prison sentence, opt for treatment. Presumably to extend the treatment period would unduly stretch resources.

Treatment centres

We have already seen [37] how the 'British System' operated for some forty years until the treatment centres were established in 1968. The use made of these centres will help to determine future British policy, and we must therefore consider this new departure, to try and discover how far it is fulfilling its original objectives and what it can reasonably be expected to achieve.

(a) *The American narcotics clinics*

The new British centres are vulnerable to the kind of criticism which led to the closure of the American prescribing clinics in the early 1920s, and which has effectively prevented attempts to re-establish such a system there. Brief mention will therefore be made of the background to that experiment and the reasons for its failure.

Under the Harrison Act of 1914, only registered physicians could legally prescribe narcotic drugs. Consequently, addicts began to flock to them in their thousands, and surgeries were turned into mass prescribing centres where it became impossible for doctors to make any pretence of catering for the real needs of the individual addict. Prosecutions followed, and in *Webb* v. *U.S.* (1919) [38] the Supreme Court held that a prescription of drugs for an addict 'not in the course of professional treatment in the attempted cure of the habit, but being issued for the purpose of providing the user with morphine sufficient to keep him comfortable by maintaining his customary use' was not a prescription within the meaning of the law.

In short, maintenance doses became illegal, and the addicts had to rely on the black market. Alarmed by this, the Treasury Department, towards the end of 1918, authorised the temporary establishment of clinics in numerous cities, to minimise exploitation and impose some degree of medical supervision. 'The clinics were never intended as a means of curing addiction, but were from the beginning conceived as emergency devices to prevent the economic exploitation of addicts by drug pedlars.'[39] Within sixteen months 44 clinics had been set up.

The Harrison Act, being a taxation measure, was initially administered by revenue officials, but after the National Prohibition Act, in 1919, narcotic and liquor law enforcement were combined under the control of the Prohibition Unit. The moralistic Prohibition campaign was extended to drugs, reinforced by sensationalist accounts in the yellow press of abuses at individual clinics. By mid-1921, all but one of the clinics had been closed by the Government.

There is not much reliable information about the way these clinics operated. That there were abuses in some of them seems clear. Especially in the larger ones, such as New York, the checks on dosage were inadequate, some addicts obtaining extra supplies by queueing up more than once on the same day. Adverse press reports facilitated the denigration of the system as a whole.

The underlying reason for the hostility which led to the closure of these clinics, so soon after being officially established, was probably an objection in principle to the notion of maintenance. This attitude was reinforced by the belief that once withdrawal had been achieved there was no sound reason for relapse. The clinics were seen as indulging the morbid craving of addicts and fostering addiction. Addiction and related offences were on the increase, and it was easy to convince people that the clinics were responsible, though in fact the increase was proportionately even greater[40] in the years immediately following their closure.

In such an atmosphere, the favourable reports of the one clinic which survived till 1923, run by Dr Butler at Shreveport, Louisiana, are all the more noteworthy. It is true that the Federal Narcotics Bureau's account of the clinics[41] is critical of Shreveport, but its general tone and motivation invite scepticism when compared with the detailed description in Terry and Pellens' classic work.[42] At the very least, as Lindesmith demonstrates, the early 1920s were characterised by two schools of thought on drug addiction[43] and on the acceptability of clinics.

There is, of course, no *intrinsic* reason why a clinic system should be unacceptable as an administrative basis for treating drug dependence. The American experience of the 1920s is important, even if one discounts the apparent achievements of Dr Butler, for its effect on subsequent American policies. Thus when the New York Academy of Medicine put forward a plan to open clinics in 1955, it was, in effect, sabotaged by the opposition of the Federal Bureau of Narcotics (then presided over by the notoriously inflexible Harry Anslinger), based on the Bureau's own dubious and coloured account of an experiment which in reality 'failed' for a reason unconnected with its administrative structure.

(b) *The new British treatment centres*

Since the second Brain report (1965) attributed the increased incidence of heroin addiction primarily to over-prescribing by a few individual doctors, it is not surprising that the Committee recommended the establishment of treatment centres, whose doctors would alone be able to prescribe for addicts.[44]

It would be a mistake to regard the consequent setting up of centres in 1968 as signifying the collapse of the 'British system'. This would only be true if the essence of the system were the right of *any* doctor to prescribe drugs to addicts. But the key elements in the British approach have really been simply the recognition that the medical profession must have primary responsibility and that maintenance treatment is in some circumstances justifiable.

In both of these respects the new centres were intended to continue previous policy, as was made clear in a memorandum issued by the Minister of Health in 1967:[45]

> The aim is to contain the spread of heroin addiction by continuing to supply this drug in minimum quantities where this is necessary in the opinion of the doctor, and where possible to persuade addicts to accept withdrawal treatment.

> The decision to supply an addict with drugs and whether to seek to substitute other drugs, the assessment of dosage, and the method of supply, rest with the clinician.[46]

By 1972, 25 treatment centres had been set up throughout the country, 16 of them in London (over three-quarters of the notifications are in the Greater London area); a few have in-patient addiction units and others are planned. There are also treatment centres in each Regional Hospital Board area.

They vary considerably in the way they operate and the range of services offered is partly dictated by existing facilities. Some have hospital beds for withdrawal, several are closely integrated with social and psychiatric services and a few pay particular attention to the addict's job situation. The vast majority require addicts to inject themselves away from the clinic, though in one or two drugs are administered on the spot.

Fairly elaborate precautions have been taken to prevent addicts from obtaining multiple prescriptions.[47] A check is made with the Home Office list of notifications whenever a centre has a new arrival. He is interviewed by a social worker and/or a psychiatrist and urine tests are taken. The procedure for obtaining supplies is that a week's prescription is posted to the local chemist, but the addict may only obtain daily doses. At first, the prescribed drug was normally heroin, but with the increasing use of methadone, by October 1972 only 25 per cent of notified day addicts were being given heroin, and of these more than half were taking it in combination with methadone.[48]

The present system has several drawbacks, though not all of them are exclusive to it. Thus the possibility of creating new addicts, and the difficulty of assessing dosage, have always existed, if not perhaps to quite the same extent.

Previously, however, addicts were at least treated by doctors experienced in the field and motivated to deal with addiction. When the clinics were introduced a far greater number of doctors, as well as nurses and social workers, many with relatively little expertise, bore this responsibility, and not presumably always through choice. Setbacks in this transitional period were only to be expected.

There is evidence from the centres of the initial hazards of diagnosis and dosage. In one clinic, 11 patients with negative urines out of a group of 52 were mistakenly prescribed opiates, mainly in reliance on false histories of illegal misuse.[49] Undoubtedly some new addicts have been created; what one wants to know is whether this inevitable danger is increased in a clinical setting. Does the doctor/patient relationship suffer materially? Do most addicts think of the centres as providing treatment or as mere distribution centres?

It is difficult to generalise on this point, as the centres themselves differ considerably in their approach, some running two or three different kinds of régime in an effort to provide individualised treatment. But this fact itself creates a further problem, by establishing an order of preference in the minds of addicts. 'Interclinic monthly heroin and methadone prescription quantities are distributed among the clinics, and this may have developed a touch of competition to stay in the range of low prescribers.'[50] Some such communication system between centres is needed to prevent multiple supply; a degree of uniformity of approach – though not to an extent which rules out innovation – is desirable to maintain an even distribution.

One feature of the present system calls into question its whole rationale – the fact that it is restricted to heroin and cocaine. The effect is to widen the already artificial distinction between heroin addiction and other forms of drug dependence by disregarding the prevalence of multiple drug abuse.[51] A policy geared to reducing heroin abuse will, if successful, lead to an increase in the misuse of drugs obtainable other than at the centres. It is easy to elevate the heroin problem out of all proportion to its overall significance and delude the public into thinking that somehow we have solved, or contained, the 'drug' problem if there are 2,000 notified addicts instead of 3,000.

To isolate the most emotive class of drugs, without reference to the environmental and personality factors which make people take them and, often, other drugs, is to place an undesirable limitation on the centres. Their present terms of reference preclude them, for example, from dealing with a spread of amphetamine abuse in a given locality.

Other shortcomings were fairly predictable. Few hospitals have satisfactory in-patient facilities, and hospital withdrawal – in the rare cases when addicts will accept it[52] – has not proved a success. The originally projected social worker/addict ratio of 1:25 has not been achieved, and 1:50 is common. 'Among all London clinics, the amount of social work time provided to addicts varies from 475 hours per week (St. Clements) to none, according to a questionnaire filled out by the clinics themselves.'[53] Nor is contact with doctors at the clinics as frequent as was hoped, once a week or once a fortnight being fairly standard.

Yet, in so far as the notification figures are a guide, heroin addiction does appear to be under control. Especially encouraging is the fall in the number of notified addicts under the age of twenty, despite the marginal increase in total numbers from 1971–73.[54] Two important qualifications must be made. The unknown number who have not been notified, or have reverted to illicit sources, makes any such assertion tentative. Some addicts fear any kind of contact with authority, whether because they are afraid of being labelled as addicts, or as a function of some personality disorder, or because they are in trouble with the law. Also, as already noted, the resort to other drugs as a reaction against stricter prescribing further diminishes the significance of the figures.

There is considerable evidence that non-opiate drug abuse increased after the centres were opened – of methedrine, until supplies were virtually withdrawn, amphetamine sulphate, and injectable barbiturates. Nor is the increase in methadone dependence – welcome to the extent that it reflects reduced heroin addiction – entirely attributable to its prescription at the centres, but is partly accounted for by the prohibitively high price of black market heroin.

On the credit side, we now have a more systematic approach towards some of the most dangerous drugs and an end to their arbitrary and irresponsible prescription. We have centres which could prove invaluable for pooling information, concentrating resources and maintaining records for research purposes. Above all, a high proportion of heroin addicts are receiving some form of continuous medical attention. This situation contrasts sharply with America, where 'Nationally, it is safe to say that well over ninety per cent of all heroin addicts are not in any treatment program at all.' [55]

We now have the opportunity to pursue an integrated approach which makes the treatment centre the focal point of a comprehensive programme. Such an approach was envisaged by Dr Owens of All Saints Hospital, Birmingham, (which has had considerable success with heroin addiction) one year before the centres became operative:

> ... any treatment centre ... newly created to deal with an established heroin problem would require:
>
> (a) a well-defined catchment area;
> (b) a system of registration of addicts for that area;
> (c) a system of identification of addicts – for example identity cards;
> (d) the co-operation of pharmacists in the area, each with an allocated number of addicts;
> (e) a drug squad (therapeutically oriented) to identify drug-takers and prevent drug abuse; and
> (f) a number of assessment beds and separate out-patient facilities.[56]

Birmingham's own programme benefits by being linked to a hostel scheme

(Granville House) whereby addicts can be resident for a one month trial period after withdrawal, while working in the general community.

Self-regulating communities

Because there is no universally accepted treatment for the various forms of drug dependence, and because results have almost always been discouraging, there is a strong case for experimentation. Several self-regulating communities have sprung up, usually modelled on the Synanon approach.

Founded in 1958, Synanon,[57] which has many branches in America, is a privately funded organisation, a kind of social movement, which combines a very rigorous régime with realistic work and rehabilitation facilities. Claims that several Houses have success rates of about 50 per cent are difficult to evaluate, since statistical information is not made available, and admission is a highly selective process, controlled by existing members of the group.

Immediate withdrawal, in the presence of the group, is followed by intensively organised activities. Non-medical use of drugs, including alcohol, is forbidden. Compulsory therapy sessions held three times a week are a key feature. It is not group therapy in the traditional sense of 'working through' problems, but rather 'attack therapy', a kind of contest with stress on honesty and immediacy of reaction, conducted by non-professional ex-addicts. Using ex-addicts for these sessions is felt to increase the motivation of the members. The aim is to liberate the individual through an outwardly merciless stripping bare of his personality to achieve a cathartic effect. Each Synanon group constitutes a close knit, almost tribal, community, demanding an exceptional degree of loyalty, seeking to provide a goal directed life.

Another American experiment run on similar lines is Daytop Village, a parole system enjoying some government support. It began in 1964 and by 1972 had four treatment centres with more than 450 residents. Ten months full time residence, which includes work in the outside community, is followed by ordinary probation. The main difference from Synanon lies in encouraging a speedier return to outside life. The success claimed[58] is open to the same qualifications as is the case with Synanon.

This is not to say that the selectivity of Synanon and Daytop and comparable institutions is open to criticism in itself. The kind of régime which they offer is obviously not suitable for all addicts and is probably too exacting for most. Nor could it function as effectively with large numbers. But those who have sufficient reserves to survive have an opportunity to build up self-respect and motivation through the responsibility of running the house, and to free themselves of their fatalism ('once a junkie always a junkie') through the therapeutic régime and sheer activity of their heavily structured day.

In the Spring of 1967, New York began its Phoenix House Program, [59] drawing heavily on the Synanon and Daytop models. Early results have proved encouraging, and the scheme, financed by private donation and the welfare money of the members, has now expanded to some 15 centres in New York with over 1,000 drug free full time residents. It is run by professional therapists and ex-addicts.

Rehabilitation involves three phases: an induction process lasting for a month, when the addict is made aware of how he rationalises his addiction, and persuaded that he has a potential for cure; a treatment phase, lasting several months, to increase understanding of oneself and build up positive attitudes, much reliance being placed on 'encounters' with other addicts and with staff and finally, re-entry into the general community.

A mere summary such as the above cannot, of course, do justice to the scale and sophistication of the scheme (and our main concern is the influence of such approaches on English schemes, rather than an examination in depth). Re-entry, for example, is a very gradual process. The addict begins by working in a detoxification ward, progresses to helping first in a Day–Evening Care Centre and then in the therapeutic community, and returns to work in the open community only after he has spent a period sharing the responsibility of leading intensive group treatment sessions.

The Phoenix House experiment has had significant repercussions in this country, providing much of the inspiration for two recently introduced programmes – the Alpha Unit in St. James' Hospital, Portsmouth and Phoenix House in London. The 'Portsmouth system' is the creation of Dr Ian Christie, who was greatly impressed by the Phoenix House methods on a visit to New York and when in 1968, St. James became the drug dependence clinic for Portsmouth, he established the Alpha Unit there on similar lines.

The régime is very exacting: 'The majority of drug offenders in the Hampshire courts opt for prison when given a choice between prison and Alpha House.' [60] The effectiveness of its approach is also difficult to evaluate. 'In the past five years, 178 people have passed through Alpha and five have graduated. Alpha also estimates that twenty-five per cent of their former residents are . . . not heavily involved with drugs.' [61]

It is not easy to convey the atmosphere of this style of community in a sentence or two. It is therefore proposed to deal with the London Phoenix House in rather more detail. It may be objected that to place such emphasis on so small scale an experiment distorts the total treatment picture and implicitly fails to do justice to other, more orthodox, methods. However, if the initial promise of some of these self-regulating communities is fulfilled in the next few years, there will be a strong case for diverting more funds to them. Also, the very nature of their régimes should promote a fuller understanding of the complexities of 'addict personalities' than is feasible in more conventional programmes.

The London Phoenix House is a residential therapeutic community for addicts which began in February 1970. Originally its three staff members were ex-addict staff of a New York Phoenix House, though the London centre is not a branch of the American programme, but part of the Community Drug Project, and has been adapted to meet the requirements of English addicts.

The régime is strict and highly organised. Drugs other than tobacco are prohibited and no physical violence is tolerated. No one is admitted unless he has been off drugs for at least a week, and the induction meeting is made deliberately challenging. In 1973/74, of 100 referrals 79 were seen, 45 admitted and 27 left prematurely against advice. The apparently high fall-out rate is partly accounted for by staff changes and shortages and the fact that many referrals are completing prison sentences when they first make contact with the House and others receive prison sentences subsequent to referral. Residents who complete the programme stay for nine or ten months on average.

The residents have usually had several years of prior addiction, and most have unsuccessfully tried more orthodox forms of treatment such as hospital withdrawal and gradual reduction of dosage in a treatment centre. This would suggest that to 'survive' the induction process and persevere reflects a determination to come off drugs and not just pre-selection of 'good risks', a charge often levelled against Synanon and Daytop.

A fundamental aim is to develop human relationships, and to this end great stress is laid on self-awareness. A typical day begins at 7.30, the day-to-day running of the House – cooking, cleaning, repairs etc. – being done by the residents. A ritualistic note is struck at the early morning meeting: 'We are here because there is no refuge finally from ourselves. Until a person confronts himself in the eyes and hearts of others he is running . . .'

Confrontation, judgement, and analysis of self and others are key elements. Progress is marked by promotion and demotion procedures; family visits, forbidden for the first three months, are a privilege, and a reward and punishment system operates. Discipline is severe – having one's head shaved, or not being permitted to speak for a week are typical punishments for serious breaches of the rules.

In the afternoon, discussions are held on a wide range of topics, and on at least three evenings a week there are 'encounter' sessions in which everyone in the group is encouraged to express his/her feelings about the others in a totally uninhibited manner. These sessions serve partly as a cathartic release of emotion, but may also enable the addict to renounce his previous self-image and grasp the need to establish personal relationships as a means towards positive living, instead of mechanically blaming the drug, as if it were the cause rather than a symptom of social inadequacy and withdrawal.[62]

The New York programmes would suggest that rehabilitation may take anything from one to three years. Again, judgement must be suspended. Some critics of self-regulating communities in general object that they are self-defeating, in that the more 'successful' they are, the less willing or able are their residents to resume life in the open community. Even if that is often the case, it is arguably a small price to pay when one considers the lamentable record of other methods, which have frequently been tried unsuccessfully by those who ultimately function adequately in therapeutic communities.

Moreover, the Synanon type of community is not an institution in the conventional sense, but typically has wider horizons which may enable members to be socially useful by helping new members. Some Synanon residents have never been addicted to drugs but simply prefer the communal life style, and the organisation encourages such membership. For people who are hostile towards traditional institutions and techniques of treatment there is a strong case for these communities, as for other therapeutic methods such as yoga and encounter groups. 'Addiction to Synanon' does occur but it is not a persuasive argument against the co-existence of such groups with larger scale projects.[63]

We need to know more about who will benefit most from a therapeutic community approach. Such information is not, however, easy to obtain, partly because thorough documentation and statistical analysis is either incompatible with, or rejected by, many groups, and partly because successful treatment is an elusive notion for which no uniformly accepted criteria exist. But a research project, including follow-up studies on the first hundred residents from Phoenix House and Alpha House, is in its final stages.

Most of the voluntary schemes are selective in their intake up to a point, and are understandably reluctant to deal with hard core addicts, who are ill-suited to any form of institutional setting. The Community Drug Project, a day centre for using addicts in Camberwell Green, provides a valuable service in coping with those who might otherwise never be reached by official means. Similarly, the organisation for the rehabilitation of metropolitan addicts (ROMA) plans to house using addicts. It is unfortunate that, in a field where funds are scarce and goodwill at a premium, there should be a measure of hostility between such organisations and those such as Phoenix House which insist on a drug free environment. Nothing will be gained by doctrinaire attitudes, especially in view of the overall lack of success in treating addicts by any methods. It should simply be recognised that different needs have to be catered for.

In the United States and Canada, this need for a variety of approaches has been met in the last few years by a vast increase in the number of unofficial social and medical agencies – running into thousands in America and over 900 in Canada. The proliferation of these 'innovative services' is partly due to dissatisfaction felt by young people with the more traditional methods of treatment and the moralising attitude of some official agencies.

These new services range from crisis centres and street clinics operating round the clock, to street community centres and therapeutic communes. The communes are distinguishable from the pioneer therapeutic communities like Synanon, in being less structured and rigorous, rather more emphasis being placed on the life style of the group as constituting 'treatment'. But it is not possible to provide a coherent picture of what are essentially small scale, often temporary, groups, where dealing with drug misuse is in many cases only one aspect of experimentation with alternative life styles.

An encouraging feature of this development is the growing co-operation with official bodies and increase in public funding. Instead of the situation in the mid-sixties, when experimental centres were almost invariably viewed with alarm, the American Courts, for example, are now much more willing to recommend them as an alternative to imprisonment or civil commitment. This seems to indicate that drug use as an expression of revolt against established institutions is giving way to a more practical concern with concrete drug problems and individual participation in communal activity.

What is really required is a cost–benefit analysis of different methods of treatment along the lines provided by the Le Dain Commission (see Appendix B).[64] Most therapeutic communities have what is, from an economic point of view, the built-in limitation that their whole ethos and much of their effectiveness depends on them remaining small scale experiments. Even granted the ability to economise by relying on ex-addict staff and voluntary workers, they fare badly on the Canadian estimate by comparison with much larger methadone programmes providing minimal services.

Nor is it necessarily the case that the most elaborate forms of treatment are the most effective. The Le Dain Commission[65] has described an experiment at Matsqui in which one group of addicts was given special treatment along therapeutic community lines, while a control group was denied this. Ironically, the superior treatment unit tended to produce a 'well-adjusted, well-educated dope fiend' who subsequently proved more successful in procuring and selling drugs in the illicit market.

At the beginning of this chapter it was suggested that, instead of applying criminal sanctions or medical treatment, in an effort to eliminate or contain drug addiction, it is also open to a society to respond by doing nothing beyond the bare minimum necessary for its own stability and the survival of the addict. The legitimacy and feasibility of legal controls must now be considered in the light of society's total response to drug use.

Notes

[1] The United States Supreme Court acknowledged this when in *Robinson* v. *California* (see ch. 3, n. 2) it held that it was unconstitutional – as 'cruel and unusual punishment' – to make it an offence merely to be an addict. It is interesting that a recent attempt to pursue the logic of this decision, and apply it to the offence of *possession* of heroin, only narrowly failed. In *U.S.* v. *Moore* 486 F.2d 1139 (D.C. Cir.) (1973), the Court of Appeals for the District of Columbia rejected the 'addiction defence' by 5 to 4. *Robinson* v. *California* was deemed to be limited to 'status' crimes as distinct from possession. A further argument based on the absence of *mens rea* was also rejected, on the grounds that the defendant's conduct was not wholly involuntary and if the defence were to be admitted it would be potentially applicable to all drug related criminal conduct.

[2] The criticism has been levelled at some of the American civil commitment schemes that they are punitive in all but name. See pp. 88–9.

Recent investigations into some of our mental hospitals highlight this problem. See e.g. Report of the Farleigh Hospital Committee of Inquiry, HMSO 1971 Cmnd. 4557; Report of the Committee of Inquiry into Whittingham Hospital, HMSO 1972, Cmnd. 4861.

[3] The Rehabilitation of Drug Addicts. Report of the Advisory Committee on Dangerous Drugs, HMSO 1969, p. 3, para. 1. Italics supplied.

[4] 'The Use of Methadone for Narcotic Blockade', *British Journal of Addiction,* vol. 63, 1968, p. 55. See also *New Society* 17 October 1968.

[5] See e.g. WHO Expert Committee on Drug Dependence, 16th Report, WHO Techn. Rep. Ser. 1969, No. 407, p. 21.

[6] See *Dealing with Drug Abuse:* A Report to the Ford Foundation, Macmillan 1972, p. 230.

[7] Ibid., p. 210.

[8] *Treatment:* A Report of the Commission of Inquiry into the Non-Medical Use of Drugs, Information Canada, Ottawa 1972, p. 10.

[9] As amended by the Mental Health Act 1959, Sched. 7, and the Criminal Justice Act 1972, Sched. 5. See H.C. Deb. vol. 808, no. 53, cols. 586–87, 9 December 1970.

[10] S. 4.

[11] S. 60(1); or, in a Magistrates' court, convicted or liable to conviction for an offence punishable by imprisonment, s. 60(2).

[12] Second Brain Report, p. 9, para. 24.

[13] H.C. Deb. vol. 808, no. 53, cols. 580–600, 9 December 1970.

[14] S. 34. Cf. The Habitual Drunkards Act 1879, which sanctioned the establishment of 'Retreats' where *non*-criminal inebriates could go for voluntary detention and treatment. The Inebriates Act 1898, made some provision for compulsory detention in State Inebriate Reformatories of habitual drunken offenders including those convicted on indictment of drink induced crime. In practice, however, the Act was a failure, and the last Inebriate Reformatory surrendered its licence in 1921. See N. East, *Society and the Criminal,* HMSO 1949, ch. 3.

The Criminal Justice Act 1967, s. 91, provided for the abolition of imprisonment for being drunk and disorderly, but the section was never brought into effect as it was contingent on suitable alternative accommodation becoming available.

[15] The American evidence is inconclusive. See e.g. J. Cole, 'Report on the Treatment of Drug Addiction', Appendix C to the *Task Force Report:* Narcotics and Drug Abuse, the President's Commission on Law Enforcement and the Administration of Justice, US Government Printing Office, Washington 1967.

[16] M. Nagahama, 'A Review of Drug Abuse and Counter Measures in Japan since World War II', *Bulletin on Narcotics*, vol. 20, no. 3, 1968, p. 19.

[17] Ibid., p. 20.

[18] He also somewhat cryptically notes: 'Cases of abuse of sleeping drugs and tranquilisers have been observed among juvenile delinquents'. Ibid., p. 24.

[19] Ibid., p. 23.

[20] The criteria used in defining relapse are not stated.

[21] See, e.g., Chein *et al.*, *Narcotics, Delinquency and Social Policy*, p. 6 and p. 159.

[22] H.C. Deb. vol. 808, no. 53, col. 598, 9 December 1970.

[23] Proposed as an Amendment to the Misuse of Drugs Bill, by Tam Dalyell MP, who also introduced a separate Bill for the purpose – the Medical Inspection (Evidence of Drug-taking) (School Pupils) Bill 1970, First Reading 9 December 1970.

[24] R. Wiener, *Drugs and Schoolchildren.*

[25] *The Times* 24 March 1971.

[26] *The Lancet,* vol. 2, 1968, p. 1239: Dr I.P. James.

[27] Ibid., p. 1350: Dr L.H. Field.

[28] R. Spiegelberg, 'Alcoholism: the hidden problem', *The Times* 13 April 1971.

[29] See P. Connell, 'Drug dependence in Great Britain: a challenge to the practice of medicine', in *The Scientific Basis of Drug Dependence,* Churchill, London 1968.

[30] A detailed summary can be found in W. Eldridge, *Narcotics and the Law,* Appendix B, University of Chicago Press 1967. Though such State legislation was condemned by the Supreme Court in *Robinson* v. *California,* 370 U.S. 660 (1962), the decision has been circumvented by charging addicts either with vagrancy or by the expedient of keeping watch on them until they can be charged with possession. See also H. Levine, *Legal Dimensions of Drug Abuse in the United States,* Charles C. Thomas 1974.

[31] G. Vaillant, 'A Twelve-year Follow-up of New York Narcotic Addicts: The Relation of Treatment to Outcome', *American Journal of Psychiatry,* vol. 122, no. 7, 1966, p. 727.

[32] See p. 95 *et seq.*

[33] See n. 30.

[34] The Civil Addict Commitment Law 1961, the Mental Hygiene Law 1962, (as extended in 1966), and the Narcotic Addiction Rehabilitation Act 1966, respectively. Several voluntary programmes were also established.

[35] Civil Commitment of Narcotic Addicts and Sentencing for Narcotic Drug Offences, Appendix D. Aronowitz, D.S., p. 151.

[36] *Treatment* (see n. 8), p. 16.

[37] Ch. 2.

[38] 249 U.S. 96, at col. 99.

[39] Lindesmith, *The Addict and the Law,* p. 142.

[40] Ibid., p. 143.

[41] *Narcotic Clinics in the United States,* Washington, D.C., US Government Printing Office 1953, pp. 12–13.

[42] *The Opium Problem,* Bureau of Social Hygiene, New York 1928. See Lindesmith, pp. 149–61.

[43] *Linder* v. *U.S.,* 268 U.S. 5 (1925), 18, in which the Supreme Court described addiction as a disease, for which a doctor acting in good faith could prescribe drugs to relieve withdrawal symptoms, is otherwise inexplicable.

[44] Para. 22.

[45] Hospital Memorandum (67) 16, The Treatment and Supervision of Heroin Addiction. Minister of Health, 7 March 1967.

[46] Paras. 8 and 10 respectively.

[47] See R. Phillipson, (ed.), *Modern Trends in Drug Dependence and Alcoholism,* Butterworths 1970, pp. 87–89, 96–97.

[48] *Drugs and Society,* October 1972, p. 1.

[49] R. Gardner and P. Connell, 'One Year's Experience in a Drug-Dependence Clinic', *The Lancet* vol. 2, 1970, pp. 455–58. See also P. Chapple and G. Gray 'One Year's Work at a Clinic for the Treatment of Addicted Patients', *The Lancet* vol. 1, 1968, pp. 908–11.

[50] *Dealing with Drug Abuse,* pp. 361–62.

[51] See M. Mitcheson *et al., The Lancet* vol. 1, 1970, pp. 606–07. In a group of 65 heroin addicts, 62 had taken barbiturates and 80 per cent had injected them at some time. See also M. Mitcheson, 'Polydrug abuse', in *ABC of Drug Addiction,* John Wright & Sons, Bristol 1970, pp. 89–93.

[52] At one clinic only 9 of 107 opioid users offered it at their first attendance accepted. Gardner and Connell, cf. note 49.

[53] *Dealing with Drug Abuse,* p. 359.

[54] See Appendix A, Tables 3 and 4.

[55] *Dealing with Drug Abuse,* p. 22.

[56] *British Medical Journal,* vol. 2, 1967, p. 501.

[57] For a detailed account see L. Yablonsky, *Synanon: The Tunnel Back,* Penguin 1967.

[58] In 1972, of 177 former residents, only 19 were considered to have failed. Thirty-nine now work for Daytop. See *Treatment,* p. 84.

[59] A similar voluntary therapeutic community, Odyssey House, was started in the same year.

[60] *Drugs and Society,* December 1972, p. 10.

[61] Ibid.

[62] Another small scale centre which has operated as a half-way house, since 1969, on broadly similar lines, and where encouraging results have been achieved is Suffolk House, near Uxbridge.

[63] No attempt has been made to describe specific forms of withdrawal treatment for addicts. A very useful survey is to be found in P. Connell, Treatment of narcotic and non-narcotic drug dependence: the need for research, ch. 2, in *Modern Trends in Drug Dependence and Alcoholism,* Butterworths 1970.

[64] *Treatment,* p. 103.

[65] Ibid., pp. 12–13.

5 The Social Response to Drug Use

The most widely used drug in the world for self-medication is aspirin. In Britain alone 'a recent survey indicated that four and a half million people took aspirin at least once a week and that half a million took more than five aspirin tablets a day.'[1] It is not widely known that aspirin is not indicated for the treatment of insomnia alone, and should never be taken for indigestion and gastric disorder. Some 7,000 people are admitted to hospital each year vomiting blood due to aspirin consumption. It is estimated that between 100 and 300 die.

These figures are not a prelude to a plea for a ban on aspirin, the overall benefits of which as an analgesic are indisputable. They do, however, usefully illustrate some of the more puzzling features of social attitudes towards drug use and in particular reveal the widespread, sometimes wilful, ignorance of the effects of even the most commonplace substances. Views on the acceptability of some drugs and the unacceptability of others are so deeply entrenched that merely to question them is to invite condemnation, often without regard to what is known.

The most compelling evidence of the dangers of alcohol, tobacco and barbiturates is either flatly disbelieved or tacitly acknowledged and rationalised in various ways; the dangers of 'new' drugs such as cannabis seem to be greatly exaggerated by a generation to whom they are alien; misconceptions abound at all levels of society, not least amongst the magistracy, whose observations on passing sentence sometimes help to reinforce the unscientific attitude prevalent in the community at large and in the mass media.

The emotive language and the image of the dope fiend are so pervasive that they are invoked to characterise all illicit drug use and all drug addicts. In consequence, even when drug taking constitutes a fringe activity it is thought, initially by others, ultimately by the user himself, to convey the user's total identity, a pattern which has been described as deviancy amplification.[2]

The prevalence of ignorance, prejudice and fear becomes most apparent when one examines the kind of arguments often deployed. For example, in the debate over the legalisation of cannabis, it is highly significant that an alleged escalation or progression to heroin has been one of the major areas of controversy. It will later be suggested[3] that whatever force the argument may originally have had, it has lost all credibility in the last few years. What concerns us here is that it should ever have achieved such pre-eminence in the first place.

Leaving aside pharmacological differences, to condemn substance X because you imagine that some who take it may then take substance Y is a crudely over-paternalistic approach, symptomatic of the panic reactions and hysteria so often encountered in discussions about drugs. Even if it is granted that, for social reasons, some kind of link exists, such a primitive form of reasoning is bound to be ineffective on the individual level, if not actually counter-productive. Meanwhile it continues to provide a handy slogan for the unthinking.

The logical inconsistencies of the present law are increasingly acknowledged at official levels, but without a corresponding change of approach. In April 1971, the then Home Secretary said: 'It is a strange anomaly that it is perfectly legal for me to drink myself to death . . . but it is not legal for me to drug myself to death. I believe this is right and I have not the slightest intention of trying to change the law on these subjects. Nevertheless, I find it extremely difficult to justify the logic of it.'[4]

The statement follows a classic pattern. It begins with the conventional fallacious distinction between drink and drugs, and proceeds to the unargued assertion that differential legal treatment is justified, while conceding it to be irrational.

When the level of debate is so crude a heavy price has to be paid. It is observable in the undoubted sense of alienation felt by those young people whose personal experience confounds conventionally accepted views about the relative harm of particular substances, and who see no reason to relate their own drug taking to a wider context. It is also evident in the stigma which even minor possessional offences sometimes attract, intensifying the alienation and sometimes damaging career prospects. Issues such as the legalisation of cannabis are artificially transformed out of all proportion to their intrinsic significance.

Above all, the highly emotive reaction to contemporary drug use is a cause for misgiving whatever one's view of the present law, for it has fostered two implacably opposed camps while at the same time obscuring the fundamental issues which divide them. What may legitimately be described as an overreaction is, in part, a genuine response to concrete and undeniable changes in the pattern of drug taking in the 1960s, characterised by increased dependence on heroin and amphetamines and a rise in the use of cannabis and LSD, without any significant fall in the consumption of alcohol and tobacco.

It is at least plausible to oppose greater relaxation of controls on 'soft' drugs as being contrary to the interests of a dynamic society, yet this and other key underlying matters are seldom adequately articulated, while attention continually focusses on essentially transient controversies. The function of this chapter is to examine issues of a general kind which, it is contended, reflect the more deeply rooted of our convictions about the propriety of drug use.

The enforcement of morality

In the Hart/Devlin controversy over which kinds of behaviour justify the intervention of the criminal law there is scant reference to drugs. The emphasis was on sexual morality since it was the Wolfenden Report [5] which precipitated the debate. But it is reasonable to suppose that in a comparable discussion a mere ten years later the appropriateness of legal sanctions in controlling drug use would have attracted far more attention. The Le Dain Committee's Interim Report,[6] and its Report on Cannabis,[7] for example, devote several pages to this theme, and it is a convenient model for examining the relevant moral issues.

Curiously enough, John Stuart Mill's *On Liberty* (1859), which provided a focal point for much of the modern argument, deals at greater length than do the contemporary protagonists with the acceptability of legal control over drugs, and the more intractable problems posed by this.

As regards the enforcement of morality generally, Mill's basic proposition is well-known: 'That the only purpose for which power can be rightfully exercised over any member of a civilised community, against his will, is to prevent harm to others. His own good, either physical or moral, is not a sufficient warrant.' [8]

Mill then qualifies this statement by saying that it '. . . is meant to apply only to human beings in the maturity of their faculties . . . .' He also acknowledges that harming oneself may indirectly harm others, citing inability through intemperance to discharge obligations to one's creditors and family as examples. But he would only impose sanctions if such a breach of duty – or serious risk of it – were shown to have occurred:

> No person ought to be punished simply for being drunk; but a soldier or a policeman should be punished for being drunk on duty. As for merely contingent or . . . constructive injury . . . the inconvenience

is one which society can afford to bear for the sake of the greater good of human freedom.'

In Chapter 5 of *On Liberty* Mill applies these general principles to particular instances, including the prohibition against importing opium into China and the restrictions on the sale of poisons. The most he would countenance as a safety measure for poisons was 'labelling the drug with some word expressive of its dangerous character', plus, possibly, a few formalities as evidence of the sale. Any further restrictions were objectionable as infringing the liberty of the prospective purchaser.

Professor Hart, who maintains that criminal sanctions restricting the supply of drugs do not necessarily signify the enforcement of morality as such, but can be explained as paternalism – 'the protection of the would-be purchasers against themselves' [9] – comments that, with regard to the sale of drugs, 'Mill carried his protests against paternalism to lengths that may now appear to us fantastic.'[10]

In fact, it is not clear that, *in this particular context,* Mill's observations were consciously anti-paternalistic. He was writing at a time when the hazards of drug dependence went virtually unrecognised, and his primary concern was that an individual who wanted poisons for 'innocent' or 'useful' purposes should not be punished merely because some people might want them in order to inflict harm *on others.* He makes no direct reference to drug taking.

However, the general tenor of Mill's argument, his emphasis on persuasion rather than sanction and his belief that people should not be discouraged from 'experiments in living' certainly suggest that he would have opposed prohibitions on drug use. His attitude typified the prevailing *laissez faire* climate. In a welfare state with a social security system and a National Health Service coping with formidable problems of priority of treatment the ambit of self-regarding behaviour is, and is seen to be, far narrower.

In supporting Mill's basic opposition to criminal sanction in matters of morality, Hart makes the point that much greater suffering is endured in the repression of deviant sexual behaviour than is normally the case in abstention from 'ordinary' crime such as theft. One might add that for the law to inflict suffering on an addict for a drug related crime is an analogous case of an evil requiring cogent justification.

In discussing the *distribution* of socially disapproved commodities, Mill put his finger on a dilemma central to contemporary discussion about the status of marijuana, namely, that many reformers appear to favour a double standard which would legalise use, yet maintain restrictions on distribution and sale. As Mill puts it: 'What the agent is free to do, ought other persons to be equally free to counsel or instigate? This question is not free from difficulty.'[11]

In principle he was opposed to restrictions on the instigator, on grounds of consistency and liberty, but admitted to being in two minds when the situation involved financial gain. Thus, while opposed to outright prohibition on liquor, he believed that, 'the interest of . . . dealers in promoting intemperance is a real evil and justifies the State in imposing restrictions.'[12] With some reluctance, he viewed indirect discouragement of drinking by means of taxation as an acceptable compromise. But the value of fiscal measures in checking alcoholism or, for that matter, cigarette smoking, is hard to discern.

Lord Devlin makes no reference to drugs in his main contribution to the enforcement of morality debate, 'Morals and the Criminal Law'[13] but does mention them briefly in a later lecture, 'Mill on Liberty in Morals': '. . . men who are constantly drunk, drugged or debauched are not likely to be useful members of the community', and again, 'Certainly no one in his senses can think that habitual drunkenness or drugging leads to any good at all.'[14]

The context of these observations is the argument that the integrity of a society is threatened if the majority sanctions, in the name of freedom, conduct which it conceives of as morally wrong and socially disruptive. Hart rejects this monistic view and it would indeed seem to be an over-simplification in an age when moral pluralism is increasingly acknowledged.

Assuming Lord Devlin's view to be what Hart terms the 'moderate thesis' – that the enforcement of morality is necessary for the preservation of society (as distinct from the 'extreme thesis' – that it is desirable for its own sake) – its superficial attractiveness in relation to drugs stems from the manner in which all drug use is commonly portrayed as a single phenomenon, and as a potent symbol of a nation in decline. Few issues exhibit so clearly the rift between 'the conventional wisdom' and 'anti-establishment' views. Few activities more readily arouse the 'intolerance, indignation, and disgust' of the juryman, which Lord Devlin[15] sees as necessary prerequisites to interference with freedom of choice.

Even if one rejects such criteria, as paving the way towards an unreasoning populism, they do provide a salutary reminder of what should be a major underlying theme in the debate, namely, how far is drug dependence generally – and cannabis use in particular – reconcilable with the social and economic ethic of an advanced technological society? For a society may embrace moral pluralism and still retain social and economic aims which are broadly accepted.

This question [16] is touched upon by Lord Devlin in the two passages quoted above, and also in 'Morals and the Criminal Law':

> You may argue that if a man's sins affect only himself it cannot be the concern of society. If he chooses to get drunk every night in the privacy of his own house, is anyone except himself the worse for it? But suppose a quarter or a half of the population got drunk every night, what sort of society would it be? [17]

His disagreement with both Mill and Hart is well brought out in a further passage from 'Mill on Liberty in Morals':

> Yet if apart from his assignable duties a man does not observe some standard of health and morality society as a whole is impoverished, for such a man puts less than his share into the common well-being. The enforcement of an obligation of this sort can be distinguished from paternalism. The motive of paternalism is to do good to the individual: the motive of the other is to prevent the harm that would be done to society by the weakness or vice of too many of its members. Mill did not overlook the distinction; he overrode it in the interest of individual freedom. [18]

And further, regarding the commercialisation of vice:

> [Mill] did not really grapple with the fact that along the paths that depart from traditional morals, pimps leading the weak astray far outnumber spiritual explorers at the head of the strong. [19]

Now it is agreed by all protagonists, and particularly emphasised by Hart, that we are here dealing with questions of degree and not absolutes. Mill himself was paternalistic towards the young and the mentally ill, and would also have imposed restrictions where 'assignable duties' were in danger of not being fulfilled. He is echoed by Lord Devlin in the context of restrictive legislation on the purchasing of alcohol and tobacco: 'An adult can look after himself and must be strong enough to resist temptation; but it is a moral duty to look after a child in this respect and keep him out of bad ways and not to indulge him unduly.' [20] Indeed this sentence could have come straight out of Mill, and is not, in its attitude towards adults, typical of Lord Devlin's general approach.

Equally, Lord Devlin acknowledges that the right to privacy must be balanced against the right to enforce morality: 'It is the old and familiar question of striking a balance between the rights and interests of society and those of the individual.'[21]

The issue then becomes one of determining what criteria should be used to decide whether or not a particular morality is enforced. In short, who has got the balance right? The 'popular' view of drug use is largely irrational and heavily laced with prejudice, reinforced by press reports which are frequently ill-informed and sensationalist. Above all, it is characterised by a blanket condemnation of all illegal drugs. Such a state of affairs affords cogent support for Hart's view that to acknowledge the existence of a popular morality does not of itself justify enforcing it by law.

Indeed, as the Wootton Committee argued, Mill's principle of minimal intervention carries even more weight today, when so many restrictions on individual liberty are deemed unavoidable. At the same time, the Committee pointed to the difficulties of distinguishing satisfactorily between purely self-regarding actions (if such there be) and those involving wider social consequences. The ambit of paternalistic legislation is in some ways arbitrary, not being invoked, for example, in respect of attempted suicide, or to prevent a sixteen year old from riding a motor cycle.

But the general formula advocated by Wootton differs little from Mill in principle:

> Every proposal to restrict the freedom of the individual in his own supposed interest must, therefore, be decided on merits, in the light of the probable severity of any damage that he may inflict upon himself, and of the risk that in damaging himself he may also involuntarily be the cause of injury to others.[22]

For a more detailed treatment of this issue one must turn to the work of the Le Dain Commission, which is particularly noteworthy for its awareness of the wider implications of drug use. Its Interim Report is a model of thoroughness and clarity in dealing with individual drugs, and also manages to convey imaginatively the wider context of drug use.[23]

Several pages are devoted to considering what role is desirable for the criminal law and three main approaches are discerned. First, there should be no legal control and the state should merely inform the people of dangers arising from the use of drugs. Secondly, distribution – but not possession for use – should be restricted by criminal sanction. Thirdly, where there is serious potential for harm, prohibition on use should also be possible. The Committee[24] found Mill's approach too *laissez faire* for modern conditions in which there are constant additions to an already proliferating supply of drugs. They stressed the importance of potential for harm to self and society as a primary criterion: 'In this sense we subscribe to what Hart refers to as the "moderate thesis" of Lord Devlin.'[25]

Regarding the dilemma posed by Mill, as to whether one could justifiably pursue different policies on distribution and use, they had this to say:

> There is no principle of consistency that requires the criminal law to be used as fully as possible, or not at all, in a field in which it may have some degree of appropriateness . . . but the appropriateness or utility of such an application must be evaluated in the light of the relative costs and benefits.[26]

It is just such a cost–benefit analysis which Kaplan has employed in his influential book arguing the case for the legalisation of marijuana – *Marijuana – The New Prohibition.*[27]

The Commission observed that the proportion of cannabis users brought to court was negligible – possibly under 1 per cent – and it was sceptical as to the value of a possessory offence as a means of preventing trafficking (of drugs generally). But in view of the attitude of law enforcement authorities, it was not disposed, at the date of the Interim Report, to discard possessory offences entirely. Two years later in *Cannabis* it recommended legalising simple possession of marijuana while retaining the prohibition on distribution; this was only a matter of a few weeks before the American National Commission on Marijuana and Drug Abuse reached substantially similar conclusions.[28] This shift in opinion reflects growing signs in America and to some extent in Britain that the police are themselves increasingly sceptical of the utility of the possessory offence, especially as regards marijuana.

But the Le Dain Commission still adhered to its basic position outlined in the Interim Report and developed the point that Mill's attitude towards self-harm was too simplistic. In particular it stressed the secondary effects of self-harm which may derive from drug use. First, there is the immediate impact on the family with possibly far-reaching effects in terms of emotional disturbance, relationships and responsibilities. Then one must consider the extra cost in medical and social service facilities, as well as the time and expertise of doctors, paramedical and social workers. Lastly, there is the imponderable general effect on the motivation and productive capacity required for a society to maintain its institutions.

In its Final Report (1973) the Commission reaffirmed its views on the acceptability of legal control. But whereas it had previously recommended that there should be no imprisonment for simple possession of *any* psychotropic drug, in the Final Report, influenced by an increase in opiate dependence, it proposed that for opiates and cocaine a sentence of up to two years should in principle be retained as a sanction.

Looking at the matter from the individual's standpoint, we cannot shirk the argument that people should be legally entitled to take their own road to perdition. In its most extreme form, this is recognised by the Suicide Act 1961. Granted that drug dependence frequently connotes an attempt to come to terms with an otherwise insupportable existence, it can also – especially with certain kinds of heroin and barbiturate dependence – represent a long drawn out suicide attempt.

'Nor can it be said that any consistent principle dictates the occasions on which the law at present intervenes to protect the individual from himself.'[29] Commonplace examples abound. We have not yet made the wearing of seat belts in cars compulsory,[30] despite highly persuasive evidence that the number of accidents would be significantly reduced. There is no law against becoming a stunt man, wall-of-death rider or fire-eater, or against engaging in any number of demonstrably hazardous activities.

Admittedly this is not a positive argument for refusing to impose legal controls on drug use, but once it is clear that any society is bound to leave a measure of freedom for self-injury, it becomes necessary to examine very closely the priorities for legal intervention.

Harm to others, as the Le Dain Commission argues, does not only arise directly through exploitation, but also indirectly from the demands made on social services. To take an extreme case, when X, during an LSD 'trip', falls through a window on to a passing car he may, as well as endangering his own life, and consequently injuring those to whom he has 'assignable duties', also directly injure the person and property of others and constitute a drain on publicly subsidised health and welfare resources already in short supply.

While one must never lose sight of the fact that the crucial question in this context is how the pressure on such resources would be affected by various possible legal régimes, the suggestion that we are dealing with purely self-regarding conduct is simply unmaintainable for all but the most patently innocuous forms of drug use.

Whether or not drug use entails a more nebulous form of harm to the social structure as a whole will be investigated at greater length. At this stage it is perhaps sufficient to reiterate Hart's warning against the dangers of assuming that a society constitutes a seamless web, remembering also that drug use itself is not a seamless web, but covers a large spectrum of behaviour which does not admit of a single, comprehensive explanation.

Above all, one is struck by the complexity both of the notion of harm and of the nature of the Law's response to it, as well as the inadequacy of an 'either/or', 'condemn/condone' approach. That legal sanction can operate at several levels is neatly illustrated by the civil case of *O'Connell* v. *Jackson,* [31] and the recent spate of cases about car seat belts.

A motor cyclist who was not wearing a crash helmet when riding his moped was thereby held contributorily negligent for injuries he received in a crash, although he was in no way responsible for the *occurrence* of the accident. His damages were reduced by 15 per cent. Here we can see how, in practice, self-harm and harm to others can merge in such a way that, while no criminal sanction is imposed, [32] the plaintiff is in effect penalised for behaviour which at first sight connotes potential self-harm only. If someone is negligently run over and his injuries are accentuated by his self-induced drugged condition, is he to be deemed contributorily negligent or should he be entitled to take advantage of the rule that the defendant must take his victim as he finds him?

We could of course abandon the attempt to formulate degrees of culpability in this area altogether, and revert to the nineteenth century approach where, as we have seen, there was virtually no control at all. Would the 'drug scene' then be materially different?

In the nature of things, the question cannot be answered with confidence. Our information about drug taking at the time is scanty; understanding of medical aspects of dependence was very limited and there was nothing to compare with the vast range of drugs and synthetics which we have today.

Initially, it is puzzling that, in the absence of controls, behaviour which is now scarcely ever out of the newspaper headlines, and can involve visibly dramatic symptoms, seems to have attracted so little attention in the documentation of nineteenth century social history. References to it pale into insignificance by contrast with the detailed information we have about alcoholism.

No doubt the explanation is primarily ignorance of the phenomenon of addiction. Since opium and home remedies containing it were standard medicines, it would indeed be strange for people to attribute illness or death to them. There is evidence to suggest that in some parts of the country opium eating was frequently indulged in. Presumably the stigma which currently attaches to drug use was far less marked, not only because of a failure to appreciate the mechanism of addiction, but also because the 'criminalising' effect of legal prohibition, reinforced by influential communication media, was absent.

But it would be incorrect to assume that no stigma at all existed. The following extracts from the Medical Times of 1873 give us a rare insight into the significance of opium-eating as seen by a medical practitioner of the time:

> . . . To begin with, one must make a distinction between the use of opium as a medicine, and as a luxury food. The line is not a very level one always, and there are many cases difficult to allot to one side or the other, but we may say broadly that whoever uses opium for the relief of pain, or to procure sleep, uses it as a medicine, even though it be used habitually. On the other hand, whoever uses it merely for exhilaration of mind, or for the enhancement of bodily comfort, uses it as a luxury. The lines between food, stimulants, or luxuries, and medicines, are often purely arbitrary, but still there are cases which can be clearly referred to one of these classes, though others are of mixed kind. The great English opium-eater – De Quincey – began the use of it as a remedy for neuralgia; just so women who are incautiously recommended to take wine or brandy as a medicine for debility, may continue it as a luxury; and the use and misuse have generally some meeting-point.
>
> Now, opium-eating is practised – as a luxury – in England; and I believe that, this, if carefully studied, will be found to give the key to the whole question in the East. In England opium-eating is a trifle; in the East it is a matter of imperial policy, – but the conditions which give rise to it in one place and the other are alike.
>
> Opium-eating is not to be found in London. Of course amongst the three millions and three-quarters there are to be found some persons here and there who take it as a luxury, though by far the greater number of those who take it in anything like quantity do so for some old neuralgia or rheumatic malady, and began under medical advice. Neither is it to be found over the agricultural or manufacturing districts, save in the most scattered and casual way. The genuine opium-eating districts are the ague and fen districts of Norfolk and Lincolnshire. There it is not casual, accidental, or rare, but popular, habitual and common. Anyone who visits such a town as Louth or Wisbeach, and strolls about the streets on a Saturday evening, watching the country people as they do their marketing, may soon satisfy himself that the crowds in the chemists' shops come for opium; and they have a peculiar way of getting it. They go in, lay down their money, and receive the opium pills in exchange without saying a word. For instance, I was at Wisbeach one evening in August, 1871; went into a chemist's shop; laid a penny on the

counter. The chemist said – "The best?" I nodded. He gave me a pill-box and took up the penny; and so the purchase was completed without my having uttered a syllable. You offer money and get opium as a matter of course. This may show how familiar the custom is . . .

In these districts it is taken by people of all classes, but especially by the poor and miserable, and by those who in other districts would seek comfort from gin or beer. But there is this remarkable characteristic about the opium-eaters. They are probably dirty, slovenly, and lazy, lying and sanctimonious, begging of the clergy and district visitors, but they are not uproarious, and do not swear. There are none of the deeds of brutal violence that are inspired by beer, and none of the foul language. Where others say "damn", they say "bless", and, in fact, you may almost know an opium-eater by his use of the word "blessed" . . .

Such are the moral effects of opium when used as a luxury in England: a state of dreamy comfort and forgetfulness of aches and pains of mind and body – a state in which people dream of virtue, and goodness and piety, and do nothing. The districts in which it is popular show the cause: the agueish, chilly, neuralgic maladies of the district, for which opium is a remedy, and which create a kind of constitutional peculiarity that tolerates opium. So that some persons who begin to take it as a medicine continue it as a comfort, and others follow their example, and take it without the original excuse. Question an opium-eater, and he or she will most likely deny the habit point-blank: if they confess it, they plead the comfort it gives.

[After a visit to a Madras opium house] When we had satisfied our curiosity, we entered with our intelligent host into the moral and political side of the question. Surely these people, we said, are pursuing a very dangerous pleasure; they will go on and lose their health and faculties, and become idiots and spectres. 'Sir', said our host, 'if people choose to do without anything of an intoxicating sort, why not? But we know they all do take something; the Englishman, he takes his rum and beer and tobacco; the Chinaman and Mussulman, they smoke opium. . . . But even if the habit be a bad one, it is better than drinking grog, for many reasons. First of all, women never smoke opium. Then, people who smoke don't smell of it as they do after grog. Then see the difference – a man takes opium and remains his own master; but grog takes him and masters him, and makes him talk nonsense and fight uproariously; while the very essence of opium-smoking is quietness. The smoker must lie down, and can't talk, and does not want to fight – he is fit for his work or to go home to his wife and family; and you can't always say this for the grog-drinker.[33]

Clearly one cannot generalise from the comments of a single, relatively well-informed observer, but it is interesting to reflect how different a picture of the fen districts would emerge from a description of the same patterns of behaviour in the modern press.

There would seem, therefore, to be some evidence – admittedly much of it of a negative kind – of an association between a lack of legal control and a relative absence of stigma. This view would also accord with the analysis by Duster[34] of the change in attitude towards drug use in America after the implementation of the Harrison Act (1914).

Whether or not the policy of very strict control adopted there has on balance had more adverse than beneficial effects is another imponderable. Certainly, several of its critics have expressed a preference for the 'British system'. According to Morris and Hawkins:

> There seems to be no doubt, however, that the policy of criminalisation and the operations of criminal justice agencies in this field have in themselves been criminogenic without measurably diminishing the extent of the drug problem or reducing the supply of narcotics entering the country.[35]

But to revert to a wholly *laissez faire* system is obviously out of the question. A degree of paternalism to protect the young and vulnerable is almost universally accepted. Most people would also acknowledge the need for controls to prevent exploitation by large scale trafficking, certainly of drugs such as heroin. Whether such controls are desirable to prevent mass distribution of less harmful drugs is more debatable, but it is important to recognise that a tolerant attitude towards private use combined with a strict control over distribution of the same drug (cannabis again being the obvious example) is only anomalous if one falls into the trap of an 'either/or' attitude. In other words, the state can legitimately condone private use while discouraging activities or consumption which on a global scale may involve both wholly disproportionate profits and medical hazards.

An obvious difficulty is that – as the American experience depressingly indicates – profitability is to a large degree dependent on illegality. As regards heroin, we have probably struck the right balance. No one would be sanguine about heroin being as available as aspirin. On the other hand, the refusal to adopt the total ban imposed in America is thought by many observers to have been an important factor in keeping the black market price too low to tempt the Mafia to try and control its supply in this country.

Once one has discarded the 'either/or' mentality and tries to picture drug use in its broader perspective, one can see the force behind Mill's view that education, persuasion and argument, rather than coercion, should be our primary considerations. The failure of Prohibition in America demonstrated the sheer impracticability of the attempt to alter, at a stroke, social patterns which had been built up and institutionalised over many generations. But even much smaller scale efforts to proscribe particular drugs have often merely served to create the pricked balloon effect, sometimes observable in a matter of months, as witness the dramatic short term changes in the nature of drug taking habits in London in the late nineteen sixties.[36]

The attempt to *eradicate* particular forms of drug use has hardly ever been successful and is invariably accompanied by adverse side effects. It is only because such an approach is still so commonly advocated that it is necessary to spell out the absurdity of expecting to remove overnight what by definition are deeply ingrained habits. More attention needs to be paid to non-coercive methods of adjusting people's attitudes to particular substances and such a process is bound to be lengthy, because no drug is simply 'taken' in the abstract, but involves a whole complex of social, institutional, and subcultural norms.

Thus it would seem pointless to try to eradicate cigarette smoking, but plausible to aim at non-smoking as a norm. A first step has been the health warning on packets. On one level this represents the ultimate absurdity; on another it must be seen as a realistic compromise in an age which tolerates special compartments for *non*-smokers on its public transport. Reports on smoking as a health hazard may have some effect,[37] though the evidence suggests that it is both very limited and transient. We cannot pretend that the whole social and economic structure which supports tobacco (or alcohol) consumption simply does not exist or could be dismantled without profound repercussions. It could conceivably be adjusted, though, as we shall see, even this is an optimistic assumption.

In the context of the debate on the enforcement of morality and its implications for drug use no apology need be made for frequent reference to alcohol and tobacco. For, pharmacological considerations apart, it is a reminder of the wide range of issues and interests involved. In this respect the 'drugs problem' is more multi-faceted than the areas more commonly featured in the morality debate. It is even less amenable than issues such as attempted suicide, abortion and homosexual relations between consenting adults to a simple 'for or against' stand on principle, yet has received the same cavalier treatment in public discussion.

The very fact that consumption of tobacco and alcohol is socially sanctioned has in fact made it impossible to sustain an argument based on the intrinsic immorality of ingesting certain substances rather than others. Few would be willing to argue that it is intrinsically morally worse to smoke marijuana than to drink alcohol. Rather they will point to the alleged adverse consequences of smoking marijuana – hence the primacy of the escalation argument – and to the social acceptance of alcohol.

Implicit in such arguments is a value judgement as to relative harmfulness – the criterion which, in an ideal world, would be the determining factor as to the acceptable measure of legal control. Our task is to apply this criterion as objectively as possible on the basis of agreed evidence as to potential for harm, but taking account of existing *mores* and making such concessions as are unavoidable given existing social structures and responses to drugs.

What needs to be stressed here is that there is a mass of 'hard' data on the dangers presented by irresponsible use of particular drugs and that much research is concerned with the fringe. The problem, for most practical purposes, of whether or not to apply controls does not derive in the main from ignorance as to the intrinsic properties of the drugs, but rather arises because of the numerous variables related to the social context in which they are taken – the mystique they have acquired (which in turn affects the user); the manner in which they are taken; the social consequences of legal control; the quantities in which they are available; the implications for a black market etc.

To pose the problem in this way certainly does not make it seem any less formidable. But it is essential to state it in some such form in order even to begin to formulate the desirable relationship between law and morality in a field which has been, and continues to be, bedevilled by dogmatic and emotive assertions.

Economic implications

It is a commonplace that modern industrial societies are geared to technological progress and productivity. One effect of this is to place a premium during our leisure hours on forms of relaxation which reflect and reinforce such goals. The pursuit of glamour, wealth and the spirit of competition are mirrored in television, bingo and sport respectively.

But an activity which is inconsistent with such values, which questions the motivation behind them, and which would substitute a radically different life style, poses a threat to the economic, as well as social, structure which is bound to be resisted. In the case of heroin, the point is obvious since, as we have seen, for many addicts the heroin subculture becomes either their total way of life, or at least, sufficiently dominant to preclude a valuable contribution to the work force.

In a sense, however, this is relatively unimportant, partly because for some a degree of heroin or other opiate dependence is a prerequisite of effective social and economic functioning but more simply because in England the number of heroin addicts is far too small to make any significant inroad into overall economic effectiveness.

By contrast, with socially accepted drugs such as alcohol and tobacco, we have gone to elaborate lengths to, as it were, build them into the structure of the working day, rationalising their use and ignoring their dangers. The very existence of pubs, the whole mythology which surrounds social drinking, the place of alcohol in business transactions, the pressures to conform, heightened by intensive advertising, are all common knowledge.

If one assumes that there are approximately 700,000 alcoholics in the country,[38] the cost to the nation in monetary terms alone must be several hundred million pounds a year, if one takes into account factors such as sickness benefit and social security as well as days lost and loss of efficiency.

Smoking has been officially described as the largest single avoidable cause of death[39] – primarily by association with lung cancer, bronchitis and coronary heart disease. In 1970, 50,000 people, constituting one in seven of all deaths before the age of seventy-five, are believed to have died through cigarette smoking.

Yet there is no evidence of a decline in the vast industries which have been built up. Alcohol accounted for 7 per cent of total consumer expenditure in 1970 (£2,178 million) and tobacco 5·5 per cent (£1,720 million). The predictable short term fall in cigarette sales following the report of the Royal College of Physicians[40] – 127,900 million in 1970, 122,400 million in 1971 – was reversed in 1972 (130,500 million), and total tobacco consumption also increased. Alcohol consumption has been steadily increasing since the war.[41] The total cost of advertising alcohol in 1967 was £25·5 million. In 1968, £52 million was spent in promoting tobacco products (including gift coupon schemes).

Any run down of industries of these proportions would have formidable economic implications. The calculation is highly complex. A ban on cigarette advertising would seriously endanger the already precarious newspaper industry. The vast loss of revenue would be partially offset by savings to the Health Service and arguably by increasing productivity. It would be substantially met by redistribution of taxation to cover substitute consumer expenditure. There would be a measure of unemployment, which would seriously affect the major plants.

In *Smoking and Health Now*[42] it was maintained that 'the government's failure to take any preventive action is based on the fear that the country can neither afford to lose the revenue derived from tobacco taxation nor tolerate the economic consequences of running down the tobacco industry.' But because these consequences would take effect gradually the report concludes that 'it is clear that if smoking of present day cigarettes were greatly reduced the ultimate economic and social benefits would be much greater than the temporary economic inconvenience.'[43]

It is true that some legal measures are now being taken to try to contain smoking – health warnings on cigarette packets and advertisements, more 'no-smoking' compartments on the underground, and reduced smoking facilities in places of public entertainment – albeit to little effect. But no comparable measures have been taken to restrict alcohol consumption.

Indeed, it is quite possible, in view of the proposals of the Erroll Committee on Licensing Reform[44] – aimed at harmonising our drinking habits with those of Europe – that the reverse will be the case. Licensing hours could very well be extended, and the legal age limit on drinking in a pub lowered to seventeen years. While it is not contended that there is a necessary correlation between drinking time and adverse effects, in so far as the 'condemn/condone' theory has any plausibility, it could be applied here just as legitimately as to the reluctance of Parliament to reduce penalties for smoking cannabis. (To put the matter at its lowest, extended hours implies a further accommodation to changing drinking habits.)

It is only realistic, then, to consider illegal drugs in a background of sustained, perhaps increasing, use of tobacco and alcohol. On this admittedly rather fatalistic view, the argument for legalising cannabis *simply because* it is not shown to be more (or as) harmful surely misses the point. There is no evidence to suggest that increasing cannabis consumption is accompanied by a decline in alcohol or tobacco consumption. The Le Dain Commission observed that 'In general, survey studies find that those who use alcohol are more likely than "teetotallers" to use cannabis, and most cannabis users still use alcohol.'[45]

In particular in the case of tobacco, where positive steps are being taken to try to check consumption – with the inference that its use might never have been sanctioned had its potential for harm been known – the argument that *since* tobacco is legal so cannabis should be has little merit. The case for legalisation of cannabis should primarily be viewed in terms of the kind of cost–benefit analysis propounded by Kaplan, rather than by a watered down version of the 'two wrongs make a right' fallacy.

The lengths we have gone to in accommodating alcohol and tobacco raises a question concerning the legal status of cannabis which will be explored further in the next chapter, but should also be touched on in the present context. Can a society which is strongly committed to economic growth maintain its competitive position if smoking cannabis becomes as socially acceptable as drinking, or smoking cigarettes?

Would the daily work routine of a Britain where cannabis was as readily available from the tobacconist as a packet of cigarettes be materially affected? It is easy to see that an underlying fear of government – amply demonstrated in the harsh drug laws of economically backward countries such as Turkey, Egypt and Iran – is that the economic utility of its work force would be undermined.

The stock response to this argument is that the consumption of relaxant drugs, such as alcohol or cannabis, is primarily a leisure time activity and that the motivation or lack of motivation to work efficiently is not causally connected with it. But it will be necessary to consider whether there are any differences between cannabis consumption and that of socially tolerated drugs which cast doubt on this assumption. More generally, the whole controversy over cannabis can be viewed as a symbol of the subconscious, but increasingly surfacing hopes and fears that we entertain about the realisation of science fiction fantasies, a step on the road to the discovery of the 'perfect' synthetic relaxant, the soma of Huxley's *Brave New World,* the ultimate rejection of our central work orientated ethic.[46]

So far we have been considering economic factors which militate against alterations to the conventionally accepted modes of drug use, and which would seem to argue against their extension. But this resistance to change coexists with a constant flow of new synthetic drugs being released on to the market by an extremely powerful pharmaceutical industry. Often these drugs are no better than those they purportedly improve on, but simply minor variations adequate to comply with patent law. A few very large companies have a vested and seemingly irreversible interest in persuading us – often by highly dubious advertising techniques – that it is necessary to swallow a pill at the slightest pretext.[47]

A cursory examination of the early history of the thalidomide disaster – without exploring the later controversy over responsibility for the drug's effects on the foetus – illustrates how undesirable it is to regard the marketing of drugs as essentially the same process as promoting any other product. When the drug first appeared in West Germany, it was glowingly advertised as being 'completely innocuous'. Soon there were reports of serious side effects – polyneuritis and nerve damage. The reaction of the company marketing the drug speaks for itself:

> Unfortunately, we are now receiving in increasing numbers reports on the side-effects of this drug, as well as letters from doctors and pharmacists who want to put Contergan [thalidomide] on prescription. From our side, everything must be done to avoid prescription enforcement, since already a substantial amount of our turnover comes from over-the-counter sales.[48]

Sales promotion was intensified. Researchers were sought to counter the adverse reports and company representatives employed in attempting to dissuade doctors from publishing their findings.[49]

Whereas nineteenth century drug abuse was virtually confined to opium and laudanum, the profusion of synthetic stimulant and depressant drugs is a modern phenomenon without a historical parallel. 'The prescription of tranquilisers, sedatives and sleeping pills is growing at four per cent a year . . . giving a total of forty-seven million prescriptions last year. Social acceptance of this mass medication seems to be increasing.'[50]

The superfluous contents of countless medicine cupboards throughout the country provide a depressing model of technological spill out. 'We live in a chemical age, and drugs are a part of our life.'[51]

The social climate

A common corollary of a dynamic industrial society is a puritanical social ethic. Until recently, the idea that people could obtain pleasure, enjoyment or gratification which was not the reward of continued hard work was roundly condemned as immoral.

Since the Second World War, however, there have been perceptible modifications of this attitude. Modern advertising, consumer affluence, the advent of the hire purchase and credit card economy – which shows every sign of intensifying,[52] have made deep inroads into the traditional and still officially sanctioned philosophy of restraint. Drug use is a barometer of social change – we 'need' stimulants to be fully alert participants in a vibrant society in which dynamism is essential to success; we 'need' tranquilisers to cope with the pressures and stresses it imposes.

Moral attitudes now cover the full spectrum from total rejection of any drugs to unquestioning acceptance of them all. The first of these extremes is really, of course, impossible in practice, unless one defines 'drug' in an unscientifically narrow way. But one can classify its adherents, in principle, as those who regard it as immoral, or perhaps demeaning, to swallow an aspirin for a headache, who eschew 'artificial' aids to relief, and whose social values in most cases were formed in the pre-war years.

The vast majority of people today are only too ready to accept drugs for relief from pain, obviously, and primarily, because it is desired as an end in itself, but partly because one can rationalise the use of artificial aids as a means to greater working effectiveness. The use of pills to create energy and vitality makes the point even more clearly. When the purpose is to enable bomber pilots to remain alert on active service, official sanction and mass acceptance are readily forthcoming; when it is to enable teenagers to stay awake in clubs on a Saturday night, popular disapproval is not solely explained by a generalised mistrust of the younger generation, but, more specifically, the pleasurable purpose which the drug is being made to serve.

There are two distinct but closely related objections here. First, the pleasure obtained by, for example, amphetamines and cannabis, is suspect because it is seen as unearned; but also because it is more or less immediate. Is it fanciful to suggest that a minor reason for drunkenness not evoking the same degree of disapproval is that it is typically a more gradual and perceptible process?

Opposition to illegal drug use on the grounds that unearned, instant pleasure is immoral may be explained in several ways. It may simply be the kind of puritanism which deprecates the pleasure of others from envy or jealousy. It may also express the psychological need to justify the rightness and propriety of one's own life style by deploring that of others. For many it doubtless does take these negative forms. But that does not preclude a more reasoned disquiet, a legitimate concern that the quality of people's lives can be eroded if taking drugs becomes a mindless activity in a vacuum, an isolated end in itself, devoid of context or framework. Perhaps an apt analogy would be the way in which advances in modern educational theory have been misconstrued by those who insist on young children being permitted total freedom of expression and require them to use their imaginative and creative powers, without providing any structure on which to build.

Even those most committed to increased use of psychoactive drugs for non-medical purposes cannot be complacent about the way in which innumerable young people, in an endeavour to follow the latest craze, latch on to multi-drug use, eagerly consuming any substance they are offered, often totally ignorant of what it contains; or, irresponsibly taking hallucinogens without taking any precautions against the possibility of a 'bad trip' and lacking the inner resources to derive benefit from their experience.

This is not to disparage life styles which concentrate on the here and now and reject deferred gratification as a matter of principle, whether it be in the field of drug use or consumer credit. The point is simply that because most people need a structure and some sense of development in their lives, and are vulnerable to commercial exploitation, experiences which are valuable for the few may overwhelm or cause widespread disillusion for the majority.

Undoubtedly a major factor in the present day controversy between what can loosely be called the 'puritanical' and 'hedonistic' schools of thought is that illicit drug use has become one of the key symbols of generational conflict. This traditional hostility may well be a psychological necessity, but making drugs the battleground serves only to foster more ignorance on the subject, as the two sides become further entrenched in their positions. However, this symbolic role has been less apparent in the last year or so. One can only hope that as time passes constant ventilation of drugs problems will ultimately have a salutary effect, making possible a franker recognition of everyone's need for a drug of some kind. Openness on the subject is not merely desirable in itself, but will in the long term be vital for psychological adjustment to the much heralded automated and leisured society which is, or was, reputedly on its way.

The influence of politics

Moving to a more tangible sphere, it is necessary to stress the importance of the attitude of politicians towards drug problems. In so far as legislation can affect the morality and patterns of drug use, the considerations which influence politicians are inevitably highly relevant.

When popular feeling on a moral issue is, for the most part rigid, as in regard to the classification of drugs, there are few votes to be won by radically challenging it. Nor do the exigencies of the parliamentary timetable augur well for investigation of such issues in depth. The reception of the Wootton Report in Parliament was as revealing as its treatment in the press was misleading.[53]

One might go further and say that several of the speeches in the Commons' Debate were little more than a refined version of the compound of ignorance and alarmism of the popular press. The blanket condemnations, the emotive language, the unsupported assertions are all there:

> The effects of cannabis are bad. It is all very well for the Hon. Member for Yarmouth to say that when it is taken in moderation they are not bad. The essential of drug taking is that one has to take more and more to have the same effect.[54]

A report which in the short time since its publication stands out as a model of moderation was ungraciously and unfairly castigated by the then Home Secretary, Mr Callaghan, who called for a halt to the rising tide of permissiveness, suggested that the Committee was over-influenced by the pro-legalisation lobby and added: '. . . eventually these remarkable conclusions emerged that it would be wrong to legalise it but that the penalties should be reduced.'[55]

The shadow Home Secretary, Mr Hogg, in the course of an impassioned speech, observed:

> When I talk to members of my profession and, often enough, to members of the medical profession, I find that, although they cannot always give figures which prove these facts, as has been the case all over the world, this drug is associated in their minds and professional experience with crime, violence and abnormality of one sort or another, but, most commonly of all, with a kind of degradation of the personality . . . We are a nation of cigarette smokers and drinkers. Are we to become a race of hashish addicts as well?[56]

In praising the Government's rejection of the Report, Mr Hogg said: 'In this case, I am convinced that the Home Secretary's *political* judgement was sound.'[57]

It is fair to say that the debates which preceded the passing of the Misuse of Drugs Act 1971 (and there were several, since the original Bill lapsed due to the change of Government) were far more constructive, though again there are numerous examples of the kind of dogmatic statement to which we have just referred.

What emerges most clearly from these debates is the recognition that the law is only one of many elements in a complex situation and that, short of the kind of radical steps which are politically unacceptable, legal modifications to the existing structure can only have a very limited effect. Thus, the 1971 Act, while it introduces some welcome improvements, is not the kind of measure which is going to influence the way people think about drugs. Indeed, as we have seen, it perpetuates some serious anomalies.

Certainly few politicians can resist the temptation which the drugs issue provides for sloganising. In introducing the Criminal Justice Bill 1971, Mr Maudling, outlining the proposals for dealing with violence, stated: '. . . I would include drug peddling, because I regard drug peddling as a violence against the human spirit equally as iniquitous as any physical violence.' [58] This may be rousing House of Commons rhetoric but, put so broadly, it does a disservice to the cause of drug education. Once again, the all purpose emotive phrase 'drug peddling' is employed. Would he include cannabis? Presumably yes, because the new maximum penalties for 'peddling' cannabis are identical to those for Class A drugs. Would he, however, consider the shopkeeper 'peddling' alcohol as perpetuating 'violence against the human spirit'?

Of course, political attitudes towards drug control are strongly influenced by international considerations and obligations. The Domino theory is not confined to international relations in the broad sense. England, with its ports and extensive international trade is vulnerable to trafficking and no country can be keen on acquiring a reputation as a drug addicts' haven.[59]

As noted earlier, Turkey and Mexico, where opium and cannabis respectively are grown in abundance, and France, which has for several years, in the Marseilles area, been a centre of clandestine laboratories, manufacturing heroin to supply the North American market, have come under intense American pressure.

Turkey is periodically urged to impose stricter control on opium production in exchange for financial compensation for its farmers. The policy has never proved very effective,[60] and threats to withhold economic aid on a much wider scale are occasionally made. 'Operation Intercept', begun in 1969, was an attempt by the American government to compel co-operation by the Mexican authorities in more intensive efforts to control cultivation of marijuana and prevent smuggling of marijuana and heroin across the border. Its 'success' demonstrated the pricked balloon effect – hashish smuggling increased, as did experimentation with other, dangerous drugs.

The Franco-American Protocol on narcotic control (1971) agreed to 'the setting up of a close co-operation between the specialised services engaged in the fight against the illicit traffic in narcotics of the two countries.' Pressure was brought to bear by the United States Bureau of Narcotics and, for several years American agents made strenuous efforts to locate illegal heroin laboratories and to break drug rings in France. Despite some spectacular hauls – for example, one of 200 pounds of heroin in October 1971 – the chances of putting an end to the traffic remain slim.

In France there has been strong evidence of police acquiescence and alleged involvement of diplomats and secret service agents. Sensitivity on issues of national sovereignty coexists uneasily with fears of economic reprisals.[61] Also, as we have seen, one result of stronger police measures has been the emergence of Brazil as a major centre.

What is true of producer countries applies equally to those consumer countries which, left to their own devices, might well take a more liberal view of drug use. To begin with, there is the whole background of international commitment – the United Nations' programme through the World Health Organisation to combat trafficking and dependence, and the Single Convention on Narcotic Drugs 1961, as well as the Convention on Psychotropic Substances (1971).

The WHO maintains a decidedly cautious approach in its attitude to control and to innovative methods of treatment. Its policies and pronouncements are primarily dictated by the appalling problems associated with the abuse of particular drugs in underdeveloped Asian countries.

Canada, for example, is a party to the Single Convention. Before contracting out, or so framing any legislation as to avoid conflict, it would have to pay very close regard to American opposition to relaxing the law. It would also, from a purely domestic point of view be loathe to encourage the influx of people with little motivation to build up its economy, a predictable consequence given the relative harshness of Drug Laws in most countries. In fact the Government has responded to the Le Dain Commission's recommendation that simple possession of cannabis be legalised only by dropping prison sentences for first offenders.[62]

Drugs and the military

Fears that extensive drug use will in some way undermine the effectiveness of the nation are not limited to civilian life. The pervasiveness of drug use generally has had its counterpart in war and military establishments. The use of drugs in war is far from new, of course, and it was quite common during the First World War for soldiers in the trenches to be sent morphine by their families and friends. But two aspects of such use today seem worthy of special comment – the extent of it by the American army in Vietnam, and the implications of drug use by military personnel with responsibility for nuclear weapons.

In Vietnam, marijuana and heroin are both extremely cheap, potent, and in almost unlimited supply. Local police control is minimal and

Vietnamese Government officials have been implicated in the drug traffic.

Heroin can be as much as thirty times cheaper than in America. It is also 94–97 per cent pure and can therefore be smoked, mixed with tobacco, unlike the 4 per cent pure American variety which is injected. As the American military role contracted troops were faced with long periods of boredom and inactivity. Knowing that it was official policy gradually to withdraw them heightened their sense of frustration and futility – caught up in a war for which they may have had little or no motivation. The social pressure among troops to smoke marijuana was intense.

There could hardly be a combination of factors more conducive to drug use had it been deliberately created. By mid-1971, it has been estimated that 50,000 of the servicemen were heroin addicts, and at least 20 per cent were using marijuana regularly. Army drug programmes in Vietnam itself were little more than a token gesture towards solving the heroin problem – conditions were wholly inappropriate, facilities poor and commanding officers unpredictable in their attitude towards establishing treatment centres. It is widely acknowledged that adequate treatment was only possible when the troops had returned home.

To the traditional problems of readjustment and employment on demobilisation was added the distressing element of large numbers of young Americans, once well-equipped to lead fulfilling lives, exacerbating the already enormous heroin problem of the big American cities. Thousands may have returned with their addiction undetected, having taken elaborate steps to fake the urinalysis tests which, from mid-1971, they all underwent on leaving Vietnam.

It would be dangerous to try to draw many conclusions from the specialised circumstances of the war in Vietnam. In fact, a follow-up study of some 500 soldiers, who had received only a thirty day period of detoxification before return to the United States, found that 93 per cent were drug free one year later.[63] It does, however, illustrate how the combination of stress and cheap, readily available drugs can lead to drug use of alarming proportions, in a situation where alertness and vitality are indispensable. It will also, doubtless, have repercussions in America going far beyond those of economic adjustment, by reinforcing public hostility towards drug use generally. One of the ironies of the 'hard-sell' anti-cannabis campaign launched for the benefit of the troops was, it seems, that many, finding marijuana relaxing and non-addictive, assumed that this was also true of heroin, particularly if it could be smoked and did not have to be injected. But the consequences are far more likely to be represented as proof of the escalation theory.

Passing from a specific war situation to military life generally, the fears associated with drug use are, if anything, even greater. In an age of nuclear power and missiles one does not have to be a crank to express misgivings about men responsible for the security of nuclear installations having access to marijuana and LSD.

Despite elaborate screening tests, several such incidents have been recorded.

> Official service investigations have confirmed cases of drug taking by men in the Navy's Polaris submarine crews, in the Air Force's Strategic Air Command, and in the Army's Nike–Hercules missile battalions . . . in each service, two key men of the crew on duty could trigger an atomic explosion.[64]

In the circumstances it is perhaps fortunate that an inquiry, which was not instituted to investigate allegations of drug use, but revealed thirty-five drug users and sellers among men assigned to a missile battalion, found that there was only one drug user per battery. When challenged about these incidents, the Pentagon's stock response is illuminating: 'What can you do? Drugs infect the society. They're bound to get into the military.'[65]

Drugs and religious practice

We have been considering some of the underlying fears that drugs constitute a threat to the dynamic functioning of a society and could so weave themselves into its fabric as to undermine social values, economic competitiveness and military security. Lastly, we might note a more abstract, but conceptually similar fear, that drug use represents a threat to conventional Western religious practice.

> Modern drug use would definitely seem to be related in some measure to the collapse of religious values – the ability to find a religious meaning of life. The positive values that young people claim to find in the drug experience bear a striking similarity to traditional religious values, including the concern with the soul and inner self. The spirit of renunciation, the emphasis on openness and the closely knit community, are part of it, but there is definitely the sense of identification with something larger, something to which one belongs as part of the human race.[66]

One must avoid falling prey to mystification. The scene outside the all-night chemist's at Piccadilly Circus before the treatment centres were set up was not most people's idea of Nirvana. But religion, too, has its share of false prophets, and to discount all forms of modern drug taking as devoid of spiritual significance is as indefensible as unquestioning, total acceptance.

The use of drugs (other than alcohol) in religious practices is characteristic of several Eastern religions or disciplines in which meditation and contemplation play a key role. There is a marked historical link with economic underdevelopment. Meditation need not necessarily imply passivity, but it is widely thought to. No Western government would welcome a pronounced shift in that direction, the spiritual counterpart of contracting out of the technological society.

The revival of interest in mysticism, the cult of the 'here and now' which, though always associated with youth, seems more prevalent than among previous generations, signifies an impatience with the institutional framework and historical strait jacket of the Church. It also reflects a disenchantment with the rationalist and scientific foundation of modern society, sufficiently far-reaching for some to discard logical positivism in favour of the Tarot cards.

Within the Established Churches, drug use as a means of satisfying spiritual hunger has found few sympathisers. It is almost invariably seen as a threat and the reasons are not hard to find. First, there is an all-too-human resistance to the possibility of an hallucinogenic short cut to states of mind otherwise attained, if at all, only after years of soul searching and exacting discipline. Can the achievement of a lifetime's work be simulated, even approximately, by popping a microdot LSD tablet into one's mouth? The sceptic's resistance is strengthened when he realises that he is being asked to use a product of the very science which is said to have blunted his religious awareness, in order to attain a state of cosmic consciousness, '. . . an extension of soulless technology to the soul itself'.[67]

Nor is he reassured by the seemingly frivolous life style of some of the more vociferous proponents of a psychedelic heaven. Certainly the life of the ascetic religious contemplative is far removed from the emphasis in the LSD experience on the use of sensory aids; though it would be a distortion of traditional forms of mysticism, in particular of Buddhism, to equate them with sensory deprivation and ascetic excess.

This sense of a 'spiritual consumer credit' evokes the same mixed feelings as its commercial counterpart. On the one hand, it is a form of religious snobbery to deny people the opportunity of a spark that might otherwise always elude them; on the other, it is legitimate to fear the traumatic (occasionally psychotic) consequences of experiencing overwhelming riches without the resources to handle them. One may feel distaste for a Billy Graham, yet acknowledge that the sudden, blinding flash of spiritual insight has been a distinctive feature of religious experience, both traditional and mystical, throughout the ages.

The assumption that there is a significant distinction between 'true' religious experience and drug induced experience is not without practical consequences. It is responsible for a conflict over the meaning of freedom of religious worship within the American Constitution which is still a live issue regarding the rites of the 125,000 Navajo Indians of the Native American Church,[68] who combine Christian and Indian beliefs. Their use of peyote (a hallucinogen which contains mescalin) for sacramental purposes is at present sanctioned by the law, within strict limits, subject to suppliers being registered and appropriate records kept.[69] In some of the western states there is still vocal opposition to what, in any other context, would be illegal drug use, though a few states have exempted peyote from their narcotics law provisions.

The First Amendment of the Federal Constitution states that 'Congress shall make no law respecting an establishment of religion, or prohibiting the free exercise thereof.' Supreme Court decisions have subsequently indicated that claims to religious exemption 'will be honored unless a substantial state interest will be frustrated in a significant way.'[70]

The only relevant drugs cases have concerned peyote, LSD and marijuana. Two main principles have emerged, namely that prohibiting the use of drugs for religious purposes is not unconstitutional where such use would involve criminal conduct – though this has on occasion been loosely defined as extending to acts contrary to peace, good order and morals; nor where there is insufficient proof of *bona fide* religious practice[71] in which drug use plays an essential part.

It is interesting that in the elaborate and very formalised ritual of the Navajo Indians, where ingestion of peyote is one element in a highly structured, institutionalised setting, – the drug itself being an object of worship – adverse reactions would seem to be exceedingly rare.[72] Such a finding is consistent with Huxley's view that the use of mescalin can be a beneficial catalyst, an aid to the attainment of states of consciousness to which relatively few can aspire through more rigorous meditative techniques.

Undoubtedly the discipline involved means that meditative practices are almost bound to remain the preserve of a minority. Moreover, for many drug users, the subtleties of possible qualitative distinctions between drug induced experience and states attained through meditation are less compelling than the fact that the former may be achieved, if temporarily, almost at once. But what may work in the close knit and heavily structured society of the Navajos may prove very elusive in our fragmented industrial societies, especially for someone who lacks precisely the kind of discipline and preparation which facilitates and enriches the experience of the mystic.

Some would go further and argue that, in any event, drug use of the kind Huxley envisaged should always be thought of as a transitional stage, to be dispensed with once higher levels of consciousness have been achieved. 'The most they can offer is momentary glimpses. Their continued use represents a form of spiritual burglary . . .'[73]

But official religious objection to drug induced spiritual experience does not rest solely on a puritanical aversion to the short cut, or, though this is doubtless a sincerely held conviction, on the belief that most people are simply not equipped to cope with it. Institutionalised religion, wedded to a hierarchical church structure, and broadly content not to present a serious challenge to the conventional social and economic order, is not surprisingly unwilling to propagate attitudes which would make people question the authority of the church or the values of the state. The dilemma is real enough, but one may still question the wisdom of the policy in the long run.

Notes

[1] D. Croft *et al.*, 'Gastric Bleeding and Benorylate, a New Aspirin', *British Medical Journal,* vol. 3, 1972, p. 545.

[2] See L. Wilkins, 'Some sociologic factors in drug addiction control', in D. Wilner and G. Kassebaum (ed.), *Narcotics.*

[3] See ch. 7.

[4] *The Times* 29 April 1971.

[5] Report of the Committee on Homosexual offences and Prostitution 1957, Cmnd. 247.

[6] See especially pp. 326–33.

[7] (1972) Information Canada, Ottawa, pp. 275–83.

[8] *On Liberty,* ch. 1.

[9] *Law, Liberty and Morality,* Oxford University Press 1963, p. 32.

[10] Ibid.

[11] *On Liberty,* ch. 5. Both the Le Dain Report on *Cannabis* – see n. 7 – and the First Report of the National Commission on Marijuana and Drug Abuse (US Government Printing Office 1972) advocate a double standard. See ch. 7.

[12] *On Liberty,* ch. 5.

[13] *The Enforcement of Morals,* Oxford University Press 1965.
[14] Ibid., pp. 106, 107.
[15] Ibid., p. 17 and see the Preface at p. viii.
[16] See pp. 119–25.
[17] *The Enforcement of Morals,* p. 14.
[18] Ibid., p. 104.
[19] Ibid., p. 108.
[20] Ibid., pp. 28–29, from 'Morals and the Quasi-Criminal Law and the Law of Tort'.
[21] Ibid., p. 15, from 'Morals and the Criminal Law'.
[22] *Cannabis,* p. 4, para. 16.
[23] See e.g. the selection of letters from private citizens in Appendix B of the Report.
[24] One member, Marie A. Bertrand, published a minority Disagreement recommending total legalisation of cannabis. Interim Report, Penguin p. 356.
[25] Ibid., p. 332.
[26] Ibid., p. 333.
[27] Pocket Books, New York 1971.
[28] But the proposal has not been implemented by the Canadian Government. See p. 173.
[29] The Wootton Report, p. 4, para. 15.
[30] Though the suggestion is currently being considered by the Ministry of Transport. It is compulsory in e.g. France, New Zealand and some Australian States.
[31] [1971] 3 All E.R. 129 (C.A.).

There is a sharp conflict of judicial opinion over whether damages should be reduced for the failure of a driver or passenger to wear a seat belt. See, e.g. *Pasternack* v. *Poulton* [1973] 2 All E.R. 74, and *Drage* v. *Smith* [1974] *The Times* 15 November, where damages were reduced; *Challoner* v. *Williams* [1974] R.T.R. 221, D.C. and *Froom* v. *Butcher* [1974] 3 All E.R. 517, where they were not.
[32] See now: Motor Cycles (Wearing of Helmets) Regulations 1973 (No. 180). As from 1 June 1973, it is an offence for a motor cyclist or his pillion passenger not to wear a crash helmet.
[33] *The Medical Times* vol. 2, 1873, p. 73.
[34] *The Legislation of Morality,* Free Press, New York 1970.
[35] N. Morris and G. Hawkins, *The Honest Politician's Guide to Crime Control,* University of Chicago Press 1970, p. 9.
[36] See e.g. K. Leech, 'The Natural History of Two Drug Cultures', *New Society* 1 June 1972.

[37] See p. 120.

[38] See p. 4.

[39] *On the State of the Public Health* 1970, p. 4.

[40] *Smoking and Health Now,* Pitman, London 1971.

[41] E.g. Beer consumption in pints per head: 1969 – 173; 1970 – 178; 1971 – 184.

Consumption of spirits and wines has increased by about 20 per cent over the same period. Ministry of Agriculture figures, July 1972.

[42] Appendix A: Economic Consequences of a Reduction in Cigarette Smoking.

[43] Ibid., p. 143.

[44] Report of the Departmental Committee on Liquor Licensing, HMSO 1972, Cmnd. 5154.

[45] Interim Report, para. 173.

[46] See M. Schofield, *The Strange Case of Pot,* Penguin.

[47] The pharmaceutical industry in Britain spends nearly £20 million a year on sales promotion as well as vast sums on research. General practitioners receive on average 7 items a day of promotional literature.

£150 million worth of medicines are prescribed each year on the National Health Service alone. According to a study of 45 drug advertisements in a medical journal, carried out in 1963, 22 contained unwarranted claims, and serious side effects or disadvantages were often not mentioned or glossed over. Wade and Elmes, 1963. Quoted, Zacune and Hensman, *Drugs, Alcohol and Tobacco in Britain,* Heinemann 1971, p. 192.

[48] See H. Sjöström and R. Nilsson, *Thalidomide and the Power of the Drug Companies,* Penguin 1972, p. 54.

[49] Ibid., ch. 3.

[50] The Prescribing of Psychotropic Drugs in General Practice. Supplement no. 4, vol. 21, of the *Journal of the Royal College of General Practitioners,* 1971. Quoted *The Times* 9 December 1971.

[51] Le Dain, *Interim Report,* para. 390.

[52] See e.g. Report of the Committee on Consumer Credit 1971, Cmnd. 4596, vol. 1, p. 366 *et seq.*

[53] See M. Schofield, *The Strange Case of Pot,* ch. 8. A perhaps surprising exception was the *Daily Telegraph,* the only national newspaper to come out wholly in favour of the report.

[54] Captain Walter Elliott, H.C. Deb., vol. 776, col. 1001, 27 January 1969. This sweeping statement might be thought peculiarly inappropriate as applied to a drug which some claim – though the evidence is admittedly slight – shows a reverse tolerance effect.

[55] Ibid., col. 959.

[56] Ibid., cols. 956, 957. The emotive distortion of the term 'hashish addicts' is not removed by his definition of an addict as someone who cannot do without something.

[57] Ibid., col. 949. Italics supplied.

[58] H.C. Deb. vol. 826, col. 967, 22 November 1971.

[59] Forty-five per cent of the adult respondents in the American National Survey on Marijuana felt that it is often promoted by people who are enemies of the United States, *Marijuana: A Signal of Misunderstanding,* 1972, p. 100. See n. 11.

[60] Turkey agreed to impose a total ban on the cultivation of opium from the middle of 1972. In 1974 the Government first repealed the ban and then, in September 1974, agreed that when cultivation was resumed, the poppies would not be lanced, i.e. they would be grown to produce 'poppy straw', not opium. UN Information Letter, Division of Narcotic Drugs: no. 11, November 1974.

[61] Any moral force behind this American pressure was seriously undermined in December 1972, when it was discovered that 179 lbs of pure heroin (worth nearly £15 million on the black market) was missing from the New York Police property clerk's offices. The missing heroin included 81 lbs from the haul in the notorious 'French Connection' case. *The Observer* 24 December 1972.

[62] *The Times* 2 August 1972.

[63] Anglo-American Conference on Drug Abuse, Royal Society of Medicine, 1973, p. 106.

[64] *Sunday Times* 5 September 1971.

[65] Ibid.

[66] Le Dain, *Interim Report,* para. 331.

[67] See R. Zaehner, *Drugs, Mysticism and Make-Believe,* Collins 1972, p. 84.

[68] See *American Journal of Psychiatry,* vol. 128, no. 6, pp. 659–99. Quoted *Drugs and Society,* March 1972, pp. 25–26.

[69] *People* v. *Woody* (1964) 61 Cal 2 d 716, 40 Cal Reptr 69, 394 p 2 d 813.

[70] *U.S.* v. *Kuch* (1968, Dc Dist. Col.) 288 F Supp, 439 35 ALR 3d 922, where the court concluded that the 'goofy nonsense, contradictions and irreverent expressions of the official catechism and handbook of the Neo-American Church indicated a sham designed to evade the drug laws.'

[71] See *Leary* v. *U.S.* (1967, CA5 Tax) 383 F 2d 851: Not unconstitutional to prevent an individual from using marijuana in accordance with the practice of a Hindu sect. *People* v. *Woody* (see n. 69)

was distinguished on the ground that in Leary's case marijuana was not essential to his faith but merely one among several aids he used for meditation.

[72] R. Bergman, in his 4 year study (see n. 68) found only one clear case of psychosis, and estimated the rate of adverse reactions as about 1 per 70,000 ingestions.

[73] R. de Ropp, in *Drugs: For and Against,* Hart, New York, pp. 217–18.

6 Towards a Rational Perspective

The more commonly articulated issues

Though it has been suggested that the economic, social, political and religious considerations referred to underpin stock attitudes towards drugs, they are not usually articulated – certainly not in any generalised form – when most people are informally asked to give their views on drug use. Reactions tend instead to follow a predictable pattern, in which it is assumed that there is a single 'drugs problem'; that drug taking is wholly to be condemned; that it diverts scarce medical expertise and resources from more deserving patients and is caused by peddlers corrupting the unsuspecting, who then turn to crime.

It is to be hoped that this, admittedly impressionistic, account is taken seriously by anyone concerned with the practical politics of reforming the drug laws. Such views are widely held not only because they embody commonplace prejudices but, in part, because they contain uncomfortable grains of truth. They are also the kind of conditioned responses which the slogans of the mass media induce, by publicising any conceivable link between violent crime and addicts. Any attempt to formulate drugs policies which pretends that they do not exist, or merely ridicules them, is doomed to failure.

We have already dealt with medical and associated problems, and the case for and against escalation theory will be considered in the next chapter. What is the nature of the relationship between drug use and crime?

Just as an individual's drug use is so potent a symbol that to the outside world it often constitutes his total personality, so the recurrent images of the 'dope fiend' and the opium den conjure up a criminal underworld, such that drug dependence is inextricably bound up with criminality. The absurdity of such an identification is readily apparent when it is acknowledged that neither phenomenon is a discrete entity. It is trite knowledge that to talk of the causes of 'crime' is as meaningless as to try to identify the causes of 'disease'. The error is merely compounded when one refers to 'drugs' as a cause of 'crime'.

The aura of criminality which surrounds drugs is obviously partly attributable to the very illegality of certain forms of drug use and prohibitions on supply and possession. In America, '. . . the addict lives in almost perpetual violation of one or several criminal laws, and this gives him a special status not shared by other criminal offenders.'[1] The process of criminalisation is reinforced in so far as addicts, identified as criminals, are compelled to rely on criminal sources for their supplies.

At the same time, the intrinsic peculiarities of drugs offences and the procedural difficulties of detecting and proving them foster a criminalising effect of a totally different kind. In what is often conceived of as a war against drugs, it is relatively easy to rationalise illegal enforcement practices and a lowering of the standards of procedural safeguards, either from distaste and prejudice or sometimes from a well-meaning, but frequently misguided, belief that prison will 'help' an addict by keeping him away from drugs.

Allegations of planting, by their very nature, cannot be reliably assessed, but abuse of 'stop and search' procedures is more open to investigation. A list of stops and searches without warrant under the Dangerous Drugs Act 1967, made by officers from three stations in the Metropolitan Police District during 1969 revealed wide divergencies:[2]

Station	Cannon Row	Sidcup	Kilburn
Stops	812	nil	45
Arrests resulting	142	nil	13

Police forces have since been requested to provide details for publication. The first such figures to be released came from the Leicester and Rutland Constabulary who, in the period from 12 July 1971, to the end of that year, carried out 62 such searches, finding prohibited drugs on 3 suspects (4·8 per cent) only. By contrast, the same force obtained positive results in 53·5 per cent of breathalyser tests administered under s. 2(1) of the Road Safety Act 1967. The Mid-Anglia force found 131 out of 359 in possession (36·5 per cent) over a similar period. In 1972, of 16,953 persons searched in the country as a whole, 5,175 (31 per cent) were found in possession; in 1973, the respective figures were 18,067 and 5,170 (28·6 per cent).

The difficulty of obtaining evidence of the sale of drugs is also a temptation to police encouragement of the offence. In America there is an established defence of 'entrapment' if it is clear that but for police inducement the defendant would not have committed the crime.[3] No such defence exists in English law.[4] Here the position is that infiltration and encouragement are permissible, in appropriate circumstances, in order to prevent crime. Evidence obtained by the police acting as *agents provocateurs,* that is, actually instigating as distinct from merely concurring in the crime, has occasionally been excluded at the judge's discretion.[5] But a recent Court of Appeal decision cast doubt on when, if at all, such evidence is admissible.[6] When it is admitted, it will at most be relevant to mitigation of the sentence.

'Entrapment' has not proved as contentious an issue in England as in America, but the stop and search powers have aroused considerable opposition. It is a chastening thought that there may be as much questionable practice in the detection of drugs offences as there is 'criminality' in their commission.

In addition to the links between drugs and crime which stem from drugs offences themselves, it is equally obvious that strict controls foster a substantial amount of 'drugs-related' crime – theft, prostitution etc. – to obtain the money needed to support the habit. While the 'British system' seems to have kept this within tolerable limits, the picture in parts of America is far from reassuring. In New York City alone it has been estimated that addicts steal $1 million worth of goods a day to finance illicit heroin use,[7] and a report commissioned by the Bureau of Narcotics and Dangerous Drugs put the total value of thefts by American addicts at $2,827 billion a year.[8]

The links between drugs and crime considered above are, by definition, merely associational. The key question, however, is whether any causal connection exists between drug taking and crime which is not drug related, except in the sense that the drug induced state, or the personalities of drug addicts, are conducive to criminal activity. An initial complication is that, quite apart from any other variables, it is not easy to distinguish between crime committed due to the need to obtain drugs and offences by addicts, or, at least, committed under the influence of drugs, wholly unrelated to such a need.

Any attempt to assess the evidence for a causal link must distinguish clearly between drugs in terms of their differing effects. The kind of behaviour patterns to be expected from heroin use differ radically from those associated with amphetamines. At the same time, it must be borne in mind that such clear cut distinctions are becoming increasingly unattainable in the face of growing evidence of polydrug use. Most recent accounts of selected groups of drugtakers reveal a pattern of multiple drug use. The ill-informed impressionable user is liable to respond to the public's hostility by attaching himself to an undiscriminating 'drug culture'.

Such evidence as we have would suggest that a causal link is most easily demonstrated with alcohol. 'In Britain the peak rate for road accidents coincides with the hour after the pubs close, when an army of incapables is loosed on to the roads.'[9]

Several surveys on problem drinking among prisoners would suggest that the connection is more than coincidental. Thus Gibbens and Silberman[10] reported that 50 per cent of 400 prisoners admitted a 'serious drinking problem' and a significant proportion of first offences were committed under the influence of drink. Edwards *et al.* (1970)[11] found that 68 per cent of 188 men claimed to have been drinking immediately before committing the offence for which they were imprisoned, 55 per cent of these being 'drunk' at the time. In 1968, 42 per cent of all murder defendants were known to have had some alcohol in their bodies at the time of the offence.[12] McClintock's study of crimes of violence[13] is also consistent with a significant causal link.

Such surveys simply bear out common experience of the possible consequences, especially on the roads, even of socially accepted drinking, often seemingly without any deep seated basis, and of the observation that drink is commonly taken to give 'Dutch courage' as a prelude to acts of violence.

As regards other drugs, it seems reasonable to assert that, apart from the shadow cast by the era of Prohibition and the notorious American gangsters, identification with violence has only become widespread and strongly pronounced in Britain since the late 1950s with the advent of large numbers of non-therapeutic addicts. It was not the case when most known addiction was either therapeutically induced or largely confined to the medical and paramedical professions.

Indeed, a moment's reflection would suggest that drugs which have a tranquilising and depressant effect are unlikely to induce criminal behaviour. Even those which disorientate and impair psychomotor functions will, at most, produce ineffective criminals.

Examining the data on heroin and related opiates, one finds that the drugs with the worst 'image' are only tenuously linked with crime. 'The non-drug offences in which the heroin addict typically becomes involved are of the fund-raising variety. Assaultive or violent acts, contrary to popular belief, are the exception rather than the rule for the heroin addict whose drug has a calming and depressant effect.'[14]

Several American studies show that a high proportion of heroin addicts have been convicted for non-drug offences before becoming addicted.[15] In his article on 'Delinquency and Heroin Addiction in Britain,'[16] Dr I. Pierce James concluded that heroin addicts in Britain, in what could be described as the 'Piccadilly junkie' category, exhibit a high degree of delinquent behaviour, but that it usually precedes their addiction (76 per cent of the men and 60 per cent of the women had prior convictions). Their crimes, when addicted, were mostly of an acquisitive or irresponsible but non-violent nature, and they were 'markedly inefficient criminals'. Few had any inclination, or indeed time, for non-drug-related crime – 'most were full time addicts whose whole daily routine was involved in "scoring" and "fixing" and this allowed little time for anything but occasional casual work.'[17] Cockett's findings[18] with a comparable category of addicts are similar and the most recent English study, *Delinquency Amongst Opiate Users* (1974),[19] concluded of a group of non-therapeutic, opiate dependent males 'that drug use, particularly opiate use, modified their criminal histories to the extent that their criminal convictions increasingly became limited to drug offences.' It is reasonable to assume that other types of heroin addicts who are more socially integrated and better able to control their drug use are much less vulnerable to delinquent patterns of conduct.

That it is possible to promote a criminogenic image for a drug intrinsically unlikely to lead to criminal behaviour is demonstrated with cannabis. The constantly publicised adverse associations have encouraged this view, despite its implausibility on scientific grounds. 'In the United Kingdom the taking of cannabis has not so far been regarded, even by the severest critics as a direct cause of serious crime . . . .'[20]

It is true that psychomotor skills are adversely affected and inhibitions lowered so that, *prima facie,* driving under the influence of cannabis presents broadly the same type of dangers as with alcohol. The initial research on this problem suggested that the degree of risk is less marked,[21] but some doubts have since been expressed. Barbiturates, too, when taken in large doses and in combination with alcohol, impair driving ability but their role in criminal behaviour (as distinct from suicide) is negligible.

More difficult to assess is the link between LSD and crime. Many of the more sensational accounts rely heavily on hearsay and are not easily verifiable, but there are well-documented reports of overt conduct and experiences under its influence which seem to be directly attributable to the drug.

In *R.* v. *Lipman,*[22] for example, the defendant gave evidence that he killed his victim in the course of a 'trip' under the illusion that he had descended to the centre of the earth and was being attacked by snakes. In *R.* v. *Wiedemann,*[23] the accused, who was acquitted of manslaughter, had jumped 120 ft from the roof of a hotel on to a passing motorist who subsequently died. Medical evidence suggested that the defendant was suffering from a delayed psychotic reaction four days after taking LSD. This delayed effect poses a formidable problem as to criminal responsibility.

Louria,[24] describing the effects of LSD intoxication on 100 patients in a New York psychiatric hospital, found that 13 exhibited uncontrolled aggression; 7 (unsuccessfully) attempted suicide or homicide; 1 in a panic jumped out of a fourth floor window, sustaining multiple fractures, and another jumped in front of a train because of LSD induced voices. Similar accounts are common:

> During the first few hours after taking the drug there may be violent behaviour; a panic stricken or paranoid patient may attack other people because he believes they threaten him . . . some . . . think they could fly from an upper window. How frequently this sort of behaviour occurs depends *inter alia* on the circumstances in which the drug is taken.'[25]

Even in the above types of situation it is difficult to identify the causal role of the drug with any precision. In the case of a Danish woman, aged twenty-five, who had received five LSD treatments and killed her lover three days after the last treatment, the psychiatric evidence was that LSD had activated already existing impulses.[26] Also, most LSD users have previously taken other drugs. At the same time, the dramatic nature of several of these incidents is significant enough to indicate that they are primarily attributable to specific 'trips', and might otherwise have taken a far less destructive form.

Where one might have anticipated a closer link with crime is in the use of amphetamines, given their ability to heighten confidence and alertness. Evidence from Japan[27] and Sweden[28] suggests strong associational connections and, in some instances, a probable causal role. But otherwise '. . . there are very few reported cases of crime directly attributable to amphetamines.'[29] Certainly the study by Scott and Willcox (1965)[30] revealed no significant difference between the frequency, seriousness and type of offence as between users and non-users. In both cases offences against the person accounted for 6 per cent of offences only.

Amphetamine use has probably increased considerably since 1965, and its dangers were greatly magnified by the sudden cult of intravenous Methedrine abuse in 1967–68, and the prescription of methamphetamine (subsequently voluntarily withdrawn from retail pharmacies) to addicts as a substitute for cocaine. Nonetheless, the DHSS report (1970) suggested '. . . that the probability of a criminal outcome from amphetamine taking is small', and here again the predominant pattern would appear to be associational rather than causal.

The broad conclusion is that, alcohol apart, over the whole spectrum, the claim that drug use is significantly criminogenic is at most an unproven assertion and at worst a facile generalisation.

A rational perspective

If it is conceded that both public opinion and the law are wedded to irrational attitudes towards drugs – a concession made even by those who are, by and large, resigned to the *status quo* – are there any practical steps that can be taken to encourage policies more in accord with current knowledge about the relative harm of various drugs?

It is submitted that a relatively objective account of the main legal and illegal drugs, to remove the major misconceptions, is feasible. The starting point of such a process of re-education is a neutral description of the physical effects of the substances in question.

It will immediately be objected that such a goal is impossible *now,* due to current controversies and our limited knowledge, and, perhaps always unattainable, in that we cannot aspire to an authoritative view. What seems definitive today is exposed as fallacious tomorrow. Tobacco and lung cancer, and the thalidomide tragedies, should be salutary lessons.

But we can at least introduce policies and legislation more consonant with what we *do* know, or have good grounds for believing. Some mistakes will inevitably be made. Thalidomide must be seen in the context of the countless modern synthetics which have saved lives and relieved pain on a vast scale. The familiar argument that it took several hundred years for us to realise the dangers of tobacco overlooks the greatly improved scientific techniques and expertise at our disposal. Such consensus as does exist needs to be effectively publicised.[31]

To begin with, we do have a sufficiently clear picture of the number of people at risk from particular forms of drug use to use as a framework for relative harmfulness. The 'numbers game' may be notoriously dangerous to play, because it conveys an appearance of certainty and scientific precision about what is in fact incalculable. We cannot know precisely how many alcoholics or heroin addicts there are because not all of them come to light, and because there are legitimate grounds of controversy over defining the dependent condition in the first place. But even with conservative estimates we can justify the 'numbers game' as a rough guide for establishing priorities and, hopefully, as an influence on policy, to demonstrate the irrationality of conventional perspectives.

The estimates in the table below must, therefore, be conjectural, but it is believed that if one takes account of the data we do have,[32] the table does not overstate current incidence of abuse (or use, as the case may be), and it is emphasised that no more is claimed for it than to give an overall picture which it is easy to lose sight of when concentrating on a single substance.

Drug	Estimated incidence in UK
Cigarettes	21,000,000 smokers
Alcohol	400,000–700,000 alcoholics
Barbiturates	80,000–140,000 dependent
Aspirin	250,000 misuse
Amphetamines (and related compounds)	100,000 dependent
Heroin (and other opiates)	4,000 dependent
Cannabis	unknown (13,827 offenders convicted in 1973)
LSD	unknown (1,491 offenders convicted in 1973)

To suggest that a conventionally accepted scale of values is misconceived is particularly unwelcome where so vital a matter as health is concerned. The patent rationalisations indulged in by heavy cigarette smokers are well known, ranging from a blatant denial of the validity of research findings to a fool-hardy or resigned defiance. Knowledge and awareness of the facts, in other words, are not enough by themselves. But it should at least be possible to present the information in a way designed to have the maximum possible impact.

There is certainly no shortage of material for dramatic presentation of alarming trends. A few examples will suffice. It has been estimated[33] that cigarette smoking kills almost as many British people each year as the total number of civilians killed by enemy action during the whole of the last war (106,927), and that the number of working days lost through illness attributable to smoking amounts to more than twenty times the number lost through industrial disputes.[34]

Prescriptions for sleeping tablets alone produce 'sufficient tablets to make every tenth night's sleep in the United Kingdom hypnotic induced.'[35] It was recently claimed that there are some 9 million alcoholics (or serious alcoholic abusers) in America (10 per cent of the total work force) and that the cost to the economy in lost work and medical expenses is in the region of $15,000 million a year.[36]

One of the most striking conclusions to be drawn from the figures available and the estimates of incidence above is that, in Britain at least, heroin (and opiate addiction generally) constitutes a relatively minor problem. The point is important in terms of a rational perspective, since heroin is constantly used as the crux in discussions of drug use. There are times when it seems that addiction is virtually equated with heroin addiction.

We can, of course, speak with more confidence about the prevalence of heroin abuse than of most drugs because of its relative visibility, the amount of research that has been done on it and the maintenance of official records. Thus we know that Home Office notifications of known narcotic addicts have never risen above 3,025.[37] It would be surprising if undetected addiction were responsible for more than another 1,000.

The importance of bearing numbers in mind can be further illustrated by taking mortality as an indicator (but by no means the only one) of harmfulness. Though the mortality *rate* among British heroin addicts is very high,[38] mortality in absolute terms is minimal. Thus of the 2,782 addicts notified to the Home Office in 1968, 61 died by the end of the year. The total number of alcohol related deaths in Britain in 1968 was 1,829. In the same year the number of barbiturate related deaths was 1,930.

The Chief Medical Officer of Health estimated in 1969 that nearly 100,000 people in Britain die each year before their time from causes related to cigarette smoking[39] and the following year said: 'It is necessary to repeat that cigarette smoking is the largest, single, avoidable cause of death in Britain today.'[40] Even on the more conservative calculation of *Smoking and Health Now,* there are between 20,000 and 24,000 premature deaths each year in men aged between thirty-five and sixty-four years caused by cigarette smoking.

In crude terms, then, alcohol and barbiturates 'kill' at least thirty times more people each year than heroin, and cigarettes perhaps 1,000 times as many. If one passes on to morbidity and social consequences it should be noted that 40 per cent of all road accidents and 50 per cent of all arrests are said to be associated with alcohol, and 26 per cent of all patients admitted to mental hospitals are alcoholics.[41] The cost to industry of smoking has already been mentioned. Ball (1970)[42] has estimated that 5,000–8,000 hospital beds are occupied each day by smokers who are in hospital only because they smoke.

It seems reasonable to conclude that, in respect of a national 'drugs problem', a schedule of 'dangerous drugs' in descending order of harmfulness would begin with tobacco. It is interesting that the NSPCC in a report listing drugs in descending 'order of danger' begins: Tobacco, alcohol, cocaine . . . and ends with cannabis.[43]

While it is easy to understand the general public's resistance to an altered perspective, the attitude of the insurance industry is more intriguing. According to *Smoking and Health Now,*[44] some insurance companies 'appear to be unaware of the large differences in the risks of smokers and non-smokers' and do not offer differential premiums. Can this be wholly explained by doubts as to the accuracy of replies? In America heavy drinkers normally pay three times the standard rate, though only a few companies offer reduced rates to non-smokers.

Whereas heroin and LSD users are uninsurable in America, the standard rate is applied for barbiturates, amphetamines and prescription drugs in general. A new development is that whereas ten years ago marijuana smokers would have been almost uninsurable, today several hundred companies will insure the 'social' smoker at 50 per cent above the standard premium if satisfied as to his risk potential in other respects.[45]

As concerns which cannot afford social prejudices which run counter to economic realities, insurance companies should provide a relatively reliable guide to the potential hazards of various forms of drug use. Their approach to heroin and LSD seems to bear this out but, leaving aside cigarettes, one is tempted to wonder whether in regard to amphetamines and barbiturates they have become victims of the 'conventional wisdom' just as their earlier response to cannabis may have been over-influenced by the excessive virulence of campaigns during the Anslinger era. At all events the experience of the insurance world should not be overlooked when re-evaluating the concept of dangerousness as applied to drugs.

It must be constantly borne in mind that any optimism about the feasibility of a more balanced perspective needs to be qualified by evidence that polydrug use is increasing and has become a distinctive feature of modern drug taking in England. In other words, even a more realistic assessment of the relative dangers of individual drugs may be of little help in dealing with individual cases. But some advances on the lines suggested should be possible, and there is a considerable body of historical and comparative material to help us.

First, it is evident that our current false scale of values is, on one level, merely a more sophisticated version of the absurd attitudes of previous generations. As Dr Griffith Edwards comments in a brilliant essay on this theme,[46] '. . . hardly any psychoactive substance has not at some time been rigorously condemned by official society.'[47] And again: 'We may indeed well conclude from a historical review that irrationality has played so important a role as to deserve pride of place in any listing of the forces which have motivated responses to psychoactive substance use.'[48] We need constant reminders of the historical continuity of drug dependence as a phenomenon, and of the hysterical reactions provoked by relatively innocuous substances such as tea and coffee. A historical perspective should also make us pause before putting too much faith in legislation as a panacea, in the light of America's experience and, to a lesser extent, our own.

Comparative material, when allowance has been made for cross-cultural differences, should also be conducive to a sense of proportion, as we are made increasingly aware of co-existing but conflicting taboos, such as the markedly contrasting attitudes towards alcohol and other drugs in many Western and Eastern societies.

So far it has been stressed that a more rational perspective is attainable, with the inference that much of the modern dilemma surrounding the 'drugs problem' is a function of our refusal to think through the concept of dependence and make a more honest appraisal. Such an analysis leaves us with several major questions to explore. How can the 'message' be conveyed in such a way as effectively to alter behaviour which is strongly resistant to change? What in particular should be done in the schools? Can the present scale of values be meaningfully adjusted within the existing social and legal structure?

Some practical problems of education

An extreme thesis would suggest that a programme of drug education carried out *within* the existing social structure would almost amount to a contradiction in terms. Misconceptions about relative dangers are so entrenched; smoking and drinking are so institutionalised, and the deviance of other drug takers so taken for granted that, it is argued, an entirely new framework and radically revised understanding of the cultural implications of drug taking today is indispensable.[49]

The case is in many ways attractive and compelling. At the very least it provides a necessary corrective to the facile assumptions commonly made. But, as so often is the case in areas of dispute which arouse deep passions, many of its proponents seem to have fallen into the same trap of doctrinaire assertion as the advocates of the *status quo,* thus encouraging an arid polarisation of views. It is depressing and faintly ominous, for example, to see drug taking referred to as a 'cause'.[50] One wonders how far indiscriminate polydrug use has resulted from the politicisation of the 'drugs problems', which is not a one way process.

Similar traces of dogmatism can be found in Young's stimulating analysis of the reasons for the hostility which drug taking evokes. Dividing people into 'absolutists' and 'relativists' in their approach to drug use – rather along Devlin/Hart lines, the absolutist seeing society as a seamless web – he sweepingly asserts that 'the therapeutic roles in clinics and hospitals are manned by doctors who *invariably* sport an absolutist perspective on drug dependency.'[51] Even if it be true that the 'absolutists' have been primarily responsible for purveying a distorted perspective on drugs, it is also true that a number of doctors have deliberately chosen what is in several respects unrewarding work precisely in order to redress the balance.

It is surely a mistake to abandon the middle ground. An approach which wholly rejects the admittedly inconsistent compromises we have made is not consonant with constructive change. In short, it is too utopian and therefore, ultimately defeatist. Depressing though the prospect may appear, we have to resign ourselves to an educational programme which frankly acknowledges the continuance of the powerful hold of alcohol and tobacco for the foreseeable future, and set our sights accordingly.

Education in schools

In the light of what has been said about deeply held prejudices and misconceptions, one may be forgiven for viewing the prospect of drug education in schools with some trepidation and a considerable measure of scepticism. What form does it in fact take at the present time, and what are its aims? Even if we manage to define them adequately, how, and by whom, can they be conveyed to maximum effect? Is the very notion of such education merely a laudable objective destined in practice to have, at best, a marginal effect, at worst, to exacerbate an already delicate situation?

Drug education, well-established in America and Sweden, is in its infancy in this country. The Institute for the Study of Drug Dependence is currently engaged on research into it and has produced a report based on a preliminary survey and a recent detailed study.[52] The Advisory Centre for Education (ACE) has also circularised all school medical officers to try to obtain some idea of present policies. As one might reasonably expect, no uniform pattern emerged. Some schools refuse to tackle the subject at all, either fearing that it would be counter-productive, or maintaining that it does not present a problem. Others have planned programmes with formal instruction, and some prefer to let individual teachers deal with the subject on an *ad hoc* basis. Until we learn more about the effects of various approaches it would be foolish to try to impose any uniformity.

There is a natural tendency to imagine that some form of drug education is desirable. Certainly the damage and suffering caused to children by ignorance about drugs must, on any reckoning, be significant. Parents tell them not to swallow the contents of the medicine cabinet; is it not mandatory for someone to tell them not to accept heroin from a stranger?

Even if, in the end, one concludes that for schools to ignore the subject totally is to shelve responsibility – there can be a questionable insularity about the attitude 'at this moment of time in my school there is no drugs problem therefore let sleeping dogs lie' – it is at least necessary to bear in mind, as Dr Birdwood has stressed,[53] that education on drugs has the *capacity* to inflict more harm than any other measures. A survey on two groups of schoolchildren, only one of which had received prior lectures on drugs, showed that a greater proportion of the group which had received instruction went on to experiment with them.[54] Without drawing any hard and fast conclusions one can see the dangers.

But a total refusal to discuss drugs in schools for fear of arousing curiosity would, in many parts of the country, constitute a ludicrous approach. Not only would it reinforce the mysterious and taboo-like nature of the subject which is partially responsible for the present situation, but it often conceals ignorance by the local authority of the extent of drug use in its area and of the drug awareness of modern children. However slight their active participation, many children of school age now identify with a pop culture which is itself closely identified – not least by their elders and the mass media – with a drugs culture.

It might also be argued that at the very time when the school leaving age has been raised to sixteen and the issue of children's rights is much in the news, an unwelcome by-product is likely to be an increase in the number of older, bored or disaffected adolescents who will fit all too easily into certain classic models of vulnerability to drug dependence. The question, then, is not whether, but how.

There is no shortage of materials at the disposal of schools for informing children about drugs. But there is much controversy as to which are the most appropriate methods, what is a suitable age and who are best fitted for the unenviable task.

This last question has been much discussed and numerous possibilities have been put forward and are already being tried. Should it be the form teacher, a specialist in health education, the head, the school medical officer, the police, or other outside speakers? Perhaps the best way to look at the matter is to think in terms of the response which one is seeking to evoke. Indeed, even to pose the question in the conventional way distorts the issue, by implying that we are exclusively concerned with imparting knowledge.

If there is anything approaching a consensus on the matter in education circles, it is that the 'scare' technique cannot work. The point needs stressing because we are dealing with a situation which is in a very real sense new for the majority of head teachers whose first thoughts may be about how best to clamp down on any form of drug use – in an environment where the contagion model of drug dependence is particularly hard to resist. But it is a matter of simple psychology that a crude authoritarianism will constitute an irresistible challenge for the daring and adventurous child, the very one most likely to be 'at risk'.

The problem of instruction is particularly acute in respect of cannabis. It is a sobering fact that many children are better versed in many aspects of drug use than their would-be educators. Dogmatic assertions about addictiveness, escalation, etc., which run counter to a child's own experience, or that of his peers, could totally destroy the impact of what is said about the intrinsic dangers of e.g. heroin and amphetamines. It is at least more plausible to explain the social background to the law and argue the case against breaking, as distinct from questioning, any individual law, where no moral issue of overwhelming importance is at stake. Drug education which lacks credibility and causes hostility may not merely arouse curiosity, but provide the impetus for a mindless, defiant polydrug abuse.

There are similar difficulties with any approach which lays nearly all its emphasis on the dangers of drug use, or indeed singles out the topic for specialised treatment. Thus, to ask the police to give talks on the subject, as a few schools do, would seem to be a misguided policy and is not encouraged by the Department of Education and Science.

Sensitive to their invidious role as upholders of the law in a contentious sphere, the police are themselves understandably reluctant to become involved in an activity for which they are not specially trained and are handicapped at the outset. If the object of the exercise is not simply to impart information, but also to win the confidence of the young and encourage frank discussion, police participation has obvious drawbacks and may also over-glamourise the issues.

Nor is there much to be said for a highly publicised outside speaker coming to give *the* talk on drugs, particularly if – as is not unknown – he is hastily contacted as a result of some isolated revelation in a school which has previously done nothing about drug education and he then disappears, so that no on-going relationship is feasible.

It is fair to say that most of the thirty schools surveyed in the ISDD exploratory study (admittedly a very small sample, comprising twenty-seven secondary and three primary or junior schools) seemed alive to the danger of stimulating undue interest, and to the need for a long term relationship. Nearly 90 per cent approved of discussion emerging naturally within the context of lessons on biology, English, liberal studies and religious instruction, while some 25 per cent had a specific health education syllabus in which drugs would be dealt with as part of a general course. No school had a policy of giving each class more than one full lesson on drugs each year. Of the 27 secondary schools only 8 employed outside speakers. Regular teachers treated the subject on an *ad hoc* basis in 20 schools, 4 used specialist teachers within the school, and only 2 had lectures by the headmaster.

The presentation varied considerably, from neutral information to warnings with various combinations, but 22 stressed the dangers of dependency and escalation. Films were used by only 7 schools, perhaps largely because most of those available were American and reflected a different situation and in some cases employed a questionably lurid and sensationalist approach. One can anticipate more use of films now that there is a greater variety of relevant British material. How valuable pamphlets are is debatable. Some of those currently available suffer from a patronising and authoritarian tone,[55] and can in any event be no substitution for personal contact and discussion.

One of the most illuminating findings was that many children were more knowledgeable than teachers had predicted and were critical of 'uninformed' and 'biased' presentation. There was in general a desire for more discussion, preferably led by young, informed teachers with whom the children had some regular contact, though several expressed misgivings about it being a teacher to whom they were directly answerable for discipline. Thus the 'consumer choice' would seem to be a liberal studies or health education teacher, or a young, expert, regular visitor.

The importance of the atmosphere in which this kind of information is given would seem to be borne out on a broader front by the impact of 'Release' as an advisory service on drugs and other social problems. It seems evident that the life style and values of its workers, as much as the expertise which it can offer, explain why it handles some 300 enquiries a week on matters for which there are far more established channels.

If any clear patterns have begun to emerge from the above survey, they are in line with the DES's basic policy that '... drug-taking should be discussed in its proper context as an aspect of health education . . . .'[56] In the later evaluation study by the ISDD in 1972/73, 4,500 pupils from 70 schools were questioned before and after lessons by their regular teachers, and 1,300 in 47 schools were re-questioned two months later. The main findings were that the effects of teaching are slight; pupils' immediate reactions are not a good guide to longer term effects; their attitudes often alter, but not normally towards a blanket approval or rejection of drugs, and lastly that there is room for improvement in teaching methods. The work of the ISDD should prove important as a guide for future teacher training. A questionnaire sent to teacher training colleges revealed that about one third had no specific instruction on alcohol or drug dependence, and just over one third gave only one or two lectures.[57]

Dr R.S.P. Wiener,[58] one of the few people to have carried out a detailed investigation of drug taking by schoolchildren in England, maintains that '. . . until more research has been carried out any educational campaign in the schools raises more problems than it is likely to solve.'[59] He cites the DES's *A Handbook of Health Education* (1968) to show that health education and school policy have had little effect in curtailing smoking and there is no reason to suppose that they would be more successful with drugs generally.

We surely have enough evidence that certain drugs are symptoms (and symbols) of adolescent rebellion and curiosity to realise that intensive preventive measures which concentrate on externals will be of questionable effect. In April 1972 the Health Education Council decided that the time was not yet ripe for a national campaign. The vast sums expended by public authorities and private companies on drug education in America have not revealed anything approaching a model drug programme. Nor is this at all likely unless the difficulties in the way of evaluation can be overcome.[60]

Indeed, the Second Report of the National Commission on Marihuana and Drug Abuse (1973),[61] went as far as to say: '. . . no drug education program in this country, or elsewhere, has proven sufficiently successful to warrant our recommending it.' It also suggested that policy makers should seriously consider declaring a moratorium on all drug education programmes in the schools pending evaluation of existing ones.

If there is some cause for concern about the problem of drug education in schools, the lack of provision of training for medical students is a far more obvious and less excusable omission. Medical students are not required to have any special practical experience of treating alcoholics or drug addicts beyond what they may encounter in their medical apprenticeship. More remarkably, they normally have no more than one or two lectures on theory in a general series on psychiatry, and it is likely to be several years before the Todd Report [62] recommendations for more training in psychiatry are implemented.

It follows that a substantial proportion of general practitioners have received scant formal education about drug taking and much of that is liable to be out of date. [63] The results can be seen by a glance at the overall picture of prescribing within the National Health Service. In 1970, 47·2 million NHS prescriptions were issued for psychotropic drugs (taken here to mean sleeping pills, minor tranquilisers and slimming pills). This in itself represents an increase of 19 per cent over the 1965 figures and they continue to rise. Comparable trends exist in countries without a National Health Service.[64]

It is not only the sheer number of pills prescribed which is alarming, but the extent to which prescribing patterns are dictated by the sales promotion techniques of the pharmaceutical companies. To take one example, appetite suppressants of medically questionable value on any long term view – and in some cases responsible for serious psychological dependence – continue to be prescribed by busy doctors whose susceptibility to the influence of advertising is partially explained by their own previous lack of relevant training. If sales promotion is so effective on doctors, it is hardly surprising that the rest of us are so readily influenced that twice as many non-prescribed medicines are taken every day as prescribed ones.

Yet the results of serious health education programmes give no cause for optimism. In 1964 and again in 1967, following the Road Safety Act, ambitious campaigns were mounted against drunken driving, with no significant improvement in road behaviour. Any initial impact that the breathalyser may have had has certainly greatly diminished though it is still regarded by the police as having made some improvement.[65]

The ban on television advertising of cigarettes had no dramatic effect and *Smoking and Health* (1962) and *Smoking and Health Now* (1971) seem to have had short lived effect only. Nor is this entirely surprising when the Government is spending a mere £100,000 to dissuade people from continuing a habit which the tobacco companies spend £50,000,000 trying to promote.

The full absurdity of the situation can be best appreciated by looking at the kind of advertisements for cigarettes commonly found nowadays in magazines. An idyllic scene of natural beauty, set on a mountain top or in the countryside or by the sea is the background to the end of a day made perfect by lighting a cigarette – 'It seemed a *natural* thing to do.' The whole, is of course, rounded off by the now mandatory sentence, 'Every packet carries a government health warning.' One could not invent a more powerful symbol of the forces in our society which hinder a balanced perspective on drug use.

Notes

[1] *Task Force Report: Narcotics and Drug Abuse.* The President's Commission on Law Enforcement and Administration of Justice, US Government Printing Office, Washington 1967, p. 10.

[2] The *Deedes Report,* p. 16.

[3] *Sorrels* v. *United States,* 287 U.S. 435 (1932).

[4] *R.* v. *Mealey and Sheridan* [1974] *The Times* 29 July.

[5] E.g. *R.* v. *Foulder, Foulkes and Johns* [1973] Crim. L.R. 45.

[6] *R.* v. *McEvilly* [1974] Crim. L.R. 239.

[7] See *Drugs and Society,* vol. 1, no. 3, Dec. 1971, p. 22. This figure would represent anything up to three times more than the actual cost of the heroin, since stolen property will fetch appreciably less than its true value.

[8] BNDD study, W. McGlothlin *et al., Alternative Approaches to Opiate Addiction Control: Costs, Benefits, and Potential,* Washington, Drug Abuse Council, Inc., May 1973, p. 3.

[9] N. Kessel and H. Walton, *Alcoholism,* Penguin 1965, p. 166.

[10] 'Alcoholism among Prisoners', in *Psychological Medicine,* vol. 1, 1970, p. 73.

[11] Drinking Problems among Recidivist Prisoners. Unpublished Report, quoted in J. Zacune and C. Hensman, *Drugs, Alcohol and Tobacco in Britain,* Heinemann 1971, p. 88.

[12] T. Morris and L. Blom-Cooper, *Criminal Homicide in England and Wales 1957–68,* Interim Report of Legal Research Unit, Dept. of Sociology, Bedford College, London, 1969.

[13] McClintock *et al., Crimes of Violence,* Macmillan 1963.

[14] *Task Force Report,* (see n. 1) p. 10.

[15] E.g. Kolb (86 per cent), Anslinger (100 per cent), *Task Force Report* (72 per cent).

[16] *British Journal of Criminology* vol. 9, 1969, p. 108.

[17] Ibid., p. 120.

[18] *Drug Abuse and Personality in Young Offenders,* Butterworths 1971.

[19] J. Mott and M. Taylor, *Home Office Research Unit Report,* HMSO 1974, p. 27.

[20] Wootton Report, p. 14, para. 56.

[21] Weil (1968), Crancer (1969). See also ch. 7, pp. 168–9.

[22] [1970] 1 Q.B. 152.

[23] *The Times* 22 March 1969, 29 April 1969.

[24] In *Adolescent Drug Dependence,* ed. C.W.M. Wilson, p. 86.

[25] *Amphetamines, Barbiturates, LSD and Cannabis,* Department of Health and Social Security, HMSO 1970, p. 26.

[26] Ibid., p. 28.

[27] H. Noda, 'The problem of amphetamine abuse in Japan', in O.J. Kalant (ed.), *The Amphetamines: Toxicity and Addiction,* Toronto 1966, p. 102.

[28] In 1968, in Stockholm, just under 50 per cent of people arrested had at some time taken central stimulants intravenously. *Bulletin on Narcotics* Jan. 1971, p. 15.

[29] DHSS Report (see n. 25), p. 7.

[30] 'Delinquency and the Amphetamines', *British Journal of Psychiatry,* vol. 111, 1965, p. 865.

[31] See pp. 146–8.

[32] See in particular Zacune and Hensman *supra,* and T. Bewley, 'Recent Changes in the Pattern of Drug Abuse in the United Kingdom', *Bulletin on Narcotics,* vol. 18, no. 4, 1966.

[33] Zacune and Hensman, p. 219.

[34] Ibid., p. 221.

[35] D. Dunlop, 'Abuse of Drugs by the Public and by Doctors', *British Medical Bulletin,* vol. 26, 1970, p. 236.

[36] Report on Alcohol and Health, US Government Printing Office, Washington D.C. 1972.

[37] In 1973. See Appendix A, Table 3.

[38] Estimated at 28 times that of the general population for comparable ages, Bewley, ben-Arie and James: 'Survey of Heroin Addicts known to the Home Office', *British Medical Journal,* vol. 1, 1968, pp. 727–30. But this was before the treatment centres were set up, and at a time when some general practitioners were prescribing large amounts of heroin.

[39] G. Godber, *On the State of the Nation's Health,* HMSO 1969, pp. 8–9.

[40] *On the State of the Nation's Health,* HMSO 1970, p. 4.

[41] *Drugs and Society,* April 1972, p. 4.

[42] 'Hospital Beds and Cigarette-smoking', *The Lancet* vol. 2, 1970, p. 48.

[43] *Drink, Drugs and the Family,* 1971.

[44] P. 129.

[45] *Drugs and Society,* March 1972, p. 24.

[46] *Unreason in an Age of Reason,* Royal Society of Medicine 1971.

[47] Ibid., p. 11.

[48] Ibid., p. 16.

[49] The argument is forcefully put by J. Young, in *The Drugtakers,* McGibbon and Kee 1971.

[50] See 'The Joint's the Thing', J. Morrison, *New Statesman* 29 January 1972.

[51] *The Drugtakers,* p. 56. Italics supplied.

[52] Exploratory study, 1971. See *Drugs and Society* June 1972, p. 21; *Evaluation of Drug Education,* B. Swift, N. Dorn and A. Thompson, ISDD 1974.

[53] Ibid., January 1972, p. 7.

[54] Dr H. Morgans, *ibid.,* May 1972, p. 5.

[55] A notable exception for children of fifth and sixth form age is P. Newark, *Connexions,* Penguin 1968.

[56] DES Handbook, HMSO 1968. See now, *Drugs and the Schools,* DES 1972, p. 16.

[57] H. Blumberg, Unpublished Report, Addiction Research Unit, London 1970. Quoted Zacune and Hensman, p. 181.

[58] *Drugs and Schoolchildren,* Longman, 1970.

[59] Ibid., p. 163.

[60] See P. Wald and A. Abrams, 'Drug Education', Staff Paper 2 in *Dealing with Drug Abuse,* Macmillan 1972.

[61] *Drug Use in America: Problem in Perspective,* US Government Printing Office, Washington, D.C. 1973.

[62] Royal Commission on Medical Education, HMSO 1968.

[63] Some 70 per cent of all drugs now being marketed in Britain were unknown or unavailable fifteen years ago.

[64] P. Parish, *Drugs and Society* April 1972, p. 11.

[65] Report of Her Majesty's Chief Inspector of Constabulary for the year 1971, HMSO 1972, p. 50. In 1971 there were 34,863 breath test convictions in magistrates' courts, an increase of 49·8 per cent over the 1970 figure. *Offences Relating to Motor Vehicles,* HMSO 1972.

7 Cannabis

Introduction

Devoting a full chapter to cannabis is not intended to imply that the drug is intrinsically more significant than the others discussed. There do, however, seem to be several reasons for treating it at greater length.

To begin with, it is hoped that a detailed examination of *one* illegal drug will underline the observations made in previous chapters about attitudes towards drugs in general. Such is the polarisation and controversy surrounding cannabis, and so extensive is its use, that it is an obvious choice for this purpose. In 1973 there were 14,119 convictions for cannabis offences. The total number of convictions in that year for offences involving controlled drugs was 22,860.

When nearly two-thirds of all drug convictions relate to one drug the importance of a fair and reasoned evaluation of it is self-evident, especially when both the legal framework for cannabis – in England, as in most parts of the world – and the attitude of policy makers generally, remain obstacles to a rational assessment, as the recent American and Canadian Reports,[1] and their official reception makes clear.

Largely for historical reasons unconnected with the issues that concern its use in England today, the legal classification and popular image of cannabis are patently misleading. There can be no justification for continuing to categorise it with the narcotics – as is still the case, for example, in international law and in thirteen American states. Moreover, though the Misuse of Drugs Act 1971 finally removed this anomaly from English law, the penal structure still betrays the influence of an unfortunate association.

Finally, on a long term view, cannabis merits a detailed analysis because of the symbolic status it has acquired. The particular substance itself may eventually recede into the background. The issues which it raises for patterns of drug use in the future will not.

Limitations on research findings

In the past, research on cannabis has been considerably hampered by the legal restrictions on its possession. A welcome feature of the 1971 Act is its inclusion of specific provisions facilitating research over a wide area. In particular, section 32 empowers the Secretary of State to '. . . conduct or assist in conducting research into any matter relating to the misuse of dangerous or otherwise harmful drugs.'

This formulation is valuable in several respects. It modifies the tendentious 'dangerous drugs' label which has been criticised earlier, and is wider than 'controlled drugs' (section 2 and schedule 2). It is also consistent with the aim of the new Act in seeking flexibility of classification in the light of changing needs. It could prove especially useful in investigating the effects of certain drugs taken in combination, at a time when multi-drug use is increasing.

Other provisions[2] require the new Advisory Council to advise on measures for promoting research to deal with social problems and to 'consider' and advise on matters referred to it by the relevant Ministers, thus enabling it to conduct its own research.

A cautionary note must, however, be struck as regards finance. As the Financial and Explanatory Memorandum to the Bill stated, '. . . the level of likely expenditure . . . is not expected to be more than £10,000 in the first year or two.' Even when every account has been taken of the difference in size of the budget and drug problems of the two countries (including that of soldiers returning from Vietnam) the Federal expenditure of $73·8 million on research for 1973 (itself a small fraction of the $492 million set aside for the whole area of drugs) provides a sobering contrast.[3]

The need for substantial funds becomes all the more apparent when one considers the pharmacological complexity of cannabis.[4] So far we have used the term 'cannabis' as an all-purpose label; in reality, there are three basic substances derived from the 'Indian Hemp' plant, namely, (in descending order of potency and using the most common, though not the only, names) hashish (mainly resin), ganja (flowering tops without the leaves), and marijuana (leaves and flowering tops). Any of these substances, in the context of an illicit market, is liable to contain impurities. The principal agent determining potency, Tetrahydrocannabinol (THC), was not identified until 1964, and analyses of its content in cannabis samples have shown considerable discrepancies.

The amount of psychoactive material in a given sample is affected by numerous variables – variations in climate and soil, time of harvest, conditions and length of storage, and method of administration – cannabis[5] is several times as potent when smoked as when ingested, and the roach (butt end) has a high THC content. Thus, conclusions drawn from scientific studies which were not rigorously conducted, and *a fortiori*, from self-reporting in surveys, are at once open to question and can be positively misleading when effectively different substances are being compared. Similarly, different reports have used different criteria for 'moderate' and 'excessive' use, while only recently[6] has adequate attention been paid to differential effects on experienced and naive users.

As well as taking account of the above drug related variables, one must have regard to other factors, familiar in criminological research generally, which limit the validity of research findings. The more obvious of these are the effects of set and setting – most studied groups of drug users are atypical, and the laboratory setting may significantly affect the expectation and response of cannabis smokers – and the dangers of extrapolating from animal studies to effects on man.

However, the overall picture is not as daunting as the foregoing might suggest. Techniques of analysis are continually being refined. There is also considerable agreement between the major modern reports and earlier ones as to some of the main effects, and differences of potency are compensated for by titration, the experienced smoker's acquired ability to regulate his intake to achieve the desired intensity. Clearly, the extent to which reliance can be placed on the findings of current research will influence the course of future policy regarding control.

The alleged medical dangers

Accumulative toxicity

The acute toxicity of cannabis is extremely low, as compared with, for example, nicotine and alcohol. But we have insufficient information about its chronic toxicity. 'No modern drug has ever been proposed for general consumption about whose safety in respect of chronic toxicity less is known.'[7]

As cannabis is a mixture of substance whose psychoactive constituents are highly fat soluble, and thus insoluble in water, they and their metabolites persist in the body. Lewin, in an article the general tone of which is broadly favourable to the drug, acknowledges that 'The details of accumulation is one of the most urgent areas of research.'[8]

Teratogenicity and chromosome damage

There has been some evidence in animal studies of teratogenic effects (effects on the unborn foetus). In a letter to the *Lancet* in 1968,[9] Persaud and Ellington reported gross malformations in 53 per cent of the offspring of pregnant rats – twenty-seven being resorbed and not born. Similar results have also been obtained with rabbits, but not with mice or hamsters. Further, in 1970, an experiment on rats by Pace,[10] using equivalent doses to Persaud and Ellington failed to reveal any congenital malformations.

Brain damage

In 1971, evidence of cerebral atrophy was found in ten males aged 18–28, who were chronic users of cannabis[11] (they had used it regularly for between three and eleven years). The researchers attributed the damage to cannabis, but this conclusion is open to doubt.[12]

Though cannabis was the subjects' main drug, they had all used LSD, eight had used amphetamines and at least five, barbiturates. Most of them also had a suspect neurological history. In the absence of supporting evidence from controlled studies or from societies with a long history of chronic use, it would be premature to draw adverse conclusions. But the area clearly deserves further research.

Bronchial and lung disease

Is it possible that chronic use could have cancer producing, or at least respiratory effects similar to those attributed to tobacco? Certainly cannabis smoke can cause 'smoker's cough', and experiments suggest that its tar yield is comparable to that of commercial tobacco cigarettes.[13]

There is no cogent evidence of a causal link with cancer in non-industrial societies – where respiratory disorders such as chronic bronchitis have been reported – nor would this be easy to ascertain as much larger quantities of tobacco are normally mixed with the cannabis when it is smoked than is the case in Western countries. The Le Dain Commission[14] did not seem unduly perturbed:

> Even if tobacco and cannabis were shown to be equally carcinogenic on a weight basis, significant differences in patterns of use would prevent clear comparisons of the cancer producing potential of these drugs. The present common pattern of regular cannabis use in North America is more analogous to intermittent social alcohol use than to the picture of chronic daily smoking presented by regular tobacco users.

But they do add a warning note:

> The deep inhalation and long retention smoking techniques . . . may

add complications, since this practice usually results in almost complete retention of all smoke particles in the lungs, as well as the absorption of the desired active compounds.

It is noteworthy that the report of a WHO Scientific Group, *The Use of Cannabis,* [15] makes scant reference to this area, beyond including bronchopulmonary diseases in a list of desirable research topics. Nor does *Signal of Misunderstanding* [16] place any stress on it. Bloomquist [17] takes a less sanguine view, but the general tenor of his work is rather polemical and tendentious.

Mental illness from moderate to heavy use

In passing from relatively identifiable forms of physical injury to the general contention that cannabis can cause mental illness, one enters a vaguely defined realm, beset with value judgements and posing intractable problems of definition and causation. Terms such as 'psychosis' and 'amotivational syndrome' are sometimes used to describe conditions allegedly caused by chronic cannabis use, but not only are the labels themselves non-specific, but, in so far as they are meaningful, a host of diverse factors may be involved, ranging from personality and pre-disposition to multi-drug use and socio-cultural considerations.

Undoubtedly, one can observe certain specific effects on the mind arising from acute use – loss of concentration, loss of short term memory and short lived delusional states, as well as impairment of psychomotor functioning. But these effects do not inflict any permanent harm on the user. Whether they constitute a significant risk of harm to others will be considered shortly. On the basis of such evidence as we have, it is reasonable to assert that in proportion to its incidence cannabis use cannot be shown, certainly in Western societies, to be a major contributor to serious mental disorder.

The above account is far from being a comprehensive survey of possible medical hazards involved in cannabis use but it does purport to outline the major areas of current concern. In the end, barring some startling and decisive medical revelation – which there is little reason to anticipate in the immediate future – social attitudes will be the determinant of future policy, and existing medical knowledge does not compel any particular solution. It was, after all, possible for three different sets of proposals to emerge from the Le Dain Commission's analysis of the mass of medical and scientific data before them, in spite of the fact that all the members were in almost total agreement as to the drug's effects. It is not the *existence* of dangers which is in issue but the degree of harm, and in particular of self-harm, which a society should permit, which in turn must be weighed against the social cost of proscribing the conduct associated with it.

Social hazards

Escalation

Variously known as 'escalation', 'progression', or the 'stepping stone' theory, one of the most influential arguments against relaxing the law has been the assertion that use of cannabis leads to the use of 'hard' drugs and, more specifically, to heroin addiction. The argument can of course take several forms, ranging from the extreme proposition that cannabis use 'causes' heroin addiction to the far less contentious view that use of one illegal drug may, for reasons entirely unconnected with the substance itself, facilitate the use of others which are more harmful.

It is easy to see how theories of progression catch the popular imagination. If an activity is viewed with disapproval, yet shows no obvious signs of causing harm when moderately indulged in, 'one thing leads to another' becomes a very tempting catchphrase. It is all the more compelling in the sphere of drug use because the phenomenon of tolerance is a defining characteristic of addiction, and many people believe that all drugs are physically addictive. Thus the perceived ambit of tolerance is extended to embrace drug use in general.

This attitude is not confined to the 'man-in-the-street' and the popular press. A former Home Secretary recently said that '. . . the evidence that soft drugs can lead users on to hard drugs is too compelling to be ignored.'[18] A London magistrate has asserted that: 'Everybody knows perfectly well that the taking of soft drugs leads to the taking of hard drugs – except, of course, the so-called experts.'[19] More importantly, Professor Paton[20] has put forward an elaborate justification of the hypothesis that 'cannabis enhances the risk of addiction to opiates', and this requires particular examination.

His argument may be summarised as follows:

1 The case histories of heroin addicts are consistent with this hypothesis in that 80–100 per cent of heroin addicts have previously taken cannabis, and that a common pattern is cannabis (and amphetamine) use at the age of sixteen or seventeen, followed by heroin at eighteen or nineteen.
2 The rise in the incidence of cannabis use runs parallel with the growth of addiction to manufactured drugs, without there being a corresponding rise in alcoholism or suicide.

3 If cannabis and heroin were totally unconnected one would expect the incidence of cannabis use among heroin addicts to be the same as that of cannabis use in the general population; but whereas only one in 2,000 of the general population takes cannabis (this being Paton's estimate for 1968), 80 per cent of heroin addicts have previously taken cannabis. The fact that all heroin addicts have previously taken coffee, etc. misses the point since, for the general population, coffee taking is very common, whereas cannabis use is very rare. In other words, the significant comparison is between the *normal* incidence of cannabis and the incidence of cannabis among heroin addicts.

4 The above data can be expressed statistically by using a Bayesian formula for calculating inverse probability.[21] Thus:

$$A = \frac{B \times C}{D}$$

where:

A = the incidence of heroin taking among cannabis takers
B = the incidence of cannabis taking among heroin takers
C = the incidence of heroin taking among the general population
D = the incidence of cannabis taking among the general population.

If one assumes that $B = 90$ per cent, $C = 5$ per 100,000 and $D = 30$–60 per 100,000, then $A = 7{\cdot}5$–15 per cent.

Paton finds support for this estimate in Dr E. Tylden's finding that in a study of 130 hashish smokers, 10 per cent were known to be taking morphine and/or heroin.[22]

Before assessing the validity of Paton's conclusions, and of the progression theory in general, it is convenient to mention two further views which he has expressed. First, he is highly sceptical of the psychopathic personality explanation of addiction:

> I would like to say how strongly I reject this approach . . . As far as I can see, there is no solid evidence yet for the view that there is a recognisable personality which you can label beforehand as liable to turn to drug addiction. *I believe it may be to a large extent a matter of chance.* [23] If a man with a successful job, who is happily married, takes cannabis, then that may be a perfectly safe episode. But let that man then lose his wife, or have some trouble with his job, or get into some major personal difficulty, then I think the chances are that the recollection that he had an escape into a drug will become more important.[24]

Secondly,

> Although it is often said that there is no pharmacological basis for such progression, this in fact exists since cannabis increases suggestibility and shares with heroin (though in milder form) the ability to produce euphoria and analgesia.[25]

The case against escalation

As has been pointed out by several critics, whilst there is no reason to doubt the relative accuracy of Paton's figures for the number of heroin addicts in the general population, or for the incidence of prior cannabis use by them, the validity of his statistical argument depends on the accuracy of his estimate of cannabis use in the general population. But 30–60 per 100,000 (i.e. roughly 25,000) was a conservative estimate even in 1968, the same year[26] that the Wootton Committee estimated the number as between 30,000 and 300,000. 'If he had taken the average of the two figures suggested in this report [i.e. 165,000 instead of his figure of about 25,000] his result would have been far less than one per cent.'[27]

At all events, whatever the incidence may have been in 1968, and though we still inevitably lack reliable figures, the fact that in 1973 11,246 persons were found guilty of offences involving cannabis[28] suggests that somewhere in the region of 500,000 users should not today be regarded as fanciful.[29] To put the obvious question bluntly: where are the missing 45,000 heroin addicts? We have already seen that the relative visibility of such addiction would preclude a discrepancy of such alarming proportions between official estimates and true incidence.

Furthermore, we know of several patterns of drug use which cast doubt on the role of cannabis as a stepping stone. First, though it is in no way probative, it is interesting to note that in Hong Kong, notorious for the highest heroin addiction rate in the world, indigenous cannabis use is virtually non-existent. Vancouver also experienced a very high incidence of heroin use before cannabis was introduced there. Conversely, in England there is considerable cannabis use by immigrant populations which is largely self-contained. The experience of the treatment centres suggests that West Indians, Pakistanis and Indians are proportionately underrepresented among known heroin addicts.

Indeed, were it not for the failure of the American campaign in the 1930s against marijuana as a 'killer drug' and the convenience of escalation as a slogan, it would be difficult to understand how the 'cannabis to heroin' theory ever took root, when one pauses to consider how arbitrary it is. What is the magical link between these two drugs –

apart from the expediency of asserting it in the contemporary situation – that has fostered such unswerving confidence in the belief that *cannabis* is peculiarly suited among drugs to lead on to heroin, or, for that matter, what are the qualities of *heroin* and the other opiates that single them out as the ultimate port of call of the cannabis smoker?

To begin with there is no compelling pharmacological relationship. That cannabis 'increases suggestibility' is a highly tenuous link, and the same could be said of several drugs. Nor is 'the ability to produce euphoria and analgesia' by any means confined to cannabis. Putting the argument at its highest, one emerges only with the truism that taking *any* drug may make one more receptive to the use of others.

But the real irony of these strained efforts to find a causal link which is inherently improbable is that it has detracted attention from far more plausible forms of association. Thus, a progression from cannabis to LSD would make much more sense,[30] both pharmacologically – as cannabis has some of the characteristics of a mild hallucinogen – and in terms of the expectations of many users. This possibility could well prove a far more cogent reason for urging caution about cannabis.

Similarly, a much better *prima facie* case exists for amphetamines than for cannabis as a stepping stone to heroin. Whereas many cannabis users express extreme distaste for heroin, it has some subcultural links with amphetamine use, especially where the symbolic and physically demanding barrier of intravenous injection has been surmounted. Numerous heroin studies testify to prior amphetamine use and Paton himself refers to it as a common pattern. It may also be argued that it is precisely the atypical cannabis user – in a custodial situation – who has also taken amphetamines and is for various reasons the most vulnerable to future heroin use, who is most frequently studied.

It is also presumably relevant to note that in western societies alcohol is almost invariably used before cannabis, and frequently at an age when its purchase is illegal. Heavy prior alcohol use is a common feature of chronic drug users generally.

As was observed when we considered the causes of drug dependence, there seems to be a marked element of chance in the initial form and subsequent pattern of drug use. The point is taken by Paton in the quotation cited earlier.[31] But, assuming it to be broadly true, surely it is damaging to the escalation argument, which, even in its less rigid forms, has a distinctly deterministic quality.

The above analysis is highly critical of the progression theory – at least in its more extreme versions – but a few qualifications have to be made. As the Le Dain Report comments:

> The attacks on a hypothesis of causation to some extent set up a 'straw man'. . . . By stimulating a taste for drug experience, lowering inhibitions about experimenting with more dangerous drugs and leading to personal associations and involvement in a pattern of life which emphasises an interest in drugs, cannabis must be reckoned as a potent factor contributing to the growth of multi-drug use.[32]

Proof of a causal link is, in the end, unattainable, but this does not preclude a strong associational connection, based on a pattern of escalation. Just as the criminologist is familiar with the juvenile delinquent for whom Borstal constitutes 'making it', so the clinician has to be on his guard against the youth for whom heroin is the ultimate status symbol in drug taking.

For the purposes of future policy, however, two points seem to be of prime concern. First, such association as exists between cannabis and the subsequent use of more harmful drugs is minimally pharmacological (with the possible exception of progression to LSD) and arises primarily for sociological reasons which derive from its classification with them as an illegal drug. Secondly, the educational impact of escalation theory, however watered down, is highly questionable.

If it is extremely difficult to persuade people to give up cigarettes because of the acknowledged danger that they will contract a specific and lethal disease, how much more difficult must it be to convince someone that he is liable to 'progress' from cannabis to heroin.

Driving hazards

In normal use, cannabis can cause significant distortions of perception, impairment of cognitive functions and adverse psychomotor effects. Short term memory, hand and body steadiness, complex reaction time and the ability to maintain concentration on routine tasks may be affected,[33] with the result that driving (or operating machinery generally) while under its influence are potentially hazardous.

Quite how serious these problems are is very difficult to judge on the basis of present knowledge. Recent research has mainly concentrated on driving skills, and on the strength of the Crancer study[34] it was originally maintained that a 'social high' caused little or no impairment, and nothing comparable to the risk from alcohol. But doubts have subsequently been expressed on several grounds.

First, the Crancer study is open to methodological criticism, and the authors themselves admit that one cannot draw any very firm conclusions from their findings. The sample was small (thirty-six regular users, and, in a less rigorous subsequent test, four naive users) and, most importantly, simulator tests were employed, so that extrapolation to actual driving performance is speculative. Marijuana from the same supply was later found to be less potent by other researchers,[35] and there is some controversy over the comparability of the alcohol and marijuana doses.

Rafaelson *et al.*[36] found that in moderate doses cannabis and alcohol had similar effects on driving skill, but that those of cannabis were less predictable. Sometimes quite small doses (200–400 mg, with 4 THC) were sufficient for the user to go through the lights at red on a simulator, and, in general, 'brake time', though not 'start time' was prolonged.

The two major recent Commission reports and other studies[37] stress our current lack of empirical evidence as to how far any impairment is causally connected with accidents. Some concern has been expressed about the additive effects when cannabis is taken with alcohol, and, to a lesser extent, about the possibility of the 'flashback' phenomenon, which is more commonly associated with LSD. The Canadian Commission was also doubtful as to whether a detection method similar to the 'breathalyser' can be devised in the near future.

Clearly this whole field needs further investigation, yet the obstacles to conducting tests in a wholly realistic setting are formidable. At this stage, one can only reiterate Le Dain: '. . . until further data are available, driving while under the influence of cannabis should be avoided.'

In the absence of empirical data, any assertions about cannabis as a possible cause of industrial injury would be merely speculative. But enough is known about impairment of psychomotor skills for it to be obvious that there is a risk potential in carrying out complex operations and even routine tasks under its influence. Research is needed particularly on the use and effects of cannabis in transportation industries.

Adolescent maturation

There is little evidence to suggest that moderate use of cannabis is intrinsically detrimental to academic achievement, but does its use and initial impact at an early age have an adverse effect on the process of maturation? The Le Dain Commission were particularly concerned by this question: 'It seems completely unrealistic to assume that adolescents, beginning as early as the age of twelve, can persistently resort to cannabis intoxication with its hallucinogenic effects without seriously interfering with development of the capacity to cope with reality that is an essential part of the process of maturation.'[38]

The argument centres on the role of drugs in evading the more painful and frustrating aspects of growing up, obscuring or delaying crises of identity, sexual maturation and decision making. Miller, writing on drugs in general, says:

> The price paid for drug abuse is that the process of sexual maturity is almost certainly inhibited. There is no evidence, if brain damage is avoided, to prove that if the habit is stopped, sexual and psychological maturity would be permanently impaired . . . most commonly [drug toxicity] appears to inhibit maturity so that some individuals appear unable to tolerate frustration and psychic pain as much as others of the same age.[39]

Again we are in an area which is beset by value judgements and ill-defined concepts, as a phrase such as 'coping with reality' suggests. It is necessary to remember that some conventionally deviant behaviour can be normative at certain ages and may itself form part of the maturation process. The point is well taken by the American Commission, who acknowledge that, on one level, experimenting with drugs is part of a 'successful' socialisation process, in keeping with the aim of encouraging independence, curiosity and a healthy self-assurance. The question of adequate controls to prevent easy access to cannabis by adolescents will be considered later.

The 'amotivational syndrome'

Linked with the question of adolescent maturation is the argument that excessive cannabis use induces what has been termed an 'amotivational syndrome'. This state is typically characterised by lack of ambition, apathy and reduced drive, inability to make or carry out long term plans, etc.[40]

Evidence for it is largely impressionistic and there are no convincing grounds for believing that such a condition is widespread, at least in industrial societies, nor, to the extent that it does exist, that cannabis is primarily responsible. Again it is partly a question of emotive labelling. If one substitutes terms such as lack of aggression, tranquility, contentment, etc., a wholly different perspective emerges.

The alleged connection with crime

As argued earlier,[41] there is no convincing evidence for the view that cannabis plays a significant role in the commission of non-drug related crime.

The alleged benefits

While the issue of legal policy is rightly concerned in the main with potential dangers, to neglect entirely the possible benefits of the drug is to present a distorted picture. The alleged benefits of cannabis use should also play some part in the determination of its legal status.

As a medicine

Cannabis has been used medicinally for some 5,000 years, notably for self-medication in India and parts of Southern Africa. European investigation of its therapeutic potential did not really begin until after Napoleon's forces had entered Egypt in 1798, and interest was awakened by the work of O'Shaughnessy[42] and Moreau de Tours.[43]

Since then it has been used in various forms of treatment – as an analgesic, to lower blood pressure and body temperature, relieve migraine and epilepsy, and as an appetite stimulant. More recently, consideration has been given to its potential in treating alcoholism, heroin addiction, burns, earache and glaucoma.[44]

But in the 20th century western medical interest in it declined for a variety of reasons – its variable potency, uncertain stability over time, water insolubility, unpredictable response to it, and the introduction of the syringe and the opiates; as well as the hostility in the 1930s which ultimately led to its proscription. Advances in isolating and synthesising certain natural cannabinoids – some water soluble – have encouraged renewed investigation of its possible therapeutic applications, and it would be unfortunate if these were not followed up because of social disapproval of the drug.

As a pleasurable relaxant

So much controversy attaches to the issue of possible harm that one can almost overlook the most obvious reason that many people use the drug, namely as a source of pleasure and relaxation. It is also worth observing that in a society where so much advertising is geared to ensuring our well-being, and we are constantly urged to take a 'tonic' to make us feel good, the traditional distinction between medical and non-medical use has lost much of its edge. For this reason, there is less force in the view often expressed by clinicians that *unless* cannabis is shown to have medical uses not provided by other drugs, no question of legalisation should arise.

If at least 8·3 million Americans are thought to be current users,[45] it is a reasonable inference that large numbers of people derive a lot of enjoyment from cannabis. As well as being a general relaxant, it is desired for its ability to intensify subjective appreciation of colour, music, food and sexual gratification.

As an aid to artistic creation

It is also contended that artistic creativity can be enhanced by cannabis. Jazz musicians have frequently claimed that their playing improved under its influence, though the evidence suggests that this is essentially a subjective experience, not borne out by tests of pitch and discrimination. Modern pop music increasingly incorporates drug terminology and owes something to both cannabis and hallucinogenic drug experiences.

The common gibe that the 'pot inspired' Shakespeare has yet to materialise would seem to be misplaced, in that verbal articulacy is known to be adversely affected. Also, the question of values intrudes. One cannot limit the concept of art to the three unities and it seems that pictorial art in particular, and especially in its less structured forms, owes something of value to the cannabis experience.

Legal status

Before examining the thorny issue of legalisation, it is convenient to glance briefly at the legal status of cannabis and at current trends in various parts of the world.

One is immediately struck by the enormous range of legal response to the drug, from the extreme of the death penalty through to legally sanctioned use. The death penalty is prescribed in several American states for sale to minors and in Iran for large scale trafficking. In several countries long term prison sentences exist for sale, and in some cases for possession. In Texas, for example, which has the harshest marijuana laws in the United States, even a first conviction for possession attracts a minimum penalty of two years and a maximum of life.

In the last few years many countries – among them Jamaica, Nigeria, Turkey, Cyprus, Mexico, Sweden and France – have increased penalties and in England, though the maximum sentence for possession has been reduced from ten to five years, the maximum for trafficking and occupation of premises where cannabis is smoked has been increased to fourteen years.[46]

On the other hand, a few countries have taken a far more lenient approach towards possession. In Denmark, for example, where possession remains illegal, a Ministry of Justice directive was issued to the police not to prosecute individuals in possession of small quantities. Holland adopts a similarly informal approach towards use and the municipality of Amsterdam has for some years been the responsible authority for a youth club where the drug is openly taken. The Dutch government recently considered introducing legislation to make use and possession a civil wrong only.[47] In the state of Oregon, since 1973, the maximum penalty for possession of up to one ounce is a fine of $100 and the national trend in America is towards reduced penalties for simple possession. Canada, as a muted response to the Le Dain recommendation to legalise simple possession, has, for first offenders only, abolished prison sentences and the maintenance of criminal records.

Similar trends are observable in parts of America and in England, notably on certain university campuses and occasionally at pop festivals when the police have let it be known that the law would not be enforced against smokers. Finally, it is of interest that in India, Pakistan and Nepal, the mild form of the drug known as Bhang (consisting of leaves only) is legal and widely taken as a drink or eaten in a confection, especially on festivals and in religious worship.

The legalisation issue

Current trends

There are several indications that some countries and one or two states in America are moving towards a form of attenuated legalisation of possession, the details of which will be considered shortly. The impetus towards this change has recently gained momentum with the publication of the American and Canadian Commission reports, but in the last few years there have been many signs of a shift in official attitudes, as indicated above, and of an increase in use.

A few examples will suffice to highlight these changes. The American tobacco industry is said to be busy making contingency plans, buying vast tracts of land where marijuana grows in Mexico, taking out the copyright on trade names such as 'Mexico Gold', and running sales test schemes. A spokesman for a San Francisco consortium commented: 'It's like the last days of prohibition, when beer trucks drove around openly.'[48]

> So widespread is its use becoming, so common its detection and so small the penalties imposed for its use, indeed, that it is not impossible to envisage a future 'tactical withdrawal' from absolute

prohibition to concentration in 'strategic prepared positions' of permitted use under strict control.[49]

A Leeds University survey suggested that 60 per cent of students have taken a drug of some sort, usually cannabis:

> 'These people have grown up in a drug conscious society. They don't conceive taking pot is either immoral or harmful.' (A doctor.)
>
> 'We have plain clothes men mingling with students in places where they gather. But we are interested in those who sell the stuff and in students who go off the rails. We're not really interested in the odd smoker any more.' (A police officer.)
>
> 'To say you haven't tried pot is a bit like a miner in a miner's club saying he's teetotal.' (A girl student.)
>
> '. . . a lot of police now believe that cannabis is not an evil drug, and feel we are banging our heads against a brick wall.' (A drug squad officer.)[50]

A significant development is the reported increase in cannabis use by middle class professionals in their thirties and over. An impressionistic but revealing account may be found in a magazine article whose very title – 'When it's harvesting time in trendy N.W.1 . . .'[51] – may have policy implications for our legislature of much greater import than the more strident tones of the underground press.

The nature of the controversy

Why has the question of legalising marijuana aroused such bitter conflict? It cannot, as we have seen, be plausibly attributed to the drug's intrinsic properties, which, at most, would argue caution and a measure of control. When we remain sanguine about artificial ingredients in food and chemical spraying processes, what is it that impels a judge in 1972 to describe cannabis as 'this vile substance'?[52]

It is submitted that the answer lies primarily in the false perception of the drug built up over the years for a whole host of reasons already examined in earlier chapters. The legal anomalies and adverse social consequences which flow in large measure from this false perception, and the extent to which it prevents a sensible approach to drug education now, and may impede a rational perspective on drug use in the future, suggest that it is the effects and degree of effectiveness of the present law, rather than nebulous concepts such as 'permissiveness', which should be in the forefront of our minds when arguing the case for and against legalisation.

Without at this stage examining possible alternatives, one can confidently assert that the present law is seriously defective for a number of reasons. As just mentioned, prominent among them is the extent to which it compromises drug education and perpetuates prejudices about the relative harmfulness of individual drugs.

But the most serious short term effect is that a substantial number of people are being labelled as criminals, in the vast majority of cases for possessory offences only.[53] The analysis of all the cannabis offences for 1967 in the Wootton Report shows that 25 per cent of all offenders and 17 per cent of first offenders were given prison or other custodial treatment. From 1969–71 the annual total of sentences of imprisonment (immediate or suspended) fell only from 17·9 per cent to 16·7 per cent of convictions. In 1972 over 700 people convicted of unlawful possession were sent to prison. Apart from the possible criminalising effect of a prison sentence and, more specifically, its potential as a source of hard drug contacts, one has to take into account the diverse ramifications which *may* ensue from any such conviction, such as expulsion or suspension from academic institutions, loss of job opportunities and miscellaneous complications with administrative agencies, as well as the more generalised stigma involved, and consequent new problems for *society* as well as for the individual.

If it be thought that such consequences are solely the burden of the young, the following cautionary, if morally ambiguous, case is worthy of note:

> A man who had been proprietor of an old people's home had his registration cancelled because of conviction at Bradford Magistrates' Court of possession of cannabis. According to the corporation's welfare executive group: '. . . he is not a fit person, having regard to his court appearance, to carry on such a home.' He had been thirty years in the field, and qualified in general and psychiatric nursing. He said he had been given a cigarette at a party, took it home and gave it to his wife, a nurse, who took it to the police. 'It is all my fault. My husband is not the kind of man who would have anything to do with drugs. I took the cigarette to the police because I thought it was the right thing to do, but it seems now that I was wrong.'[54]

The last sentence hints at a more intangible consequence, namely a reduced respect for the law in general, which has tended to widen the generation gap. It would of course be naive to suggest that the drug laws are a major cause of inter-generational hostility, which is to be expected in any event; on the other hand, they do seem to exacerbate it needlessly.

It is not simply the legal proscription of cannabis which is in issue here, but the relative severity of the law in matters of evidence, procedure [55] and sentencing. It is unsatisfactory to point to the fact that maximum sentences are rarely imposed. They are meant to indicate gravity and, in consequence, merely confirm the suspicions of those who are already hostile. Particularly in the case of possession they are surely still too high, even if a criminal law framework is to be retained. This would matter less were the area less emotive and not so susceptible to disparity in sentencing. It involves an added danger in that penalties for possessing amphetamines have tended to be less severe, [56] which could encourage the belief that they are less harmful.

The mere classification of cannabis as illegal to some extent carries with it the risk of entry into a drug subculture, more especially in the context of increasing multi-drug use, and encourages commercial exploitation and adulteration. It is, however, important to realise that these problems are common to any solution which fails to legalise distribution as well as possession.

Turning from effects to effectiveness, it is readily apparent that the financial cost and administrative burden of the existing system far outweigh the returns. In America, it is acknowledged that the police simply cannot cope with the amount of work that would be involved in extensive enforcement, the total cost of actual enforcement in California alone being estimated at over thirty million dollars a year.

The sheer inability to control such a widespread abuse of the law accentuates the risk of arbitrary and/or discriminatory police methods, discernible to a degree in the Deedes Report and also in some Chief Constables' reports. A wholly disproportionate amount of police time is diverted from other urgent areas of law enforcement, and police morale suffers, in that they are still expected by the general public to maintain effective control in an area where it is plainly impracticable and in the face of growing doubts within the force itself as to the value of the exercise.

Even if the law could be rigidly enforced, and the traffic in cannabis was severely restricted, the lesson of 'Operation Intercept' – the pricked balloon effect – remains. It is easier to produce amphetamines than to smuggle cannabis.

Lastly, there is a cogent economic argument for treating cannabis as a potentially lucrative source of revenue. This would be no more cynical an approach than that already adopted for alcohol and tobacco. Where the law has visibly failed with proscription, solace of a kind might be derived from taxation.

The case for retaining the present law

Any relaxation of the current law, and more especially legalisation of supply, would inevitably increase use. The majority view on the Le Dain Commission was that, '. . . it is likely that under the stressful conditions of modern life an increasing number of people will take to smoking cannabis daily, and even several times a day.'[57] Even Marie Andree Bertrand, who recommended full legalisation, thought that the number of users would then double, though she doubted whether the rate of growth would be maintained. It follows that there would be a greater chance of increased harm of the kinds already described.

The young, the weak, the ignorant and the vulnerable might suffer. Certainly if a policy of full legalisation were adopted one could foresee great difficulties in this respect, and they would be immeasurably increased if a private enterprise system of distribution, with commercial advertising, were introduced.

It can also be argued that it is unrealistic to view cannabis control in isolation. If, as seems evident, a key element in the public's response to drugs is to lump them all together, then any form of legalisation could prove to be the thin end of the wedge, interpreted as implying a tacit condonation of drug use in general. But this view seems unduly defeatist, as it precludes the possibility of ever achieving a more balanced scale of values.

The point sometimes made by the police that, assuming distribution is not legalised, the possessional offence should be retained as an aid to the prevention of trafficking, is open to question. Its chief weakness, as noted by the American Commission, is that most cannabis users are 'simply too low in the distribution chain to help very much.'[58] The time saved by abolishing the offence of possession would more than compensate.

There is also the somewhat Machiavellian logic that one should deliberately retain the illegal status of a relatively harmless drug so that youth can rebel by taking it rather than a more dangerous one. Not only is this a distasteful, patronising and anti-educational attitude, but it suggests, without justification, that illegality is a stronger incentive for using cannabis than enjoyment.

The technical dispute over the precise implications of international law for any change in domestic approach will be considered later.[59] There remains, however, one issue which requires more attention than it normally receives when legalisation (especially of supply) is discussed, namely the imponderable social consequences if cannabis were to become as freely available as alcohol or tobacco.

The question is occasionally touched on but rarely pursued. Thus Paton:

> . . . such a comparison [with alcohol] requires a major effort of the imagination. To estimate the probable result of treating cannabis like alcohol one must suppose it to be as readily available, with equivalent advertisement and promotion, in an equivalent range of potencies, and used by a comparable proportion of the population. [60]

Similarly, the Le Dain Commission:

> If cannabis products were made legally available we could expect them to be offered as an alternative intoxicant at cocktail parties and other social gatherings. Regular supplies would undoubtedly be kept on hand in just as casual a way as alcohol is today. [61]

Certainly there are good grounds for supposing that easy availability would have a disruptive effect in the short term, but largely, one would imagine, for the very reason that its present illegal status means that it has not been socially accommodated or widely used in the community at large.

There is an analogy here with the experienced and inexperienced drinker. It is common knowledge that 'holding one's liquor' and ability, within limits, to predict the alcohol level at which one can function effectively, are skills that can be acquired through practice. The same principle can operate with control of the marijuana 'high'. That the effects of cannabis may differ considerably depending on whether one is an experienced or naive smoker helps to explain why so many give up the drug, having failed to find the initial attempt pleasurable.

In a period of transition, however, one would expect the novelty of being able to purchase freely a hitherto taboo substance – especially given the mythology surrounding it – to lead to initial abuse. The long term picture is far more difficult to visualise. In particular, does cannabis have any effects which would appreciably affect working habits in ways different from or more disruptive than alcohol?

It is broadly true to say that reaction to smoking cannabis is less predictable than is the case with alcohol, and that more variation of mood is likely on any given occasion. Also, an experienced smoker will often get an almost instantaneous 'high'. Does it follow that the 'liquid lunch' is more amenable to self-imposed restraint than lunch time 'turning on'?

On the whole this would seem unlikely, at least for the experienced smoker. Psychomotor skills are in general less adversely affected, and the marijuana 'high' is probably easier to turn off consciously than is a comparable state of drunkenness. Nor does it leave a 'hangover'. It is also possible that unpredictability of effects is partly a function of illegality, in that subconscious fears may be at work and/or there is variability in the potency and quality of the substance.

What has to be stressed is that legalisation implies a great deal more than a change of status. When it is discussed, it is usually in regard to what form of administrative regulation seems desirable. But some thought should also be devoted to the kinds of behaviour patterns which could emerge and the steps needed to cater for them. This is all the more necessary because signs of cannabis use are far less visible and, as yet, far less effectively detectable, than alcohol.

Possible alternatives to the present law

Any decision to alter the existing law must naturally depend on how it compares with all the other available choices. It is submitted that there are six possible lines of approach, though three of them may be dealt with summarily. We could:

(i) impose stricter controls;
(ii) legalise possession and distribution with no restrictions;
(iii) retain the *status quo;*
(iv) reduce criminal penalties for possession;
(v) abolish criminal penalties for possession; or
(vi) legalise possession and distribution on a regulatory basis.

These propositions will now be considered.

(i) *Imposition of stricter controls* A case could be made out for a stricter policy only if it could eradicate trafficking in cannabis. Similar policies were implemented, seemingly with a considerable measure of success, for heroin and amphetamines in Japan, but proved a singular failure in America's 'Operation Intercept' against cannabis.

Even if it could succeed, which is unlikely in the extreme, the hostility which it would arouse and the diversion of already overworked law enforcement resources would be wholly disproportionate to any conceivable gain.

(ii) *Unregulated legalisation* Even Mill recognised the need for some restrictions to protect the young and others unable to exercise free choice, and on this ground alone such a course is unacceptable. Most proponents of some relaxation in the law also consider it desirable that a measure of disapproval of cannabis use be expressed by the law, in however attenuated a form.

(iii) *Retention of the status quo* It is possible to maintain, especially after the passage of the Misuse of Drugs Act 1971, that the present balance is about right and that no formal change in the law is needed in order for cases to be dealt with adequately and fairly. It is suggested that on the basis of the account given in this chapter, current legal provisions are not satisfactory.

This is not to say that the law has no place in controlling cannabis use, merely that a classification so strongly influenced by narcotics legislation is inappropriate, and that the 1971 Act has not done enough to free it from this strait jacket.

A stronger argument for maintaining the *status quo* is that it is undesirable to effect any change which might alter social attitudes towards cannabis use pending further investigation of its potential for harm. But from what has been said earlier, it should appear that the present social perception of the drug is so divorced from what we do know about its effects, when used in moderation, that relaxation of the law on *private possession* is indicated in any event. It would then follow that we have three possible courses of action – reduced penalties, legalised possession and full legalisation subject to regulation.

(iv) *Reduced penalties for possession* This approach was suggested by Ian Campbell in his dissent from the majority recommendations of the Le Dain Commission, when he proposed that rather than full legalisation of possession, the maximum penalty both for possession and for cultivation for purposes other than trafficking should be a small fine.

One reason advanced for this solution is that legalised possession, especially in the polarised situation which obtains today, would inevitably be misinterpreted to imply approval or condonation. However, it could equally be said that reduced penalties would be misinterpreted. When the Wootton Committee reported, 'soft on pot' was a typical headline, and it is still commonly believed that it advocated legalisation. There was a similar reaction when the Le Dain Commission published its Interim Report. Alternatively it can be argued that if distribution remains illegal there is little danger of serious misinterpretation.

Respect for the law in general, Campbell argues, acts as a deterrent for many. But there is little evidence of this as far as the marijuana laws are concerned. The American Commission's survey finding that at least 24 million people in the United States have taken cannabis once and some 8·3 million are current users surely leaves room for doubt. The Le Dain Commission itself estimated that the total proportion of convictions was well below one per cent of Canadian users,[62] and a comparable figure would be perfectly feasible for England. One might add that the kind of person who would feel thus constrained is unlikely either to end up as one of the tiny minority of chronic smokers under a system of legalised possession or to 'progress' to more dangerous drugs which are still proscribed.

Difficulty of detection, as has been noted, is another factor which counsels caution, and is a strong argument for not taking precipitate, irreversible action. But it is still a debatable issue as to whether, on this point alone, the difference between a system of reduced penalties and legalised possession would be crucial.

A consideration which does argue in favour of reducing penalties only is that there could then be no question of a breach of the Single Convention on Narcotic Drugs 1961. It is necessary therefore to consider both the implications of such a breach and also precisely what obligations the Convention does impose.

The United Kingdom is a signatory to the Single Convention. The Convention, by aligning cannabis with the narcotics, both for historical reasons and because in some areas of the world cannabis use is viewed as a social problem of epidemic proportions, constitutes an obstacle to a rational policy in countries where this is not the case. As the American Commission points out, the absurdity of the original international classification was compounded by the inclusion of THC (but not cannabis) in the Convention on Psychotropic Substances, 1971.

The first point that might be made is that the Single Convention makes provision for denunciation by any signatory,[63] so that the full force of the stigma attached to abandoning treaty obligations would not be felt on withdrawal. On the other hand, such a course would be both politically and diplomatically ill-advised, and additionally inopportune when Britain has just committed herself to a co-operative effort by Common Market countries to counteract drug abuse. The ramifications of trafficking are such that it is unrealistic to withdraw unilaterally from the international framework.

Secondly, the Convention makes provision for its own amendment,[64] though this again is implausible without a greater consensus than at present obtains. Is it then possible to implement the Convention without imposing criminal penalties for simple possession? If so, this would clearly be the most expedient and least damaging approach.

It should be said at once that orthodox opinion maintains that criminal sanctions are required. However, the Convention nowhere says so in terms. To take a preliminary point, its definition of cannabis is as follows: 'The flowering or fruiting tops of the cannabis plant (excluding the seeds and leaves when not accompanied by the tops) from which the resin has not been extracted . . .'[65] The Le Dain Commission comments on this provision: 'It is generally considered that the above definition of "cannabis" in the Convention would permit the legalisation of a form of marijuana which consisted of the leaves of the cannabis plant . . .'[66]

Admittedly, Article 28, para. 3 states that: 'The parties shall adopt *such measures as may be necessary*[67] to prevent the misuse of, and illicit traffic in, the leaves of the cannabis plant.' But *penal* measures are not expressly mentioned, nor is the word 'misuse' entirely free from ambiguity.

However, as will be suggested later, legalisation of the mildest form of the drug alone would be an unrealistic compromise, given the existence of a substantial market in stronger varieties, the possibility of their cultivation, and the administrative costs of determining the dividing line in individual cases.

Article 4 provides for '. . . such legislative and administrative measures as may be necessary . . . to limit exclusively to medical and scientific purposes the production, manufacture, export, import, distribution of, trade in, use and possession of drugs.' Again there is no express requirement of penal sanctions. It is arguable that whereas penal provisions are deemed 'necessary' to prevent traffic, official discouragement could suffice for possession for personal use.

Article 36 requires parties to 'adopt such measures as will ensure that the cultivation, production, manufacture, extraction, preparation, possession, offering, offering for sale, distribution, purchase, sale, delivery on any terms whatsoever, brokerage, dispatch in transit, transport, importation and exportation of drugs contrary to the provisions of this Convention . . . shall be punishable offences when committed intentionally . . .'

The orthodox interpretation of Article 36 is that 'possession' there includes possession for use as well as possession for trafficking, since Article 4, as we have seen, restricts lawful possession to medical and scientific purposes. The American Commission has challenged this view: 'However, from a comparative study of the history of the Convention, the Commission has concluded that the word "possession" in Article 36 refers not to possession for personal use but to possession as a link in illicit trafficking. This interpretation is bolstered also by the failure to include use in Article 36 even though it has been included in Article 4.' [68] Might it not also be argued that by applying a *noscitur a sociis* construction to the word 'possession' in Article 36 (i.e. interpreting it in the context of the surrounding words) one would reach the same conclusion? Le Dain notes that the context is one of distribution rather than use, as the French version *détention* would seem to indicate.

Finally, one should mention that Article 33 states that: 'The parties shall not permit the possession of drugs except under legal authority.' The American Commission took the view that even if Article 4 does not require penal sanctions, it could imply that cannabis would have to be designated as contraband in order to comply with Article 33, and they incorporate this requirement in their recommendations.

Niceties of interpretation are not, in the final resort, what is at issue here. It is of interest to recall that in the plenary discussions prior to the Single Convention, the United Kingdom and France both made it plain that cannabis was of little concern to them, and that they were not in favour of its prohibition or of mandatory restrictions. True, a decade later, the climate of opinion has changed and cannabis use is of concern to both countries. At the same time, a political consensus, stimulated by the American and Canadian reports and the other developments described earlier might be favourable to a more radical interpretation, or, in the alternative, to amendments which would effect it. The purpose of the Convention was, after all, according to the Preamble, to prevent 'addiction to narcotic drugs'. There is no justification today for keeping cannabis in that category, and the American Commission recommended its removal from the Convention. [69]

The case for limiting change to a reduction in penalties is sometimes also put on the basis that the public is not ready to accept legalised possession, much less legalised distribution. This argument, of course, has implications extending far beyond drug use. The public, one might hazard, was not 'ready' for the abolition of capital punishment in 1965, the Sexual Offences Act 1967, or the Abortion Act 1967.

The American Commission summed up its National Survey finding as follows: '. . . roughly one quarter of the American public is convinced that criminal sanctions should be withdrawn entirely from marijuana use. Another fourth of the public is equally convinced that existing social and legal policy is appropriate and would jail possessors with the exception of young first offenders.' [70] The remainder were confused about the meaning of marijuana and ambivalent about what society ought to do about its use.

Of course these are only limited survey findings from another country.

There is, however, no good reason to suppose that popular attitudes here would favour a more punitive line. This would argue at least as much 'readiness' for legalised possession as existed for the legislation mentioned above.

(v) *Abolition of criminal penalties for possession* This approach, which is favoured, though with some differences of detail, by both the American and Canadian Commissions is sometimes described as the vice model. In other words, use of the commodity in question is to be discouraged, but the purveyor, not the consumer is to be penalised.

Under the Canadian proposals the prohibition against simple possession would be repealed. Cultivation would not be punishable unless it was for the purpose of trafficking. [71] Giving, without exchange of value, by one user to another of a quantity of cannabis, which could reasonably be consumed on a single occasion would not constitute trafficking. The police would have power to seize and confiscate cannabis wherever found, unless possession or cultivation had been expressly authorised for scientific or other purposes. [72] But this would not make unlawful cultivation for use, which is in effect classified with simple possession.

Amongst other things the American scheme would legalise possession for personal use, but marijuana possessed *in public* would remain contraband, subject to summary seizure and forfeiture. There would be a small fine if the amount exceeded one ounce. Casual distribution in private of small amounts for no or insignificant remuneration not involving profit would no longer be an offence. In public, it too would attract a small fine. [73] Cultivation would remain a criminal offence, presumably as part of the policy of discouraging use.

To avoid needless repetition, it will suffice at this stage to state summarily the advantages of a vice model: [74]

1 It retains an element of discouragement.
2 It makes the marijuana issue less emotive.
3 It allows *non*-legal methods of control to be pursued unhindered.
4 It removes the stigma of a criminal offence and of imprisonment.
5 It relieves the pressure on the courts.
6 It allows flexibility in the event of new information arising.

A major criticism is that such an approach is inconsistent, by virtue of its differing attitudes to possession and supply. Two points may be made here. First, the existing system is inconsistent in its whole attitude towards drug use generally and cannabis classification in particular. Secondly, as the American Commission points out, the approach would only be truly inconsistent if their attitude towards use were one of approval or neutrality. In fact, they make it abundantly clear that their general policy would be one of disapproval, to be actively pursued by non-legal means: 'The individual is being allowed to make his own choice. Hopefully, he will choose not to use marijuana. If he chooses to do so, however, he will have to do so discreetly and in private.' [75] This partly meets the charge of condoning use, a charge which the prohibition on distribution and the contraband provision are also designed to refute.

It is submitted that the two major defects of this 'partial prohibition' model are the problems it raises in respect of public use, and its retention of the disadvantages entailed in illegal distribution. Both Commissions support a policy of discouraging use. [76] It would presumably follow that public use should either be banned or reduced to a minimum. The American proposals are at least consistent in this respect: Le Dain, surprisingly, does not recommend any special limitations on public use.

More consideration must surely be given to the concept of private use, unless a licensing system is to arise, as it were, by default, along the lines of private theatre clubs. The Appendix to the American Report briefly touches on the matter;

> 'Use in public' should be narrowly construed to mean smoking or otherwise ingesting cannabis in a public place. Public places do not include homes, apartments or hotel rooms, though exact definitions would probably have to await development of case law on the issue. [77]

One can foresee the kind of demarcation disputes that are constantly arising over the definition for legal purposes of a 'public place'. [78] Would one, for example, ban use at the cinema, on the grounds of causing offence to a substantial proportion of the audience and of encouraging widespread use, yet by the same token condone it at pop festivals? How would the law view the converse case of a well-stocked 'pot cellar'?

Perhaps the weakest element in 'partial prohibition', however, is that illegal distribution and its attendant ills – exploitation, lack of control over price, quality and potency, and criminalising effects – would remain. It is largely this drawback, admittedly less objectionable if casual transfer is legalised, which provides the main attraction of the licensing model, the case for which is cogently argued by Kaplan in *Marijuana, the New Prohibition.*

(vi) *The licensing model* Again, we may summarise its potential benefits thus:

1 control over price, quality and potency;

2 a source of revenue;
3 a step towards a credible drug education policy, through a visibly consistent approach;
4 eliminating the costs, both financial and social, of criminalisation.

There would thus be formidable gains, but what would be lost?

First, such a system would obviously maximise use, and make a policy of containment or non-legal discouragement barely credible. The only significant qualifications to this would be that for many alcohol would remain the drug of choice and that many experimenters would probably cease use. 'The most striking of the use patterns revealed in the National Survey is that forty-one per cent of the adults and forty-five per cent of the youth who have ever used marijuana reported that they no longer use the drug.'[79]

A serious difficulty in practice would be to prevent availability for adults from extending to minors, as the examples of alcohol and tobacco indicate. Whatever system of distribution were decided upon – and most proponents of licensing agree that it would have to be government controlled to prevent serious exploitation – it is not easy to see how this problem can be satisfactorily overcome.

It is precisely on this issue that Kaplan's arguments carry least conviction. He simply asserts that the price could prove prohibitive for many young people; that law enforcement could be concentrated in this area – this hardly seems desirable – and, surely somewhat optimistically, that introduction by adults to use of the drug could be beneficial and help to eliminate its current mystique.

There would also be considerable expense involved in operating a regulatory system, with all its concomitants of licensing applications, hearings with objectors, inspection, etc. Nor, to the extent that it was administratively restrictive, would it interfere substantially with a continued black market.

It is submitted that to take such a radical and virtually irremediable step *now* is not justified. Medical and scientific advances may be made in the next few years, for example, in regard to driving hazards, which could be accommodated far more easily under any system short of legalised distribution. As a general principle, gradual change is likely to be the least socially disruptive overall, and is, in any event, probably the only politically attainable goal at the moment. It must not be forgotten that the Canadian government's response was broadly negative; that President Nixon immediately rejected the American Commission's proposals out of hand, and that a Labour government in this country poured scorn on a

Committee which had not even proposed legalising possession.

Perhaps the only clear conclusion to be drawn from the above account is that the evidence does not point strongly in any one direction. The existing law is inadequate, and the obvious alternatives are open to attack on various grounds. Political expediency will at most stretch to a reduction of penalties for simple possession of cannabis.

At the same time, our main concern on this issue is not cannabis use as an isolated phenomenon, but its significance in the overall pattern of non-medical drug use today, and as it is likely to develop in the future. This concern argues for a radical change, but one which is not irreversible. It is submitted that 'partial prohibition', along the lines advocated by the American Commission, is the policy most appropriate at the present time, and the one best suited to harmonising the legitimate conflicting interests at stake, though it will require a close study of the meaning and implications of prohibiting public use.

Notes

[1] See ch. 5, n. 11. From hereon, *Signal of Misunderstanding* and *Cannabis* respectively.

[2] S. 1(2) (e) and s. 1(3), respectively.

[3] Between 1969 and 1974 the annual Federal drug abuse, treatment, rehabilitation and prevention budget increased from $46 million to $542 million.

[4] An excellent account of the pharmacology and effects of the drug can be found in *Cannabis.*

[5] The term 'cannabis' will be used throughout this chapter to cover all the various forms of the drug.

[6] See e.g. H. Becker, *Outsiders,* op.cit., and N. Zinberg and A. Weil, 'A Comparison of Marijuana Users and Non-users', *Nature,* vol. 226, 1970, pp. 119–23.

[7] W. Paton, *Student* vol. 2, no. 2, 1969, p. 47.

[8] R. Lewin, *New Scientist* 8 June 1972, p. 552.

[9] Vol. 2, pp. 406–7.

[10] University of Mississippi, December 1970.

[11] A. Campbell *et al., The Lancet* 4 December 1971, p. 1219.

[12] Ibid., p. 1240–1.

[13] E.g. R. Magus and L. Harris, Paper presented at Federation of American Societies for Experimental Biology, Chicago 1971.

[14] *Cannabis,* p. 115.

15 WHO, Tech. Rep. Ser. 1971, No. 478, p. 26.

16 See n. 1.

17 E. Bloomquist, *Marijuana: The Second Trip,* Glencoe Press 1971, pp. 99–101.

18 Reginald Maudling, quoted, *Sunday Times* 4 April 1971.

19 J.D. Purcell, Clerkenwell Magistrates' Court, quoted, *The Times* 17 November 1970.

20 'Drug Dependence – a Sociopharmacological Assessment', *Advancement of Science,* vol. 25, 1968, pp. 200–12.

21 See Schofield op.cit., p. 106.

22 'Cannabis taking in England', *Newcastle Medical Journal,* vol. 30(b), 1968, p. 533.

23 Italics supplied.

24 *The Listener* 14 November 1968, p. 643.

25 *Drugs and Society* June 1972, p. 19.

26 Though not published until January 1969, the Wootton Report was completed in July 1968. Schofield, op.cit., p. 86.

27 Ibid., pp. 106–7. Both the Wootton Report and Paton appear to be referring to any use of cannabis, however transient or irregular.

28 The figure of 14,119 in Appendix A, Table 5 represents the number of convictions.

29 In August 1973, a BBC survey based on a sample of 12,000 people estimated that 3,812,000 people in Britain have used cannabis at some time.

30 See E. Goode, 'Multiple Drug Use among Marijuana-Smokers', *Soc. Probs.,* vol. 17, 1969, pp. 48–64.

31 See p. 165.

32 *Cannabis,* p. 271.

33 See the findings of the 'La Guardia Report: Mayor's Committee on Marijuana. The marijuana problem in the city of New York', Jacques Cattell Press, Lancaster, Penn. 1944. Confirmed in several subsequent reports, e.g. L. Clark *et al.*, 1970; G. Kiplinger *et al.*, 1971; A Weil *et al.*, 1968; cited in *Cannabis* at pp. 345, 356 and 375, respectively.

34 A. Crancer, Jr. *et al.,* 'The Effects of Marijuana and Alcohol on Simulated Driving Performance', *Science* vol. 164, 1969, pp. 851–4.

35 'The Marijuana-induced "Social High": Neurological and Electroencephalographic Concomitants', *Journal of the American Medical Association* vol. 213, pp. 1300–2.

36 'Cannabis and alcohol: Effect on simulated driving'. Paper presented at 5th World Congress of Psychiatry, Mexico City, November 1971.

37 *Cannabis*, pp. 63–4, 269; *Signal of Misunderstanding*, pp. 78–9,

and e.g. J. Waller, Drugs and Highway Crashes, *Journal of the American Medical Association* vol. 215, no. 9, 1971, pp. 1477–82; L. Nichols, 'Drug use and highway safety: A review of the literature', Rep. DOT-HS-012-1-019 US Dept. of Transportation, Nat. Highway Traffic Safety Admin. Washington D.C. 1971.

38 *Cannabis,* p. 268.

39 D. Miller, 'Sexual Conflict and Drug Abuse', *New Society* 16 September 1971, p. 512.

40 See W. McGlothlin and L. West, 'The Marijuana Problem', an overview, *American Journal of Psychiatry,* vol. 125, no. 3, 1968. pp. 126–34.

41 See ch. 6.

42 W. O'Shaughnessy, 'On the Preparations of the Indian Hemp, or Gunjah *(Cannabis indica):* Their Effects on the Animal System in Health, and their Utility in the Treatment of Tetanus and Other Convulsive Diseases', *Provincial Medical Journal and Retrospect Medical Sciences,* vol. 5, 1843, p. 343.

43 J. Moreau de Tours, *Du haschisch et de l'aliénation mentale*, Masson, Paris 1945.

44 Even research on its hibernation powers as a battlefield aid for mass casualties has apparently been carried out in America – one injection of pure marijuana put dogs into a state of suspended animation for up to eight days. (*The Times* 16 April 1971).

45 'A Nationwide Study of Beliefs, Information and Experiences', a National Survey sponsored by the American Commission, see *Signal of Misunderstanding,* p. 7.

46 Misuse of Drugs Act 1971, Sched. 4. For an example of particularly severe new legislation see the South African Abuse of Dependence-Producing Substances and Rehabilitation Centres Act 41 of 1971. *Justice of the Peace* vol. 136, no. 1, 1 January 1972, p. 8.

47 *The Times* 3 July 1972.

48 *Observer* 10 January 1971.

49 *Justice of the Peace* vol. 135, no. 21, 22 May 1971, p. 352.

50 *Observer* 2 May 1971.

51 Ann Leslie, *Nova* August 1971.

52 *The Times* 7 March 1972.

53 In 1973, of 14,119 convictions, 11,911 (84 per cent) were for unlawful possession.

54 *The Times* 17 April 1971.

The case illustrates a further peculiarity of drug offences, in that the wife, too, could have been prosecuted for possession. (Cf. as regards amphetamines, *Warner* v. *Metropolitan Police Commissioner* [1969] 2 A.C. 256, at pp. 304–5, *per* Lord Pearce.) The Misuse of Drugs Act 1971, s. 5(4), provides a new defence for someone who delivers a controlled drug 'into the custody of a person lawfully entitled to take custody of it.'

[55] See ch. 2 for a discussion of the burden of proof and powers of arrest and search.

[56] For an analysis of comparative penalties, see D. Thomas, *Principles of Sentencing,* Heinemann 1970, pp. 162–7.

[57] *Cannabis,* p. 267.

[58] *Signal of Misunderstanding,* p. 163.

[59] See pp. 181–3.

[60] *Drugs and Society* June 1972, p. 20.

[61] *Cannabis,* p. 284.

[62] *Cannabis,* p. 290.

[63] Art. 46.

[64] Art. 47. Also, by Art. 3, a Party or the WHO, may propose a change to the Schedules, including the deletion of a given drug from a Schedule.

[65] Art. 1, 1(b).

[66] *Cannabis,* p. 209. Compare the definition in the Misuse of Drugs Act 1971:s. 37(1) '. . . the flowering or fruiting tops of any plant of the genus *Cannabis* from which the resin has not been extracted, by whatever name they may be designated.' This definition has been held to include the leaves: *Harding* v. *Hayes* [1974], *The Times* 15 October.

[67] Italics supplied.

[68] *Signal of Misunderstanding,* p. 165.

[69] Ibid., pp. 173–4.

Indeed, it has been argued that this incongruity is a ground for invoking the international law doctrine of selective denunciation, provided for by the Vienna Convention, 1969, (not yet in force) Article 44, if the article in question is clearly separable and not of the essence of the Parties' consent to the treaty as a whole.

The requisite ground for such denunciation could be either error of fact (Vienna Convention, art. 48), or fundamental change of circumstances (Vienna Convention, art. 62), though these grounds have in practice been invoked only for physical changes to boundaries etc., as distinct from changes in the state of medical knowledge. It is also true that evidence existed well before 1961 to the effect that cannabis was not addictive.

For a fuller exploration of international law issues see M. Leinwand, 'The International Law of Treaties and United States Legalisation of

Marijuana', *Columbia Journal of Transnational Law,* vol. 10, no. 2, 1971, pp. 413–41.

[70] *Signal of Misunderstanding,* p. 103.

[71] Once cultivation was established, the onus would shift to the defendant to raise a reasonable doubt as to intention. *Cannabis,* pp. 302–3.

[72] Ibid.

[73] *Signal of Misunderstanding,* pp. 152–4.

[74] Ibid., p. 150.

[75] Ibid., p. 162.

[76] For the Le Dain Commission view see *Cannabis,* p. 301.

[77] Appendix to *Signal of Misunderstanding,* p. 1175.

[78] A potentially far-reaching change has been made in the Criminal Justice Act 1972, s. 33, which substitutes for the definition of 'public place' in the Public Order Act 1936, s. 9(1): ' "Public place" includes any highway and any other premises or place to which at the material time the public have or are permitted to have access, whether on payment or otherwise.'

Thus the definition is no longer confined to 'any open space': See *Cooper* v. *Shield* [1971] 2 W.L.R. 1385.

[79] *Signal of Misunderstanding,* p. 34.

8 The Paradox of Drug Control

In almost any area of social concern there is a persistent demand for solutions or, worse, *the* solution to *the* problem. In criminology this 'itch for uniformity' has expressed itself at various times in claims to have unearthed the 'cause' or causes of 'crime', as well as the universal 'cure'. But whereas considerable inroads have been made into the popular notion of crime as a discrete entity, the same is not true of attitudes towards illegal drugs.

We have seen how the emotive effect of the word 'drug' and the fact of illegality have encouraged this all-embracing approach. That a substantial number of young people currently use drugs unfamiliar to their parents serves to reinforce it – youth provides a central focus; the novelty of the substances is a barrier to differentiating them, and their sudden widespread use is inevitably perceived as a 'new' phenomenon.

It is not surprising then that the media frequently allude to 'the drugs problem' and how to solve 'it'. Not only does this obscure the fact that there are several different patterns of drug taking, but it tends to over-emphasise the intrinsic dangers of the substances divorced from the psycho-social context in which they are taken.

Clearly there are several drug 'issues', some of which it is fruitful to perceive as 'problems' – where individual well-being and social stability are demonstrably endangered. These issues admit of various approaches, but few, if any, solutions, save the kind of 'solutions' which entail new problems – the 'pricked balloon' effect previously referred to.

The relative ineffectiveness of the legal response is easy to understand, once it is grasped that harmful drug use cannot be dealt with as a problem in isolation, because, in itself, it is not a problem so much as a misguided attempt at a solution. We cannot explain drug taking if we divorce it from the total social and economic context in which it occurs. Yet this is precisely what the criminal law tends to do, because it is not geared to ameliorating social problems. It cannot provide the social and economic alternatives – the jobs, the recreational activities, the sense of involvement – which are most likely to reduce the incidence of irresponsible use and minimise its harmful consequences.

To the extent that society expects the law to solve what it perceives as the drug problem it is pursuing an unrealisable dream. The most that the law ought sensibly to aim at is to make some inroad into drug trafficking; to penalise demonstrably anti-social behaviour, and, more positively, to act where appropriate as the point of entry to agencies such as treatment centres, probation and community service.

As regards drug *trafficking,* the outlook is rather bleak. A United Nations estimate is that '. . . ten per cent at the most of drugs smuggled in a country are seized.' [1] Even if economic subsidies are provided on an immense scale to producer countries such as Turkey, the chances of cutting out excessive production on a long term basis are – on the strength of past experience – slim. But there is no obvious alternative to a continuation of present international policies.

In respect of drug *use,* we need a franker acknowledgement of the inadequacy of criminal sanctions, and of their inappropriateness as a response to what is frequently a combination of drift and behavioural problems. We should be reluctant to imprison people for the simple possession of *any* drug. Even if it is thought desirable to retain liability to imprisonment as an expression of the seriousness with which certain kinds of drug use are viewed, as with opiates, the emphasis should still be on the value of the court as a means of diversion to non-punitive institutions or agencies. In the particular case of cannabis, if legalisation of possession for private use, as suggested in the previous chapter, is at present politically unacceptable, surely nothing of value would be lost by the immediate abolition of liability to imprisonment. This would at least be a step towards a more balanced view of potential for harm. Similarly, if judges and magistrates feel constrained to express concern about drug taking on passing sentence, it is to be hoped that they will avoid doing so in a way that merely reinforces public ignorance and prejudice.

One of the disadvantages in giving pride of place to legal measures is precisely that this tends to minimise the vital role of non-coercive community responses, whether in the form of local liaison schemes, voluntary restraints on medical prescribing, youth clubs or simply family influence. As Freedman has put it: '. . . drug abuse is not the drug problem. Rather our solutions have been the problem . . .' [2]

In so far as British policy has been relatively non-coercive in the past, the concentration of resources on education, prevention and treatment entails a far less radical change of perception than, for example, in America; yet, particularly in regard to education, we seem to have lagged far behind. [3] The current American disenchantment with educational programmes does not imply that we should take no steps in this direction. Even without embarking on any grandiose or controversial campaigns, there is much that can be done which could hardly fail to be beneficial.

The lack of adequate training for medical students and of instruction in teacher training colleges are gaps that ought to be narrowed without delay.

One of the most pressing needs, as Freedman has observed, is to devise within the social services, at local community level, some means of counteracting the traumatic effects which must so often follow when parents discover that their children have been taking illegal drugs. 'In my experience, you can show people what *not* to do as a first step – how not to panic, how to begin to look at themselves, at their own community . . .'[4] This would not necessarily require a formal school counselling system throughout the country, but it does imply that, ideally, all local authority areas should have someone who is well-informed on the subject of drug use in general (and about local treatment facilities in particular) whom both children and parents could confidently approach.

Yet there is no justification for believing that more research and more emphasis on education will provide us with 'solutions'. Undoubtedly both are very necessary. The scientific accuracy of much of the early research has been questioned and investigation of illicit drugs has been hampered by their illegal status. The potential value of educational efforts has already been noted. But without disparaging the importance of either, we must beware of creating 'the drug abuse industrial complex' to which the United States National Commission drew attention in its final report.

What must ultimately be faced up to is that the lack of effective solutions is really implicit in the very activity of using drugs. For the inescapable paradox about the forms of drug use that cause the most disquiet is that their actual, or in some cases assumed, central feature – dependence – is an ambivalent attribute of the human condition in general. In its more benign aspects, dependence shades off into protection, comfort and well-being; in its more disturbing manifestations it can be 'cured' only by the substitution of a hopefully less damaging form of dependence.

Unfortunately, the more emotive and dramatic the issue, the greater is the impulse to demand total solutions – in this case the 'eradication of the scourge of drug abuse'. But herein lies a double irony, for not only is dependence the very question at issue, but one can confidently predict that experimentation, the creation of new synthetics and refinement of existing drugs will rapidly develop. In *Marijuana, a Signal of Misunderstanding,* much emphasis was placed on the possibility that cannabis use is a passing fashion and therefore should not be given the stamp of social approval. Even if this does prove to be true, the 'pharmaceutical revolution' has achieved so much in the last forty years that cannabis (and

LSD) could easily, within a generation, be seen not as a passing fashion, but rather as precursors, as primitive models; the science fiction of today becoming, in some measure, the reality of tomorrow. In any event, politicians will continue to implement short term measures,[5] though they may be at odds with plausible predictions of future needs.

Social cohesion necessitates the belief that we can control our environment. Current concern about pollution, including the proliferation of drugs – and predictions of ecological disaster – reflect the anxiety that man at the apparent height of his scientific mastery over nature is in fact losing control. We fear that the drug which is sought as a form of relief and protection is in reality a form of enslavement; protection purchased at the expense of loss of control over our destiny.

Much of the irrationality to be found in attitudes towards drugs begins to dissolve, then, or is at least explicable, if it is recognised that a society is justified in both encouraging and discouraging drug use of various kinds. The paradox remains that drugs may be taken to cure, relax, or stimulate, yet may lead to addiction, lack of motivation, or aggression. Most societies want to promote both productivity and relaxation. They want to encourage independence of mind, experimentation and creativity,[6] but prevent the resultant harm to the vulnerable; to dissuade from socially disruptive use, yet encourage medical research.

Above all, perhaps, most societies aim to promote drug use of a kind which will not blur the distinction between work and leisure, and in this respect they reflect the psychological mechanisms that most people use in order to avoid confronting themselves. We seek the perfect relaxant but resist its discovery in the name of the preservation of organised society.

These ambiguous and seemingly abstract implications of drug use are not solely the concern of the artist or philosopher. It is equally vital for the policymaker to reflect on drug use as a symbol of the human condition, for only then can he appreciate the built-in limitations of legal measures as an effective and acceptable means of control.

Notes

[1] V. Kusevic, *Drug Abuse: Nonmedical Use of Dependence-Producing Drugs,* S. Btesh (ed.), Plenum Press 1972, p. 277.

[2] Anglo-American Conference on Drug Abuse, 1973, p. 9.

[3] It is interesting to note that the first DES pamphlet specifically devoted to drugs, *Drugs and the Schools,* was not published until September 1972, and though sensitive to the issues it is not particularly

informative about individual drugs or the teacher's role.

[4] D. Freedman, in *Drug Abuse: Nonmedical Use of Dependence-Producing Drugs,* p. 157.

[5] Such as the Misuse of Drugs Act 1971, despite the undoubted improvements it makes possible.

[6] See G. Claridge, *Drugs and Human Behaviour,* Allen Lane, The Penguin Press 1970, pp. 111–13 for an account of how an architect drew on an LSD experience in designing a hospital suited to the needs of the mentally ill.

APPENDIX A

Table A.1

Estimate of number of drug 'misusers', United Kingdom, 1966

Type of misuse	Comment	Total no. in UK (very approx.)
Hallucinogens	Small amount of illicit use of LSD	Less than 500[1]
Cocaine	Almost entirely used in combination with heroin	1,000
Morphine	Majority heroin addicts	2,400
Cannabis	Illicit use without dependence	24,000
Amphetamines	(a) Slight dependence on prescribed amphetamines	80,000
	(b) Illicit use of amphetamines	80,000
Barbiturates	(a) Regular use with dependence	100,000
	(b) Regular use without dependence	500,000
Alcohol	(a) Obvious and chronic alcoholics	70,000
	(b) Alcoholics without deterioration	230,000

[1] This figure relates to 1965.

Source: Derived from T. Bewley, *Bulletin on Narcotics*, vol. 18, no. 4, 1966 with amendments. See also Drug Addiction, Office of Health Economics, 1967, p. 15.

Table A.2

United Kingdom statistics of drug addiction and criminal offences involving drugs

Drug addicts	1958	1959	1960	1961	1962	1963	1964	1965	1966	1967	1968	1969 [1]	
												Year Total	As at 31.12.69
Total number	442	454	437	470	532	635	753	927	1349	1729	2782	2881	1466
Drugs [2]													
No. taking heroin	62	68	94	132	175	237	342	521	899	1299	2240	1417	499
methadone	12	60	68	59	54	55	61	72	156	243	486	1687	1011
cocaine	25	30	52	84	112	171	211	311	443	462	564	311	81
morphine	205	204	177	168	157	172	162	160	178	158	198	345	111
pethidine	117	116	98	105	112	107	128	102	131	112	120	128	83
Origin													
No. of therapeutic origin	349	344	309	293	312	355	368	344	351	313	306	289	247
non-therapeutic origin	68	98	122	159	212	270	372	580	982	1385	2420	2533	1196
unknown origin	25	12	6	18	8	10	13	3	16	31	56	59	23
Ages													
Under 20	–	–	1	2	3	17	40	145	329	395	764	637	224
taking heroin [3]	–	–	1	2	3	17	40	134	317	381	709	598	221
20 – 34	–	50	62	94	132	184	257	347	558	906	1530	1789	897
taking heroin [3]	–	35	52	87	126	162	219	319	479	827	1390	1709	872
35 – 49	–	92	91	95	107	128	138	134	162	142	146	174	116
taking heroin [3]	–	7	14	19	24	38	61	52	83	66	78	101	69
50 and over	–	278	267	272	274	298	311	291	286	279	260	241	204
taking heroin [3]	–	26	27	24	22	20	22	16	20	24	20	46	40
Age unknown	–	34	16	7	16	8	7	10	14	7	82	40	25
taking heroin [3]	–	–	–	–	–	–	–	–	–	1	43	26	13

H

Sex													
No. of male addicts	197	196	195	223	262	339	409	558	886	1262	2161	2295	1067
No. of female addicts	245	258	242	247	270	296	344	369	463	467	621	586	399
Total from professional classes (medical or allied)	74	68	63	61	57	56	58	45	54	56	43	43	26

1 It will be seen that the statistical data from 1969 is presented differently from the preceding years. Previously these statistics had been based on the total number of addicts coming to the notice of the Home Office during the course of the year. New recording procedures have made it possible to give details of those addicts known to have been receiving supplies of drugs at the end of the year as well as the total number of cases coming to notice during the year.

2 These figures refer to drugs used alone or in combination with other drugs. Thus an addict using both heroin and cocaine will be included under both drugs, and it must be pointed out that the majority of the cocaine addicts shown are also using heroin.

3 From 1969 this figure is for addicts to *heroin and/or methadone.* The reason for this is that as a result of a deliberate policy adopted by hospital clinics in the treatment of heroin addiction by weaning patients from heroin on to methadone, methadone has supplanted heroin as the drug most commonly used by addicts.

Source: The Home Office (Drugs Branch)

Table A.3

Drug addicts	1970 Year total	1970 As at 31.12.70	1971 Year total	1971 As at 31.12.71	1972 Year total	1972 As at 31.12.72	1973 Year total	1973 As at 31.12.73
Total number	2661	1430	2769	1555	2944	1619	3025	1818
Drugs[2]								
No. taking heroin	914	437	959	385	868	339	866	380
methadone	1820	992	1927	1160	2171	1280	2247	1440
cocaine	198	57	178	58	178	46	194	51
morphine	346	105	346	103	292	90	268	84
pethidine	122	80	135	73	98	59	81	50
Origin								
No. of therapeutic origin	295	231	265	218	244	180	207	174
non-therapeutic origin	2321	1177	2457	1313	2659	1413	2631	1505
unknown origin	45	22	47	24	41	26	187	139
Ages								
Under 20	405	142	338	118	279	96	253	84
taking heroin[3]	365	136	304	111	260	95	226	83
20 – 34	1813	959	2010	1123	2262	1221	2368	1415
taking heroin[3]	1705	921	1912	1088	2178	1195	2262	1375
35 – 49	158	112	156	112	178	120	185	137
taking heroin[3]	95	69	94	73	126	87	129	95
50 and over	253	195	226	179	204	165	214	181
taking heroin[3]	50	39	47	35	42	36	49	42
Age unknown	32	22	39	23	21	17	5	1
taking heroin[3]	18	10	19	9	7	5	3	1
Sex								
No. of male addicts	2071	1053	2134	1135	2272	1197	2345	1371
No. of female addicts	590	377	635	420	672	422	680	447
Total number from professional classes (medical or allied)	38	26	44	22	33	23	29	15

[2,3] See Table A.2

Source: The Home Office (Drugs Branch)

Table A.4

Ages of addicts under 20 known to Home Office

	14	15	16	17	18	19	Total
1960	–	–	–	–	–	1	1
1961	–	–	–	–	1	1	2
1962	–	–	1	–	–	2	3
1963	–	–	2	2	2	11	17
1964	1	–	1	8	11	19	40
1965	–	8	5	19	42	71	145
1966	1	17	26	68	111	106	329
1967	–	3	38	82	100	172	395
1968	–	10	40	141	274	299	764
1969 Total	–	–	24	83	218	312	637
31.12.69	–	–	6	33	73	112	224
1970 Total	–	1	9	49	117	229	405
31.12.70	–	1	1	18	30	92	142
1971 Total	–	–	10	45	114	169	338
31.12.71	–	–	2	13	34	69	118
1972 Total	1	1	7	27	85	158	279
31.12.72	–	–	3	13	24	56	96
1973 Total	–	–	7	39	78	129	253
31.12.73	–	–	2	9	24	49	84

Table A.5

Offences involving drugs controlled under DDA, 1965

	Cannabis	Opium	Manufactured drugs	Drugs (Prevention of Misuse) Act 1964
1945	4	206	20	–
1946	11	65	27	–
1947	46	76	65	–
1948	51	78	48	–
1949	61	52	56	–
1950	86	41	42	–
1951	132	64	47	–
1952	98	62	48	–
1953	88	47	44	–
1954	144	28	47	–
1955	115	17	37	–
1956	103	12	37	–
1957	51	9	30	–
1958	99	8	41	–
1959	185	18	26	–
1960	235	15	28	–
1961	288	15	61	–
1962	588	16	71	–
1963	663	20	63	–
1964	544	14	101	–
1965	626	13	128	958[1]
1966	1119	36	242	1216
1967	2393	58	573	2486
1968	3071	73	1099	2957
1969	4683	53	1359	3762
1970	7520	66	1214	3885
1971	9219	55	1570	5516
1972	12611	98	2068	5284
1973	14119	244[2]	8497[3]	

From 1945 to 1953 inclusive the figures relate to prosecutions
From 1954 onwards the figures relate to convictions

[1] This figure is in respect of the period 31 October 1964 to 31 December 1965

[2] Includes medicinal opium

[3] Includes offences under the Dangerous Drugs Act 1965, the Drugs (Prevention of Misuse) Act 1964 and the Misuse of Drugs Act 1971 which came into force on 1 July 1973 and which repealed the 1965 and 1964 Acts

APPENDIX B

Cost estimate of a treatment complex

(From *Treatment: A Report of the Commission of Inquiry into the Non-Medical Use of Drugs,* Information Canada, Ottawa (1972) p. 103.)

The Commission has undertaken a comparative study of costs *(per diem)* of the different methods of managing or treating a person dependent on opiate narcotics in institutional settings. These are the relative daily expenditures:

in a half-way house without a special programme		$ 7·50
in a therapeutic community		10·00
in a Federal penitentiary		16·30
in a prison (Quebec)		20·54
in a correctional institution with	(men)	24·00
a remedial programme (Matsqui)	(women)	66·00

Simple methadone maintenance without an adjuvant treatment and rehabilitation program would probably cost about $1,000·00 a year per person ($2·75 *per diem*).

The operating cost of a fully equipped treatment complex using methadone or antagonist maintenance for persons dependent on 'hard' drugs (opiate narcotics, and, in the future, possibly speed or cocaine) in a centre which could care for about 50 patients living in the community can also be estimated. To be able to cover the full range of acute and follow-up diagnostic testing (medical, psychological and chemical), acute and chronic treatment and rehabilitative aftercare, such special centres would require at least the following staff: 1 psychiatrist, 2 nurses, 1 clinical psychologist, 2 social workers, 1 job rehabilitation officer, 1 occupational therapist, 1 pharmacist. The treatment centre should be located in a building equipped with offices, an infirmary with four beds, a laboratory, a dispensary, a lounge and a workshop. The operating cost for such a centre is estimated at about $125,000 *per annum.* A sufficient number of centres to care for 1,000 drug-dependent persons would cost about $2,500,000 per year.

Based on this estimate, the cost of providing therapeutic care for a drug-dependent person in such a centre would be $7–10 per day – a figure which compares favourably with the cost of therapeutic communities and is well below the cost of imprisonment in penal institutions.

Bibliography

Adams, E.W., *Drug Addiction,* Oxford University Press 1937.
Advisory Committee Report on Drug Dependence, *Cannabis,* HMSO 1968. (The Wootton Report.)
Advisory Committee Report on Drug Dependence, *Rehabilitation of Drug Addicts,* HMSO 1969.
Advisory Committee Report on Drug Dependence, *The Amphetamines and Lysergic Acid Diethylamide* (LSD), HMSO 1970.
Advisory Committee Report on Drug Dependence, *Powers of Arrest and Search in Relation to Drug Offences,* HMSO 1970. (The Deedes Report.)
de Alarcon, R., Paper to the Royal Medico-Legal Association, *The Times* 7 May 1969.
Anglo-American Conference on Drug Abuse, Royal Society of Medicine 1973.
Anonymous, *The Medical Times,* vol. 2, 1873, p. 73.
Bean, P., *The Social Control of Drugs,* Martin Robertson 1974.
Becker, H.S., 'Becoming a Marihuana User', *American Journal of Sociology* vol. 59, 1953, p. 235.
Becker, H.S., *Outsiders,* Free Press, 1963.
Bergman, R., 'Navajo Peyote Use: Its Apparent Safety', *American Journal of Psychiatry* vol. 128, no. 6, 1971, p. 659.
Bewley, T.H., 'Recent Changes in the Pattern of Drug Abuse in the United Kingdom', *Bulletin on Narcotics* vol. 18, no. 4, 1966, p. 2.
Bewley, T.H. *et al.,* 'Survey of Heroin Addicts known to the Home Office', *British Medical Journal* vol. 1, 1968, pp. 727–30.
Bewley, T.H., 'Control of Drug Dependence', *Medico-Legal Journal* vol. 37, part 1, 1969, p. 7.
Black, J.R., 'Advantages of Substituting the Morphia Habit for the Incurably Alcoholic', *Cincinnati Lancet-Clinic,* vol. 22, 1889, p. 537.
Bloomquist, E.R., *Marijuana: The Second Trip,* Glencoe Press 1971.
British Journal of Psychiatry, News and Notes Supplement, 'Dangerous Drugs and the National Health Service', June 1972, p. 8.
British Medical Association, *The Drinking Driver,* BMA 1965.
Brittain, V., 'How the Drug Clinics Work', *The Times* 18 August 1970.
Brittain, V., 'Teenage Heroin Epidemic that has alarmed U.S.', *The Times* 13 March 1970.

Btesh, S. (ed.), *Drug Abuse: Non-Medical Use of Dependence-Producing Drugs,* Plenum Press 1972.

Departmental Committee on Liquor Licensing (Report), HMSO 1972, Cmnd. 5154. (The Erroll Report.)

Departmental Committee on Morphine and Heroin Addiction (Report), HMSO 1926. (The Rolleston Report.)

Department of Education and Science, *A Handbook of Health Education,* HMSO 1968.

Department of Education and Science, *Drugs and the Schools,* HMSO 1972.

Campbell, A. *et al.,* 'Cerebral Atrophy in Young Cannabis Smokers', *The Lancet* vol. 2, 1971, p. 1219.

Card, R., 'The Misuse of Drugs Act, 1971', *Criminal Law Review* 1971, p. 744.

Chapple, P.A.L. and Gray, G., 'One Year's Work at a Centre for the Treatment of Addicted Patients', *The Lancet* vol. 1, 1968, p. 908.

Chein, I. *et al., Narcotics, Delinquency and Social Policy,* Tavistock Publications 1964.

Claridge, G., *Drugs and Human Behaviour,* Allen Lane, Penguin Press 1970.

Cloward, R.A. and Ohlin, L.E., *Delinquency and Opportunity: A Theory of Delinquent Gangs,* Free Press, 1960.

Cockett, R., *Drug Abuse and Personality in Young Offenders,* Butterworths, 1971.

Commission of Inquiry into the Non-Medical Use of Drugs (Interim Report), Ottawa, Queen's Printer 1970; Penguin 1971. (The Le Dain Report.)

Commission of Inquiry into the Non-Medical Use of Drugs (Report), *Treatment,* Information Canada 1972.

Commission of Inquiry into the Non-Medical Use of Drugs (Report), *Cannabis,* Information Canada 1972.

Commission of Inquiry into the Non-Medical Use of Drugs (Final Report), Information Canada 1973.

Commission of Inquiry into Whittingham Hospital (Report), HMSO 1972, Cmnd. 4861.

Connell, P.H., 'Drug dependence in Great Britain: A challenge to the practice of medicine' in H. Steinberg (ed.), *The Scientific Basis of Drug Dependence,* Churchill 1969.

Crancer, A., Jr. *et al.,* 'The Effects of Marihuana and Alcohol on Simulated Driving Performance', *Science* vol. 164, 1969, p. 851.

Croft, D. *et al.,* 'Gastric Bleeding and Benorylate, a New Aspirin', *British Medical Journal* vol. 3, 1972, p. 545.

Department of Health and Social Security, *Amphetamines, Barbiturates, LSD and Cannabis, Their Use and Misuse* (Reports on Public Health and Medical Subjects, No. 124), HMSO 1970.

Department of Health and Social Security, *On the State of the Public Health, (1969),* HMSO 1970.

Department of Health and Social Security, *On the State of the Public Health, (1970),* HMSO 1971.

De Quincey, T., *Autobiography and Confessions of an English Opium Eater (1822),* Penguin 1971.

De Ropp, R., in *Drugs: For and Against,* Hart, New York 1970.

Devlin, P., *The Enforcement of Morals,* Oxford University Press 1965.

Dole, V.P. and Nyswander, M.E., 'The Use of Methadone for Narcotic Blockade', *British Journal of Addiction* vol. 68, 1968, p. 55.

Downes, D., 'Drug Takers and the Community', in *Behind the Drug Scene,* British Medical Association 1969.

Drug Abuse Survey Project, *Dealing with Drug Abuse:* A Report to the Ford Foundation, MacMillan 1972.

Dunlop, D., 'Abuse of Drugs by the Public and by Doctors', *British Medical Bulletin* vol. 26, 1970, p. 236.

Duster, T., *The Legislation of Morality,* The Free Press, New York 1970.

East, N., *Society and the Criminal,* HMSO 1949.

Edwards, G., *Unreason in an Age of Reason,* Royal Society of Medicine 1971.

Eisenlohr, L., *International Narcotics Control,* Allen and Unwin 1934.

Eldridge, W.B., *Narcotics and the Law,* University of Chicago Press 1967.

Farleigh Hospital Committee of Inquiry (Report), HMSO 1971, Cmnd. 4557.

Federal Narcotics Bureau, *Narcotic Clinics in the United States,* US Government Printing Office 1953.

Fort, J., 'Heroin addiction among young men', in J.A. O'Donnell and J.C. Ball, *Narcotic Addiction,* Harper and Row 1966.

Frankau, Lady, 'Treatment in England of Canadian Patients Addicted to Narcotic Drugs', *Canadian Medical Association Journal* vol. 90, no. 6, 1964, p. 421.

Gardner, R. and Connell, P.H., 'One Year's Experience in a Drug-Dependence Clinic', *The Lancet* vol. 2, 1970, p. 455.

Gibbens, T.C.N. and Silberman, M., 'Alcoholism among Prisoners', *Psychological Medicine* vol. 1, 1970, p. 73.

Goode, E., 'Multiple Drug Use among Marijuana-Smokers', *Soc. Probs.* vol. 17, 1969, p. 48.

Goodhart, A.L., 'Possession of Drugs and Absolute Liability', *Law Quarterly Review* vol. 84, 1968, p. 382.

Goulding, R., 'The Statistics of Drug Addiction', *Medicine, Science and the Law* vol. 8, no. 4, 1968, p. 266.

Harris, D.R., 'The Concept of Possession in English Law', in Guest (ed.), *Oxford Essays in Jurisprudence* Oxford University Press 1961.

Hart, H.L.A., *Law, Liberty and Morality,* Oxford University Press 1963.

Hayter, A., *Opium and the Romantic Imagination,* Faber and Faber 1969.

HM Chief Inspector of Constabulary (Report for the year 1970), HMSO 1971.

HM Chief Inspector of Constabulary (Report for the year 1971), HMSO 1972.

HM Government Report to the League of Nations for 1935: *Traffic in Opium and Other Dangerous Drugs,* HMSO 1936.

Hewetson, J. and Ollendorf, R., 'Preliminary Survey of 100 London Heroin and Cocaine Addicts', *British Journal of Addiction* vol. 60, 1964, p. 109.

Home Office, *The Duties of Doctors and Dentists Under the Dangerous Drugs Act and Regulations,* DD 101, 6th ed., 1956.

Huxley, A., *Brave New World,* Chatto and Windus, 1934.

Imlah, N., *Drugs in Modern Society,* Geoffrey Chapman, 1970.

Interdepartmental Committee on Drug Addiction (Report), *Drug Addiction,* HMSO 1961. (The 1st Brain Report.)

Interdepartmental Committee on Drug Addiction (Report), *Drug Addiction,* HMSO 1965. (The 2nd Brain Report.)

James, I.P., 'Delinquency and Heroin Addiction in Britain', *British Journal of Criminology* vol. 9, 1969, p. 108.

Kahn, E., 'The New Dependence-Producing Drugs Act', *Justice of the Peace,* vol. 136, no. 1, 1972.

Kalant, O.J. (ed.), *The Amphetamines: Toxicity and Addiction,* University of Toronto Press 1966.

Kaplan, J., *Marijuana – The New Prohibition,* Pocket Books, New York 1971.

Keniston, K., 'Drug Use and Student Values', in *Drug Awareness,* Avon Books 1970.

Kessel, N. and Walton, H., *Alcoholism,* Penguin 1965.

Laurie, P., *Drugs,* Penguin 1968.

Leech, K., 'The Natural History of Two Drug Cultures', *New Society* 1 June 1972.

Leinwand, M., 'The International Law of Treaties and United States' Legalisation of Marijuana', *Columbia Journal of Transnational Law* vol. 10, no. 2, 1971, p. 413.

Leslie, A., 'When it's harvesting time in trendy N.W.1 . . .', *Nova* August 1971.
Levine, H., *Legal Dimensions of Drug Abuse in the United States,* Charles C. Thomas 1974.
Lewin, R., 'Marijuana on trial', *New Scientist* 8 June 1972, p. 552.
Lindesmith, A.R., 'The British System of Narcotics Control', *Law and Contemporary Problems* vol. 22, 1957, p. 142.
Lindesmith, A.R. *The Addict and the Law,* Indiana University Press 1967.
Lindesmith, A.R. *Addiction and Opiates,* Aldine Publishing Co. 1968.
Linstead, H.N., *Poisons Law,* Pharmaceutical Press 1936.
McClintock, F.H. *et al., Crimes of Violence,* MacMillan 1963.
McGlothlin, W.H. and West, L.J., 'The Marijuana Problem: an Over view', *American Journal of Psychiatry,* vol. 125, no. 3, 1968, p. 126.
McGlothlin, W.H. *et al., Alternative Approaches to Opiate Addiction Control: Costs, Benefits and Potential,* Bureau of Narcotics and Dangerous Drugs Study, Washington, Drug Abuse Council, Inc. 1973.
MacSweeney, D. and Parr, D., 'Drug Pushers in the United Kingdom', *Nature* vol. 228, 1970, p. 422.
Magus, R.D. and Harris, L.S., Paper presented at Federation of American Societies for Experimental Biology, Chicago 1971.
Matza, D., *Delinquency and Drift,* J. Wiley 1964.
May, E., 'Narcotics Addiction and Control in Great Britain', in *Dealing with Drug Abuse:* A Report to the Ford Foundation, MacMillan 1972.
Mayor's Committee on Marijuana. *Report on the Marijuana Problem in the City of New York,* Jacques Cattell Press 1944. (The La Guardia Report.)
Menninger, K., *Man against Himself,* Harcourt, Brace 1938.
Mill, J.S., *On Liberty,* 1859.
Miller, D., 'Sexual Conflict and Drug Abuse', *New Society* 16 September 1971, p. 512.
Minister of Health, *Hospital Memorandum* (67)16: 'The Treatment and Supervision of Heroin Addiction', 7 March 1967.
Mitcheson, M., 'Polydrug Abuse', in B. Lucas (ed.), *ABC of Drug Addiction,* John Wright and Sons, Bristol 1970.
Mitcheson, M. *et al.,* 'Sedative Abuse by Heroin Addicts', *The Lancet* vol. 1, 1970, p. 606.
Moreau de Tours, J., *Du haschich et de l'aliénation mentale,* Masson, Paris 1845.
Morris, N. and Hawkins, G., *The Honest Politician's Guide to Crime Control,* University of Chicago Press 1970.

Morris, T.P. and Blom-Cooper, L., *Criminal Homicide in England and Wales, 1957–68,* interim report of Legal Research Unit, Department of Sociology, Bedford College, London 1969.

Morrison, J., 'The Joint's the Thing', *New Statesman* 29 January 1972.

Mott, J. and Taylor, M., *Delinquency Amongst Opiate Users,* Home Office Research Unit Report, HMSO 1974.

Nagahama, M., 'A review of Drug Abuse and Counter Measures in Japan since World War II', *Bulletin on Narcotics* vol. 20, no. 3, 1968, p. 19.

National Commission on Marihuana and Drug Abuse (1st Report), *Marihuana: A Signal of Misunderstanding,* US Government Printing Office 1972. (The Shafer Report.)

National Commission on Marihuana and Drug Abuse (2nd Report), *Drug Use in America: Problem in Perspective,* US Government Printing Office 1973.

National Society for the Prevention of Cruelty to Children, *Drink, Drugs and the Family,* 1971.

Newark, P., *Connexions,* Penguin 1968.

Ng, K.C., *The Chinese in London,* Oxford University Press 1968.

Nichols, L., 'Drug Use and Highway Safety: A Review of the Literature', Rep. DOT-HS-012-1-019, US Department of Transportation, National Highway Traffic Safety Administration, Washington D.C. 1971.

O'Callaghan, S., *Drug Addiction in Britain,* Robert Hale and Co. 1970.

Odier, D., *The Job: Interview with William Burroughs,* Jonathan Cape 1970.

Office of Health Economics, *Drug Addiction,* OHE 1967.

Office of Health Economics, *Medicine and Society: the Changing Demands for Medical Care,* OHE 1972.

O'Shaughnessy, W., 'On the preparations of the Indian hemp, or Gunjah *(Cannabis indica):* Their effects on the animal system in health, and their utility in the treatment of tetanus and other convulsive diseases', *Provincial Medical Journal and Retrospect Medical Sciences* vol. 5, 1843, p. 343.

Owens, J., 'Integrated Approach', in a symposium: 'Centres for Treatment of Drug Addiction', *British Medical Journal* vol. 2, 1967, p. 501.

Parish, P., *Drugs and Society* April 1972, p. 11.

Paton, W.D.M., 'Drug Dependence – a sociopharmacological assessment', *Advancement of Science* vol. 25, 1968, p. 200.

Paton, W.D.M., 'Drug Dependence', *The Listener* 14 November 1968, p. 643.

Paton, W.D.M., *Student,* vol. 2, no. 2, 1969, p. 47.

Paton, W.D.M., 'Guide to Drugs: Cannabis', *Drugs and Society* June 1972, p. 19.

Phillipson, R.V. (ed.), *Modern Trends in Drug Dependence and Alcoholism,* Butterworths 1970.

President's Commission on Law Enforcement and Administration: *Task Force Report, Narcotics and Drug Abuse,* US Government Printing Office, Washington D.C. 1967.

Rafaelson, O.J. *et al.,* 'Cannabis and Alcohol: Effect on Simulated Driving', Paper presented at 5th World Congress of Psychiatry, Mexico City, November 1971.

Rodin, E.A. *et al.,* 'The Marijuana-induced 'Social High': Neurological and Electroencephalographic Concomitants', *Journal of American Medical Association,* vol. 213, 1970, p. 1300.

Royal College of Physicians (Report), *Smoking and Health Now,* Pitman 1971.

Royal Commission on Medical Education (Report), HMSO 1968. (The Todd Report.)

Schofield, M., 'Background to the Drug Scene', in *Behind the Drug Scene,* British Medical Association 1969.

Schofield, M., *The Strange Case of Pot,* Penguin 1971.

Schur, E.M., *Narcotic Addiction in Britain and America,* ABP Ltd. 1962.

Scott, J.M., *The White Poppy: A History of Opium,* Heinemann 1969.

Scott, P. and Wilcox, D., 'Delinquency and Amphetamines', *British Journal of Addiction,* vol. 61, 1968, nos. 1/2, p. 9.

Sjöström, H. and Nilsson, R., *Thalidomide and the Power of the Drug Companies,* Penguin 1972.

Spiegelberg, R., 'Alcoholism: the Hidden Problem', *The Times* 13 April 1971.

Steinberg, H. (ed.), *The Scientific Basis of Drug Dependence,* Churchill 1969.

Stengel, E., *Suicide and Attempted Suicide,* Penguin 1964.

Stimson, G., *Heroin and Behaviour,* Irish University Press 1973.

Swift, B., Dorn, N. and Thompson, A., *Evaluation of Drug Education,* ISDD 1974.

Teff, H., 'The Meaning of Possession in Drugs Cases', *Modern Law Review* vol. 34, 1971, p. 582.

Teff, H., 'Drugs and the Law: the Development of Control', *Modern Law Review* vol. 35, 1972, p. 225.

Thomas, D.A., *Principles of Sentencing,* Heinemann 1970.

Trocchi, A., *Cain's Book,* Calder & Boyars, Jupiter Books, London 1966.

Tylden, E., 'Cannabis taking in England', *Newcastle Medical Journal* vol. 30, no. 6, 1968, p. 533.

United Nations Commission on Narcotic Drugs, *Summary of Annual Reports of Governments relating to Opium and other Narcotic Drugs,* Geneva, E/NR 1955/Summary, 1955.

United Nations Division of Narcotic Drugs, *Information Letter,* No. 11, November 1974.

Vaillant, G.E., 'A Twelve Year Follow-up of New York Narcotic Addicts: The Relation of Treatment to Outcome', *American Journal of Psychiatry* vol. 122, no. 7, 1966, p. 727.

Waller, J.A., 'Drugs and Highway Crashes', *Journal of the American Medical Association* vol. 215, no. 9, 1971, p. 1477.

Weil, A., *The Natural Mind,* Jonathan Cape 1973.

West, D.J., *The Young Offender,* Penguin 1967.

Wiener, R.S.P., *Drugs and Schoolchildren,* Longman 1970.

Wilkins, L., 'Some sociologic factors in drug addiction control', in D. Wilner and G. Kassebaum (ed.), *Narcotics,* McGraw-Hill, New York 1965.

Wilner, D.M. and Kassebaum, G.G. (ed.), *Narcotics,* McGraw-Hill 1965.

Wilson, C.W.M. (ed.), *Adolescent Drug Dependence,* Pergamon 1968.

World Health Organisation, Technical Report Series, No. 287, 1964.

World Health Organisation, Technical Report Series, No. 478, 1971.

Yablonsky, L., *Synanon: The Tunnel Back,* Penguin 1967.

Yeger, S., 'Weekend Junkies', *New Society* 19 February 1970.

Young, J., *The Drugtakers,* McGibbon and Kee, 1971.

Zacune, J., and Hensman, C., *Drugs, Alcohol and Tobacco in Britain,* Heinemann 1971.

Zaehner, R.C., *Drugs, Mysticism and Make-Believe,* Collins 1972.

Zinberg, N.E. and Weil, A.T., 'A Comparison of Marijuana Users and Non-users', *Nature,* vol. 226, 1970, pp. 119–123.

Index

Indexer's note: If a page reference given in the index cannot establish the subject, readers should turn to the notes at the end of the chapter for a lead.

The Author

Harvey Teff graduated in law, from the University of Oxford. He was called to the Bar in 1965 (Middle Temple), and in 1973 was awarded a doctorate by the University of London for his thesis on the legal and social aspects of drug dependence. He has written a number of articles on the law relating to drugs and on the pharmaceutical industry. Dr. Teff is at present Senior Lecturer in Law at the University of Durham.